An Imp on Either Shoulder

An Imp on Either Shoulder

...Working on our Temperaments

Gilbert Childs, PhD

The acts of supersensible beings
can be described as good or bad;
the beings themselves, never!

Rudolf Steiner
Initiation, Eternity and the Passing Moment

A catalogue record of this book is available from the British Library

ISBN 1 900301 00 8

Published by Fire Tree Press
Bisley, Stroud
Gloucestershire GL6 7BL
England

1995

Cover design and Artwork by
Sylvia E Childs and Allmut ffrench

This book has been typeset in Palatino 11 on 13pt by Imprint Publicity Service of Crawley Down, Sussex and printed and bound by Woolnough Bookbinding Ltd, Irthlingborough, Northants

Contents

FOREWORD

Hidden Realities

There is, of course, much that is *hidden* behind what manifests to our senses in outer nature. We can perceive only symptoms and phenomena, and then endeavour to integrate into our existing body of knowledge what is meaningful to us. There is a fundamental urge in us all to make sense of what is going on around us – to *understand* it, so that we may preserve the essential integrity of our own personal world, the world of our own creation existent in the universal scheme of things. At the same time, we know that many aspects are, and may remain, hidden from us; but this should not deter us from striving towards their being revealed to us. We may not be capable of actually apprehending the original percept, but we may comprehend as concept that which we are able to grasp with our mental powers. Even where outer material phenomena are concerned there is often little agreement among those who perceive them. Observations may be subjected to repeated scrutiny, and the correctness of these confirmed, yet it is their *interpretation* that is of paramount importance. This may well be different, according to individual understanding, but there can never be any argument about the facts themselves; for these must, by definition, be *true*. Apprehension of material phenomena is of course the proper concern of our bodily-material senses, and there is usually no substantial disagreement as to these. Explication of these is often difficult enough; but when it comes to phenomena which are inaccessible to these senses, and therefore *hidden*, the problem of getting to the truth of the matter becomes enormously expanded.

The difficulty becomes even more compounded when the observations of supersensible phenomena are taken into account, as in the case of Rudolf Steiner's pronouncements concerning his spiritual-scientific researches. For most people, these have to be taken on trust; and on the principle that everything must be believed before it can be understood, such trust can, in the long run, be justified. Any body of knowledge must be able to be put to the test in ways that make its credibility progress to feasibility, from possibility to probability, and thence in gradual stages to viability and practicability, and thus as close to certainty as can possibly be determined.

Steiner's insistence that spirit is primary and matter secondary is often a reason for a certain hesitancy upon first acquaintance. His assertion that orthodox materialistic scientists will never understand matter until they realise that spirit is constantly at work in it at once raises the necessary contention that behind every material phenomenon there is a complementary spiritual phenomenon. Where animated beings are concerned, philosophers, psychologists and physiologists may endlessly discuss the visible consequences of invisible incitements as being parallel, coincidental, causative, reciprocal or whatever, but they cannot deny that they are inter-connected.

Chapter One
An Imp on Either Shoulder

There is indeed an intermediary between what is thus brought over from earlier lives on Earth and what is provided by heredity. This intermediary has the more universal qualities provided by family, nation and race, but is at the same time capable of individualization. That which stands midway between the line of heredity and the individuality is expressed in the word "temperament".[1]

Rudolf Steiner
The Four Temperaments

The Devil and Satan

We all learn very soon in childhood that life is real, life is earnest, and that we certainly are born to trouble, as the sparks fly upward. (Job 5:7) Most of us have the vague feeling from time to time that we are somehow being "got at", and not really in charge of ourselves. We frequently learn that what seemed a good idea at the time leads to our realisation later on that we may be rather too inclined to "give way" to whatever enters our mind in the way of idea, impulse, stimulus, fancy, whim or other inclination to act in this or that manner. How often do we act in haste, but repent at leisure!

The dictionary definition of an imp is "a little devil or spirit characterized by its mischievous disposition"; and the notion that there is one sitting on either of our shoulders is not quite as fanciful as it may seem. Perhaps the definition itself may not be entirely accurate, but the notion is reasonably sound. By long tradition we have two tormentors who were sent by God to enable us to become perfect, even as He is perfect: on our left we have the Devil, also known as Lucifer, and on our right is Ahriman, also known as Satan. The Devil is the Tempter, and it is he and his minions who "promise the Earth", who inspire enthusiasm and ardour, and fascination, enchantment and enticement, usually in that order, are the devices employed by them to go just that little bit too far – and into trouble. Satan is the Evil One, who with his impish assistants seeks to entrap and beguile us by employing lies, half-truths, and deceitful wiles of every kind. Whereas Lucifer would whirl us away into the very heavens themselves, Ahriman would foster our self-interest, and by cold but suspect logic bind us fast in matter and turn us into automatons, ossified in body and mummified in mind.

Lucifer and Ahriman, of which much more will be said in due course are, strictly speaking, collective nouns employed for all spiritual beings of Diabolic or Satanic nature, although it is not a case of mere personification, for there does exist one of each dynasty who has taken on the role of leader. It is the rank and file, so to speak, who do the actual mischief, albeit in a manner that is not altogether without sound motives from the point of view of cosmic history. It may be helpful, in attempting to discern which influences are active, and how and where they are at work, to ponder the fact that Ahriman, in Zoroastrian times, was regarded as the spirit of darkness (and by inference, of evil), whose antagonist was Ahura Mazda, as representative of light and goodness. However, Lucifer must not be identified with Ahura Mazda, but must be regarded as possessing some of his qualities.[2]

As we know, Lucifer is especially active in our astral nature, our medium for feelings and emotions of all kinds. The very word *Lucifer* means "light-bearing", and it bears connotations of the *light of consciousness*, for it was Lucifer who infiltrated the human astral body, the vehicle of our consciousness. By contrast, Ahriman is entrenched in our etheric body, in which we are, for the most part, only dimly, darkly conscious. Reminders of this dichotomy in human nature, as our "lower nature" comprising physical and etheric bodies as *corporeal,* and our "higher nature" consisting of our astral body and ego as *soul-spiritual,* are to be found in the methods of spiritual training practised by the Essenes.[3] Lucifer and Ahriman are better known in Christian religious circles as the Devil (as Tempter) and Satan (as the Evil One) respectively. However, in modern times these two are becoming increasingly regarded as two aspects of the same entity, or more abstractly as two aspects of the same principle that works in opposition to Good. This whole concept is nicely brought together by Thomas à Kempis:

> *When a good man is afflicted, tempted, or troubled with evil thoughts; then he understandeth better the great need he hath of God, without whom he perceiveth he can do nothing that is good.*[4]

Delusion and illusion

Ahriman is the master of *delusion,* whereby we become subject to falsehoods and misapprehensions, and our perception of reality, particularly *inner* reality, becomes warped and unreliable. Very often, the darkest depths of the personality are plumbed repeatedly and consistently, the mental processes becoming closed, and ever more concentrated in self-interest and egotism. Beelzebub or Mephistopheles, according to Goethe, is "the father of lies", and is generally of a negative nature – the spirit that denies. However, no entity can be entirely negative in the absolute sense, for as Mephistopheles himself recognizes, he is "Part of that Power, not understood, Which always wills the Bad, and always works the Good".[5] Moreover, it is easy to understand that, as Steiner pointed out, Ahriman is the god of hindrance. Self-delusion all too easily paves the way to pessimism and dark moods, melancholy and self-absorption, during which time it is difficult for the sufferer to make decisions which may generate a swing away from depression and apathy to optimism and action.

Lucifer, on the other hand, is the master of *illusion*, by which we become induced to perceive what is imaginary or nonexistent in the *outer* world. Our feet do not, so to speak, touch the ground, and we tend to become whirled away into the realm of daydreams and exaggerated expectations, unrealistic hopes, wishes and desires, and over-optimistic attitudes generally. Strength and energy are squandered in fatuous, nebulous and trifling initiatives and activities of all kinds in efforts to catch "shifting shapes", tenuous and illusive.

Our etheric body and time

We know that our temperaments are established in our etheric body, and Rudolf Steiner averred that the "various members of our etheric body are differentiated according to the different temperaments: the upper part is inclined to the melancholic temperament, the central part alternates between phlegmatic and sanguine, and the lower part is inclined to the choleric".[6] In this statement, made in 1913, we are already able to discern indications he made several years later, when he published his findings concerning mankind's fundamentally threefold nature.[7] Briefly, he pointed out that our *head*, with its brain and supporting nerves/sense system, serves our faculties of *thinking*; that our *rhythmic system* of heart and lungs, occupying our chest cavity, serves our life of *feeling*, and that our *metabolic/limbs system* sustains our forces of *willing*.

Just as our solid, physical-material body exists principally in the element of *space*, our etheric body likewise endures through that of *time*. In our "lower", corporeal being we are "dwellers all in time and space", and the two vehicles abide synchronously and co-incidentally. As long as an organism is alive, the physical and etheric vehicles must be sufficiently well integrated to allow of its continuation in the vital state. Should either of these two principles for some reason find purchase of the other impossible to maintain, partition occurs, and what we call death ensues. Thereupon, the mineral body returns its constituent substances to the material world, and the etheric body its particular forces to the etheric world diffused around us.

From this it would be reasonable to deduce that, with regard to the element of time which is always associated with the etheric body, memory and the melancholic temperament is concerned mainly with what is *past*. The rhythmic system and in terms of temperament, sanguines (outer concerns) and phlegmatics (inner concerns) are concerned mainly with what is going on in the *present*. The metabolic/limbs system is associated with the choleric temperament, and by inference the will with its propensity for *future action*.[8] Steiner states that for melancholics past experiences resonate within their inner nature for a long time, and they often have difficulty in "letting them go". Sanguines alternate between past and present considerations, whereas phlegmatics float along steadily with the flow of time. Cholerics, however, have the tendency to resist the approach of future time.[9] These indications in themselves give much food for thought and contemplation according to individual needs and circumstances.

However, it should never be forgotten that the essential quality of all etheric forces is that of *form-giving*, and a reminder of this is Steiner's own term for the etheric body, namely *formative-forces-body* (bildekrafteleib). It is the primary attribute of the etheric, certainly in the human, animal and plant kingdoms. At the age of six or seven, children shed their deciduous teeth, and it is then that a considerable proportion of their etheric forces changes function. Hitherto mainly engaged upon forming their own bodily natures (which they have modelled on the physical bodies inherited from their parents), the etheric forces thus liberated begin increasingly to serve the soul-spiritual nature of the children, that is to say, their powers of thinking, feeling and willing.

The etheric principle supplies the basis for the forming of ideas and concepts, and a conceptual memory capable of handling abstractions now develops in addition to the pictorial kind proper to the stages of infancy and early childhood. Our thoughts, ideas, notions, judgements, opinions, beliefs, viewpoints and other mental structures have by definition to be *formed*, and the forces employed in the fashioning or construction of these are etheric forces. Thinking is a constructive process, and in this operation the brain is merely the organ for it – in no way can it *originate* mental processes. From what before the shedding of the milk teeth in children was a kind of *sensitive chaos* now gradually emerges a *sensitive cosmos* – the embryonic thought-world now set to expand as directed by the all-important incarnating ego.[10]

The philosopher Immanuel Kant was of the firm opinion that people possess one temperament only, but one is tempted to deduce from this contention that he must have had one temperament that was inordinately dominant. Of course, when we take the whole notion of the temperaments seriously, we soon get to know which one is our main one. Rudolf Steiner recommended that, in order to gain mastery over our main temperament rather than be a slave to it, that we turn it against itself.[11] Thus, individuals who are thoroughly melancholic should take care to practise self-criticism, and adopt hostile or contemptuous attitudes toward themselves.[12] This way they will look at themselves more objectively, and self-appraisal may well become a regular habit from which everyone in the household will benefit.

Sensitive Chaos: in his book of this title, Theodor Schwenk opens the chapter *Water, Nature's Sense Organ*, with this statement:

> *The formative boundary surfaces in flowing movement prove to be areas of sensitivity. They respond to the slightest changes in their surroundings by expanding, contracting or making rhythmical waves. Water creates an infinite variety of these surfaces and is therefore not merely an inert mass, as we usually think. It is interwoven with countless sensitive membranes, which are prepared to perceive everything taking place in its surroundings. Water is not enclosed within its inner surfaces, but open to its surroundings and to all the stimuli and formative impulses from without. It is the impressionable medium par excellence.*[13]

Here again is a depiction for reflection and contemplation. The outer manifestation of the etheric is, of course, water, though this should be understood in the sense of Ancient Greek science as anything of a fluid nature. We ourselves are liquid rather than solid, and this can be said of practically every living thing. Fluids are by their very nature adaptable to whatever they are contained in or by, but this reflects only the *externality* of the principle of containment. Within its confines, contained fluids are hardly ever entirely static, and when accommodated within the cells and tissues of living organisms, never anything but dynamic, bearers as they are of various solid particles necessary for the maintenance of the life process.

It may be of some help in all this if we ponder in imaginative ways the fact that the phlegmatic temperament is on its own ground, so to speak, in being based in the etheric body. As representative of water, it is always seeking its own level, and this in whatever circumstances, and so is the very manifestation of equilibrium, and even stability in a dynamic rather than a fixed mode. Water is essential to all forms of earthly life, and warrants special consideration because of its proximity to solid, mineral matter on the scale that may be designated as being "below", and immediately "above" is the whole gaseous sphere, which it is capable of interpenetrating and permeating also. All three realms and human principles – mineral (physical), watery (etheric) and airy (astral) – are capable, whether in single state or mixed with either or both elements together – of being pervaded and affected by the "upper" element of fire or heat (ego). Thus, in human constitutional terms, the picture is made complete. The "fire" of the ego, with its peculiar status of freedom and ability to invade the other principles, when in contact with water results either in the creation of steam or its own demise by being extinguished!

Our temperament is, in the main, entrenched in our etheric body, as mentioned earlier. It is, so to speak, built into us, into our very constitution; and this is why certain bodily characteristics are manifest in us all, in our very physiognomy, according to temperament. The essentially *formative* function of the etheric body ensures this; for in a very real sense the physical and etheric bodies are fully identified with each other. This is why the melancholic and phlegmatic temperaments are so much alike in many ways. People who have these as their main temperament share the same qualities characteristic of passivity, conventionalism, restraint, discretion, conservatism, and even narrow-mindedness. The matter of actual body build is an interesting one, for whereas melancholic people are in the main leptomorphic (tall and thin), phlegmatics are eurymorphic (short and thickset). It is as if the solid (bony) nature of melancholics constitutes a concentration of matter in a centrifugal way, whereas the phlegmatic build is suggestive of centripetal, expansive influences. This view is supported by the fact that the forces of *gravity* are strongly evident in the melancholic physiognomy, and those of *levity* in that of phlegmatic types.

This in turn is underlined by the notion that melancholics are related to the earthly forces, whereas phlegmatics possess rather a cosmic nature. Phlegmatics live, as it were, in their body fluids, more particularly in their glandular system, and in this respect represent a comparatively early stage of human development. The bony system, centrally placed as it is in the organism, is the very last physiological structure to be "precipitated" or even "crystallized out", hardened and fully formed from mineral substances, and which remains mainly lifeless. The presence of bone marrow with its blood-forming propensities, represents the exact polar opposite of the blood, which is the most spiritual – or *spiritualized* – of all our organs. As might be expected, this polarity is reflected in the heat of the blood, with its connotations of fire and choler, and the solid mineral, earthy skeleton which does not possess blood-vessels, lymphatic support, glands and suchlike, and is relatively "cold" – as are melancholics in a soul/spiritual sense. The blood is characteristic of much that is Luciferic in nature, and the skeleton much of what is Ahrimanic.

This is an example of what can happen when, say, melancholic folk, weighed down as they are by Ahrimanic gravity, take steps to engage the Luciferic forces which reside in their blood, and warm themselves through and through with them, to their very bones. This will then result in their becoming compassionate, benevolent and charitable, with sympathetic and empathetic qualities far beyond the innate capabilities of the other temperaments. Their fellow-feeling, kindness, consideration, tenderness and so on which they have hitherto lavished *upon themselves* in an egotistical way will then be shared in ever greater measure with others. They will take on properties of expansiveness, generosity and magnanimity, much after the fashion of Scrooge after his change of heart.[14]

The temperaments and their polarities

In the case of the temperaments which share the qualities of activity, liberalism, progressiveness, permissiveness and broadmindedness, again we are faced with a kind of inner polarity. Typical cholerics will get the task done even if it kills them, whilst sanguines will walk away from the job upon (early) lack of interest. Again, we have one eurymorphic (choleric) and one leptomorphic (sanguine) type; but as both strongly incline towards the soul-spiritual in nature, there is little to "anchor" them. It is therefore not surprising to find that if a person possesses a main temperament that is identifiable as being in the one category, he or she may well have a secondary temperament that belongs to the other. A good instance of this is the choleric/melancholic pairing, which gives rise to the typical manic-depressive type of behaviour, or the sanguine/melancholic mixture, resulting in swings of mood between optimism and pessimism. Contraction and expansion, reductionism and pluralism, even weeping and laughing, are only a few examples of what can, respectively, be said to be Ahrimanic or Luciferic in character, and as always a degree of equilibrium should be sought.

Rudolf Steiner asserted that stability, imperturbability and equanimity are highly desirable qualities to cultivate in all circumstances of life, and essential for steady progress along any path of personal or esoteric development. Mainly because of this, but also because phlegmatic people are in any case highly sensitive to changes within their own constitution, bodily and soul-spiritual, they – if their interest in spiritual development is sufficiently aroused, of course – are already at advantage in that they possess many of the qualities that are pre-requisite for esoteric training. Steiner, who could never be accused of any kind of bias, had this is to say: "The phlegmatic type whose soul develops is therefore the best material for serious anthroposophical development".[15]

We all possess characteristics of the *phlegmatic* element in due proportion in relation to our other temperaments, all of which go to make up our own individuality. Furthermore, *every single temperamental quality is rooted in the etheric body*, irrespective of the fact that, in the main, choleric traits are essentially expressible through the heat of our blood; sanguine qualities through the airy nature of our rhythmic system; phlegmatic propensities via our glandular system, and melancholic attributes by means of all we manifest in terms of rigidity and solidity, namely our skeleton. These are typically associated with the traditional elemental characteristics of fire, air, water and earth respectively. In a fully functioning human being, all these qualities and attributes are necessary for their smooth operation; that is to say, everything must work in harmony to the extent that all functions are co-ordinated so as to impart the sense or feeling of integrality, unity and wholeness. It is the paramount function of any etheric organization to achieve harmony above all, and the temperament most characteristic of this is without doubt the phlegmatic.

Nature is for the most part investigated by scientific methodologies and interpreted by materialistic philosophies, and these are obviously associated with the typically Ahrimanic qualities of forming and structuring, in this case logically conceived and systematically presented concepts proper to our soul-faculty of *thinking*. With equal validity the whole of Nature could be regarded as the result of the workings of the cosmic *will*, manifesting as a colossal work of art which provides the sphere for reciprocating acts of will in the form of action. This involves the Luciferic attributes of inciting the desire for deed, energetically deployed for the most part in the selfish interests of the doer.

The principle of *feeling* arises between these two poles of soul-activity, thus giving rise to opportunities for the exercizing of sympathetic subjectivity (Lucifer) as well as antipathetic objectivity (Ahriman). Of great assistance in this is the undoubted advantage to be gained by regarding the whole of Creation artistically. By application of investigative methods involving the cultivation of the kind of aesthetic perception based on appropriately trained feelings, artistic methods of investigating the world are seen to be entirely valid. It is the balancing principle innate in our soul faculty of feeling that endeavours constantly to stabilize and bring into harmony our faculties of thinking and willing, so that we become increasingly capable of wisdom-filled deeds. By reason and virtue of this process, we shall inevitably progress on our path towards perfection.

> Patience *attracts the treasures of higher knowledge; impatience repels them. In the higher regions of existence nothing can be achieved by haste and unrest. Above all things, desire and craving must be silenced, for these are qualities of the soul from which higher knowledge quietly withdraws with aversion. Valuable as all higher knowledge is, we must not crave for it if it is to come to us.*[16]
>
> Rudolf Steiner
> *Knowledge of the Higher Worlds and Its Attainment*

Chapter Two
Tension between Opposites

In addition to the etheric and astral bodies, we bear another spiritual element in us – the "I". We know how complex this I is, and that it continues from incarnation to incarnation. Its inner forces build the garment, so to speak, that we put on with each new incarnation. We rise from the dead in the I to prepare for a new incarnation. It is the I that makes each of us a unique individual. We can say our ether body represents, in a sense, everything birth-like, everything connected with the elemental forces of Nature. Our astral body symbolizes what brings death, and is connected with the higher spiritual worlds. And the I represents our continual resurrection in the spirit, our renewed life in the spiritual world, which is neither Nature nor the world of the stars, but permeates everything.[18]

Rudolf Steiner
Towards Imagination

L'Allegro and *Il Penseroso*

As we know, the four temperaments can be classified in various ways according to particular aspects and viewpoints.[19] It is clear that there are only two main somatotypes, or types of bodily conformation, and they are exemplified by those people who are short and thickset (eurymorphic), and those who are tall and thin (leptomorphic). These correspond respectively in terms of temperament to those who are introverted in behaviour and convergent in their ways of thinking, namely either melancholics or phlegmatics, and those who are manifestly extravert in demeanour and divergent as far as their mental processes are concerned, as represented in the sanguines and cholerics. Taking their relative characteristics further, we perceive that we are able to classify the first group as *conservative* in nature, and the second as *liberal;* roughly speaking, those who tend to have "closed" natures and those who have "open" natures. The list of characteristics, attributes, propensities, preferences, pre-dispositions, tendencies, aptitudes and inclinations that denote this kind of polar opposition could go on and on, but in general principles they all point either to the qualities often called Ahrimanic or Luciferic.

The main aspects of their several attributes are typified in the language of the poet John Milton, "L'Allegro" and "Il Penseroso" respectively, and the first few lines of each are worth quoting:

Hence loathèd Melancholy
    Of Cerberus and blackest midnight born,
In Stygian Cave forlorn
    'Mongst horrid shapes, and shrieks, and sights unholy.
Find out som uncouth cell,
    Where brooding darkness spreads his jealous wings,
And the night-Raven sings;
    There, under Ebon shades, and low-brow'd Rocks
As ragged as thy Locks,
    In dark Cimmerian desert ever dwell.
But com thou Goddes fair and free,
In Heaven ycleap'd Euphrosyne,
And by men, heart-easing Mirth...

Here is ample material for contemplation, and there should be no need to point out the various indications, except perhaps to mention that Rudolf Steiner, born some 250 years later than Milton, asserted that Ahriman flees away in the presence of laughter!

Hence vain deluding joyes,
    The brood of folly without father bred,
How little you bested,
    Or fill the fixèd mind with all your toyes;
Dwell in som idle brain,
    And fancies fond with gaudy shapes possess,

As thick and numberless
    As the gay motes that people the Sun Beams,
Or likest hovering dreams
    The fickle Pensioners of Morpheus train.
But hail thou Goddes, sage and holy,
    Hail divinest Melancholy,
Whose saintly visage is too bright
    To hit the Sense of human sight…

As in all cases of polarities, opposing qualities meet in the area of tension between them; and often the boundaries between them are paper-thin.

In any case they are complementary, often contradictory, and almost certainly paradoxical. The shift in Milton's thinking is quite clear, and the fact that he was able to eulogize on these sets of opposites, and be able to appreciate the positive and negative characteristics of both, should be a source of encouragement to everyone in their attempts to balance out their own temperaments.

Poles apart: It can be very revealing deliberately to jot down lists of significant or important sets of polar opposites, and then proceed to divide them into those that are Luciferic in nature and character, and those which are archetypally Ahrimanic, and ponder how their respective qualities and attributes react upon each other. An interesting one is the polarity of *blood and nerve* in the human organism, a particularly illuminating one described by Rudolf Steiner himself. Our nerves-senses system serves our astral nature, our soul nature with its surging emotions and our individual sympathies and antipathies which are in constant oscillation. As the very word *astral* implies, our astral body is our starry body. Contrary to scientific belief, it is actually in the far reaches of the star-strewn space that its affinities lie. Expansiveness in human soul-spiritual terms is the gift of Lucifer, with its connotations of freedom, levity, openness and extension in all forms, and thoroughly centrifugal in action. However, once these forces enter the domain of Ahriman, that is to say, the realm of gravity, contraction and density, form and structure are seen to operate. His is the empire of the earth, the underworld, the lifeless, and as one would expect, our nervous system in terms of physiology is dead.

In polar opposition to our nervous system is our vascular system, or more precisely our blood itself, with all its life-giving and life-sustaining properties. Blood and nerve meet in our senses, and the presence of both is necessary for our sense-organs to function effectively, facilitating our earthly consciousness and our bodily awareness, with all its manifold sense-impressions and sensations. If we have the courage to read the book of Nature in this way, in terms of polarities, we should not be surprised to learn that the origin of our red blood cells (and some white blood cells) lies encased in the hardest, most contracted and most mineralized components of the human body – the bone-marrow. In a sense, the living is called forth from the dead, just as in the case of the nerves, that which is dead is precipitated from the life-giving forces of the starry worlds.[20]

Where Lucifer and Ahriman do battle

We not only have an imp on either shoulder, Lucifer on the left one and Ahriman on the right, we have, in a certain very real sense, been "taken over" by these two opposing spiritual factions. This knowledge can at first be alarming and disturbing, for when it dawns upon us that we are a kind of battlefield for their machinations, designs, schemes and stratagems, we feel far from comfortable. However, they all have become, over long ages of time and many generations, part of our very nature, corporeal and soul-spiritual, so the idea should not seem so very frightening. In fact, we benefit greatly from their presence within ourselves as part of our very nature and being. Lucifer is our benefactor in very many ways, primarily as the bestower of our will, which enables us to be doers of deeds, of being creatively active in innumerable ways. Ahriman, on the other hand, has endowed us with all the powers of the intellect that we take for granted. All the formative power we need to shape our thoughts and ideas we owe to him, as well as the power of memory.

We gain much of insight into the opposing dispositions of Lucifer and Ahriman by reflecting on the fact that they are as it were resident in our astral and etheric principles respectively. They have been responsible, over many generations throughout the millennia of evolution, for the formation and function of our actual bodily organs. Lucifer in very fact influences the left hand side of our organism, whilst Ahriman's authority is down our right side. The asymmetry that we manifest in our constitution, particularly in our chest and abdomen, is very much due to their opposing influences. It is no accident, for example, that the human heart, as the traditional (and actual) seat of our life of feeling, is placed slightly to the left, namely in the sphere of Lucifer; and in this we may immediately recognize the astral principle involved. Our stomach is also placed slightly to the left, whereas that important organ the liver is located to the right. Recognition of this fact, Rudolf Steiner asserted, could provide useful pointers to physicians, physiologists and the like. Space does not permit further elaboration along these lines, and interested readers are referred to his main indications.[21]

A few words to the wise: As mentioned just now, our *willing* processes are strongly connected with the

Luciferic influences, and our *thinking* operations with Ahriman, so it is in these areas we must look for negative as well as positive forces. Knowing this, we are enabled to become aware of the source of all kinds of aberrations in these areas, and how to deal with them. This is of course very much to our advantage in terms of self-knowledge as well as our understanding of our fellow human beings and their behaviour. As we know, behaviour patterns may be roughly characterized by reference to the four temperaments and their various admixtures.[22] Each of our temperaments may be in a different stage of development, and in any assessment of the behaviour of various individuals this should be taken into account. It follows that the more experienced we become in our observation of the diverse symptoms and phenomena manifested in other people's behaviour, the more accurate our conclusions.

The most obvious example of thought deviation is that of the *lie*. Our thoughts themselves are merely instruments in the structuring of our thinking processes themselves. The science of logic governs the laws of thought, but these were themselves arrived at by examination of what we think, how we think it, and testing the validation of the whole process by practical application. Lies invariably result in confusion piled on confusion, for as we all know: "O what a tangled web we weave, when first we practise to deceive". The arch-deceiver is of course Ahriman, ruler of the icy realms of strict rationality, and master of abstract intellectual endeavour. By implication, his sphere of greatest influence is that of science, more particularly materialistic science, for the world of matter is his kingdom, and proper domain. Science strives for the *truth*, yet paradoxically enough scientists seek it in the sphere of Ahriman, and the question arises as to whether their efforts can ever meet with genuine success.

Of course, scientists proceed along the strictest possible lines of empirical methodologies in their efforts to arrive at the facts, and as far as they are concerned facts cannot be called facts unless they are *correct*. But such facts may be stated as being correct only because they are construed as such by interpretation and deduction *in the light of their state of knowledge at the time*. In other words, they may be correct, but are they *true*? Truth is – or should be – compatible with or even synonymous with *wisdom*. In this connection Steiner had this to say:

> *Plato called the ideal of "wisdom" by a word which was in common use when man still possessed the ancient wisdom, and it would be well to replace this by the word* truth, *for as we have now become more individual, we have withdrawn ourselves from the divine, and must therefore strive back to it... We are now in the fifth post-Atlantean age. We are still far from the time when the wisdom instinctively implanted in humanity as a divine impulse, will be raised into consciousness. Hence in our age people are liable to err ... and it is now particularly necessary that the great dangers to be found at this point should be counteracted by a spiritual conception of the world, so that what humanity once possessed as instinctive wisdom may now become conscious wisdom.*[23]

To materialistic science must be added spiritual science, as necessary and complementary, in order for valid truth and genuine wisdom to be established as fully viable, indisputable and incontrovertible.

The struggle for balance: A commonly held view is that possessors of a sound phlegmatic disposition are to be pitied rather than envied. They personify the blandness of the taste of water itself – but it is fortunate for us all that we are able to energize our phlegmatic propensities in that regard, and never tire of its flavourlessness! Apparently unresponsive to many a stimulus that would excite people endowed with rather more lively qualities, the dull and apathetic phlegmatics are in fact highly sensitive to atmosphere and environment as well as the "presence" of others. The dislike of their own equilibrium being disturbed is usually extended to others, so reluctance on their part to react should not offend. Internal and external harmony is paramount. The conditions necessary for progress on the path of self-development are well known to students of spiritual science, and these are achievable by anyone, temperament notwithstanding. In this case, virtue is indeed its own reward, for who does not wish for anything but harmony within and without?

A companion temperament to the phlegmatic, even if for the sole reason of being the other with innate "Ahrimanic" propensities, is the melancholic. A prominent characteristic of those of this disposition is their readiness to criticize and call to account – themselves if they are so disposed, but also other people. Self-centred as they generally are, melancholics are well placed for self-examination and even genuine self-knowledge. They are apt to turn in on themselves the qualities of contrariness, self-inflicted misery, rigidity and their innate sense of being someone rather special, unequalled in their near martyr-like sufferings for the benefit of others. Depth of character is a definite asset to melancholics, unless, of course, they dive so deeply into themselves that they find it difficult ever to surface. When they do, they should endeavour to make for the shallow end of themselves, and try to have a little fun – just a bit to start with, naturally. A little unfamiliar activity of a Luciferic nature – and there are plenty of ventures to choose from – could sharpen them up and help them discover latent talents.

Choleric people believe that changing themselves in any way is not only unnecessary, but a definite disadvantage. They are self-confident and self-assured, and have plenty of drive and ambition: the will to succeed at almost any cost is built into them. It is not for them to change – the world must change to suit them; and what is more, they have the urge to change it. Lucifer is a consummate inspirer of the *will*, and with it the hot-bloodedness for it to become action. Ahriman is the master of reason, of the laws of *thought*, and seeks to persuade us that our inner world is the only real world.

Those happy-go-lucky folk with sanguine temperaments are not worried one bit that their nerves are out on stalks, because generally they do not even realise that this is the case. Their inability to concentrate on anything for long is helped (or hindered) by Lucifer, for theirs is the airy realm. The image of butterflies is a superb one where sanguines are concerned. Their flight may seem erratic, irregular and unpredictable, but they very often settle on the finest of flowers. They may find it very difficult to balance themselves in the orthodox fashion, but never underestimate them. On the difficult path of self-knowledge we all find it difficult to strengthen our will, whatever mixture of temperaments we possess.

However, we should not of course rely on our temperaments alone, for we must resist any tendency to become enslaved to them. Rather should we do all we can to strengthen our ego in order to *command* whichever is appropriate in a given situation, and bring them into harmony by exercizing our *will* in a *wise* manner. As we know, our will pole is Luciferic, comprising as it does our choleric and sanguine proclivities; ideally, we should be ever sensitive and alert to the appropriateness of any action we carry out, so that what we do should ultimately be in the service of the divine powers. Lucifer would have us be good and moral, but act out of a kind of spurious freedom of the kind associated with compulsive knee-jerk reaction prompted by sentiment rather than genuine, self-effacing love.

Our Ahrimanic pole, consisting of our phlegmatic and melancholic propensities, serves our powers of thinking, the means by which we obtain knowledge. This necessarily forms the basis of wisdom, which is none other than knowledge permeated by genuine altruistic love. Our aim should always be to "think with the heart", thus combining *will* and *wisdom* in all our dealings by harnessing the powers of Lucifer and Ahriman in a thoroughly Christian way. The human heart (feeling) acts as balancing agent between our head (thinking) and our metabolic/limbs system (willing). Indeed, the whole world is a result of the working of countless manifestations of the working of balance.

> *Through wise self-knowledge it is possible, in the course of esoteric development, to repair the damage done by the predominant temperament. One begins to feel convinced that this damage can be repaired by bringing about modifications with the other temperaments; one must be aware of the effect of the transformations in relation to the other temperaments.*[24]
>
> Rudolf Steiner
> *Effects of Spiritual Development*

Chapter Three
Balancing our Temperaments

It is utter nonsense to believe that Earthly existence should be valued lightly... Like all the other phases of human development, Earthly, physical existence has its purpose. We reap permanent, eternal gains from what the soul experiences by having a physical body and by way of what we experience under the influence of memory and habit, which are gifts of the physical body. Gradually, in the course of repeated Earth-lives, we acquire these gains.[25]

Rudolf Steiner
Riddle of Humanity

The forces of sympathy and antipathy

Strictly speaking, the soul finds existence as a result of the tension between the body on the one hand and the spirit on the other, and its nature is determined in terms of *feeling*. The spirit-filled ego finds its function almost entirely in terms of action, which is the archetypal attribute of the *will*. It is characteristic of the will to unite itself with the deed or action that it brings about by the agency of the physical body, our corporeal nature. This is a highly significant quality, for it necessarily involves the generation of karma or self-created destiny according to how meaningful the relevant action is.[26] The deed could not be accomplished without the doer, and the necessary element of *unity* is invoked, a kind of "flowing over" into the action itself, upon which the ego of the doer has stamped something of his or her own individual character, at the same time bringing about some kind of change in the world, whether significant or trivial.

Now we know that it is Lucifer who is the instigator

of willed action. The instrument for that action is the dark, dense, and relatively – at least outwardly – inert physical body. In any deed two factors are at work: the ego as *agent*, and the corporeal principle or vehicle as *patient*. (The ever-present third factor representing the "tension field" between the two poles is of course the deed itself.) Here we have the paradoxical situation whereby a Luciferic influence (the soul-spiritual agent) is seen to be making use of what is fundamentally Ahrimanic (the corporeal patient.) This is how it is: there can be no other way.

As Steiner has asserted on many occasions, it is by virtue of our physical body that the sense of egoity or selfhood is experienced and for the most part generated, principally by the factor of *resistance* or pressure necessarily involved. This process necessarily involves the principle of *objectivity*, and by very definition, *antipathy*. Whatever we are united with is bound to be, *ipso facto, subjective* to us. This being so, *thinking* engages feelings – largely unconscious in this case – of *antipathy*. Unless we are able to objectify our thoughts they remain unformed and indeterminate, and our ideas lack coherence and structure. Thinking, therefore, is an Ahrimanic activity, and this we know. This propensity is seized on by the ego, as integrator of all *experiences* in the form of feelings, sense-impressions, memories, mental images and so on – whatever presents itself to our field of consciousness.[27]

Thoughts *per se* are dead, as befits products with strong Ahrimanic attributes. Concepts, definitions, logic and so on must by nature be rigid and fixed, otherwise the ego would not be able to handle them if they were mobile or semantically unsound. Much of our mental or intellectual life is spent employing as needful and appropriate procedures that are essentially *analytic* and/or *synthetic* in operation, and these are purely mechanical activities, which are enervating and fatiguing. We need only reflect on the liveliness, mobility and rapid changes we experience in our life of feeling to realize that intellectual processes must be lifeless. This is why we need to educate children through their feelings rather than through lessons intellectually conceived and delivered. We are able to control our thoughts, perhaps, but not our feelings; and in this connection ponder the fact that it is much easier to find feelings for our reasons than reasons for our feelings!

The heart as an organ of balance

Psychologists, educationists and others would do well to study the implications of Rudolf Steiner's observation that feeling is thinking in reserve, and also willing in reserve.[28] The life of the soul is lived in the experiencing of thinking, feeling and willing. Equidistant between the two behavioural poles, willing (Luciferic) and thinking (Ahrimanic), lies feeling, which is representative of purely human behaviour. Thinking ossifies and hardens; feelings in a positive sense are rejuvenating, and by means of artistically creative teaching methods, not only are children's aesthetic propensities fostered, but the rejuvenating effects can extend themselves into the realm of healing. From its central position between thinking and willing, feeling is of course nicely placed to be influenced by, and in turn to influence, both of these opposite soul-qualities, and this is achieved by the exercise of the faculties of sympathy and *antipathy*, which are in ceaseless oscillation whenever we are in a state of conscious awareness.

Ahriman's abode in us is centred in the brain and central nervous system which supports it as our organ of thinking, and our bony framework. Lucifer's domain is for the most part our vascular system and metabolic/limbs system, upon which our life of will is focused. Neither faction is present in a directive capacity in our rhythmic system which lies between the other two systems and is, by long tradition and in fact, the seat of our life of feeling. The heart, with which is connected the life-sustaining blood, has obviously important associations with the metabolic system, and hence the sympathetic, subjective will-nature, and the lungs bear antipathetic, objective relationships with the outside world by reason of the air we breathe. All this is necessarily so, and the interrelationships are not difficult to discern.

The heart is known to be a kind of inner "sense-organ" for the whole human organism; and part of its function is, organically and in soul-spiritual terms, to strive for a balance between the head system and the metabolic system, between thinking and willing, and – at least as far as this is possible – between sympathy and antipathy! The heart, with its centrally placed zone of power, is therefore ideally placed for counter-influencing them in turn within its ability, perhaps enhancing them or diminishing them. The modifying influence of the heart as a balancing agent tends to resist excessively Luciferic temptations. At worst, these take the form of giving expression to the kind of actions that manifest an unreasonably high proportion of egotistical *will*-activity, such as excessively headstrong and domineering behaviour, perhaps incorporating unrealistic schemes, extravagant ambitions and exaggerated selfish actions of all kinds.

Where Ahriman is concerned, it is the *thinking*-activity that becomes subject to various aberrations. This may well manifest itself in speculative thinking, excessive emphasis on purely intellectual issues and such stock-in-trade as abstractions, dubious hypotheses, pedantry, over-dependence on purely empirical research, thinking along logical-positivist or deterministic lines, and suchlike. It is virtually impossible for Ahriman, bereft of any kind of feeling, even to comprehend what stirs in the human heart. Lucifer knows very well that every kind of passion and emotion reside there: love, hate, lust, envy, jealousy, fear, courage, hope, devotion, joy, sorrow, despair, gloom, optimism, pessimism, depression, elation, enthusiasm, anger and so on. Any of these – and countless other soul-sensations – when taken to excess spells trouble.

Cold fire – an unholy alliance: Considered objectively, there is little doubt that the most influential and indeed powerful factor in modern civilization is television, and its very sinister "down-side" will become increasingly apparent during the coming decades. These downside effects will be seen to have truly devastating consequences on social life, first in the West, and later in following cultures. Socialization and education by means of television is practically the norm in many domestic scenarios, and babies and young children are being conditioned to violence and crime by means of it. The medium is becoming increasingly recognized as the anti-social influence that it is, and this fragmenting of social and family life is another insidious Ahrimanic trait, which is dis-uniting and reductionist in its influences.[29] A further Luciferic inclination is towards unification of all kinds, and the implementation of this is, for example, that the image of the same news-reader in action is seen and heard in countless millions of homes all over the globe. This extends to sport, entertainment and many other programmes reaching all parts of the world by means of satellite tele-communication. This makes for conformity, and thence to uniformity, so that the various cultures are being eroded and tendencies towards the homogeneous fostered and promoted.

These are a few of the many dangers that have accompanied the universal massification and levelling out of the nations of the world. But too many people are thoroughly hooked on the television drug for it ever to be abandoned, in spite of the growing realization that it is a curse as well as a very mixed blessing. Lucifer's hold is far too firm, and Ahriman is more than happy to oblige: both are set to profit from it in an extraordinarily equal degree. It seems that we have to live with it, just as we do every potential danger.

In the case at issue, with both the Devil and Satan making up a kind of unholy alliance, it is difficult, if not impossible, to play one off against the other, to harness the forces of one in opposition to those of the other, as it is so often possible to do. "The acts of supersensible beings," declared Steiner, "can be described as good or bad; the beings themselves – never!"[30] In any case, there is no point in withdrawing from the manifest consequences of the influences of either Lucifer or Ahriman: they must be faced and dealt with – but how? Rudolf Steiner supplied the answer in one brief statement: "It is a matter of finding the way towards understanding the spiritual world with the very same powers as we also use to understand the outside world".[31]

> *Through our body we hold together what is really seeking to become "ideal" in the universe. But while we go through life and retain memories of our experiences, we leave behind in the World something still further behind our memories. We leave it behind us in the course of time, and must experience it again as we retrace our steps... Our Earthly memories are transient, and become dispersed through the universe. But our Self lives behind them; the Self that is given us again from out of the spiritual world, that we may find our way from time to eternity.*[32]
>
> Rudolf Steiner
> *Anthroposophy and the Inner Life*

Chapter Four
Christ – the One who Intercedes

Even though Lucifer towers above, it must be shown that the Christ raises his hand in compassion. Lucifer is not supposed to be toppled by the power of Christ, but plunges down by his own power because he is unable to bear the radiance of the Christ nearby, and the Christ looks up and raises His brow toward Lucifer. Similarly, Ahriman is not conquered by any hatred from Christ, but because he feels he cannot stand the forces emanating from Him. The Christ, however, towers in the middle as the One who... not through His power, but through His very being, induces others to overcome themselves, rather than being overcome by Him.*[33] *

Rudolf Steiner
Christ in Relation to Lucifer and Ahriman

Back to the Old Testament

Rudolf Steiner repeatedly pointed out from many standpoints that world history is becoming increasingly involved with Ahrimanic influences. As mentioned elsewhere, the time is ripe for this in terms of historical necessity. Lucifer, throughout all the Ages of the Post-Atlantean aeon, has bestowed on humankind significant and valuable gifts, more particularly our freedom of choice, as typified in the biblical story of Adam and Eve. As the Tempter who enticed them to eat of the fruit of the Tree of the Knowledge of Good and Evil, Lucifer brought it about that our remote ancestors came to know the difference between them. Hitherto, living in the Garden with God himself, they had known only the Good; Evil was necessarily entirely absent. By

* This extract refers to the sculpture known as The Group.

long tradition, the fruit of the Tree was the *apple,* ancestor of the species *Malus floribunda* – but the acid "crab" variety rather than our modern delectable cultivars. The Latin word *malus* is an adjective meaning *bad* or *wrong,* and by implication and association, *ill,* more particularly in the soul-spiritual sense. The Hebrew word translated as "evil" in most bibles is *ra,* but it could equally well be translated as "bad", and this is the more obvious term expressive of polarity to "good".[34]

In his *Verses and Meditations,* Rudolf Steiner includes two short *sprüche* which refer to the two pillars at the entrance before King Solomon's Temple. The right hand one Solomon named Jachin (Hebrew: foundation) and the left hand one he named Boaz (Hebrew: fleetness, strength) (2 Chronicles 3:17).

J
In pure Thinking thou dost find
The Self that can hold itself.

Transmute the Thought into Picture-life
And thou wilt know creative wisdom.

B
Condense thy Feeling into Light:
Formative powers are revealed through thee.

Forge thy Will into deeds of Being:
So shalt thou share in World-creation.[35]

Steiner states that we enter Earthly life through Jachin, assured that what is there outside in the macrocosm now lives in us, that we are a microcosm; for the word Jachin signifies "The divine poured out over the world is in you". Similarly, what is contained in the word Boaz means something like "What I have hitherto sought within myself, namely strength, I shall find poured out over the whole world; in it I shall live". Boaz, he asserts, is the entrance into the spiritual world through death; moreover, life is only to be found in the balance between the two.[36] Interestingly enough, discernible in these verses are references to Ahriman to our right in J (foundation), with its connotations of Word/Wisdom/Thinking, and Lucifer to our left in B, (strength) with obvious references to Feeling and Will, qualities within us for which he is accountable. Material for meditative reflection indeed!

"The Representative of Mankind"

Rudolf Steiner's well-known sculpture, to which he gave this title, came to be known in familiar terms as merely "The Group". The representative of humanity is taken here to be the Christ, who is modelled as the central figure and whose gesture apparently is one of holding off Lucifer from above, and Ahriman from below, but this is not actually the case. Howbeit, this pose may be construed as indicative of *balance;* and the message for us all is abundantly clear: Lucifer and Ahriman are to be understood as being *realities*, actual, valid and substantive, and not merely as *abstractions*, metaphorical, symbolic or allegorical. This sculpture stands as a permanent reminder that we, too, must strive to hold Lucifer and Ahriman in balance. Furthermore, whether we accept and understand this or not, they are inextricably entangled in our very nature and constitution, and have to be reckoned with. Those who remain ignorant of these facts are obliged to conduct their lives according to their instincts, impulses, abilities and predispositions, more or less letting themselves drift on the tides of circumstances, vaguely hoping for better things: to become better people, and leave the Earth all the better for their sojourn on it.

All this means that we should make every effort to discover just how we ourselves relate to Lucifer and Ahriman, and take their influences into consideration by means of greater and more discerning self-knowledge. The problem here is that of *subjectivity*. Try as hard as we may, it is virtually impossible for anyone to remain entirely *objective* about himself or herself, and this is why a thorough knowledge of the temperaments, as representing various points of reference, is strongly to be recommended. Every attempt to be as objective as possible about one's own main and secondary temperament by means of reflection and self-criticism, employing "backward review" techniques and the like, is never lost. It can only be to our advantage in terms of spiritual development if we practise re-tracing, in imagination, our actions during the day, but in reverse order; that is to say, from the time of preparation for sleep at the end of the day back to the moment of waking that morning. It is all too easy to "wallow" in our personal characteristics, blaming them for our shortcomings, foibles and weaknesses, when we know only too well that these should be resisted; or worse still, blaming others for our own deficiencies.

Not I, but Christ in me

Those who tread the path of personal development and take into account this profoundly esoteric statement will, without difficulty, arrive at the consideration that almost every person we meet can say it, too! In other words, when we exercise our ego-sense whilst confronting another individual, we are, either consciously or unconsciously, seeking to espy – and acknowledge – the Christ in that person. With The Group in mind, it will be incumbent on us to strive to discern in each fellow human being a *representative of mankind* in the sense of the quotation above. With enhanced perceptivity gained as a consequence of whatever knowledge of the temperaments we are able to accumulate, we shall be able to perceive how a particular individual is succeeding in maintaining a balance between the Luciferic and Ahrimanic attributes inbuilt into his or her whole being. We shall then be in a position to determine what, in terms of sympathy and antipathy in the light of our understanding of the temperaments, how best to approach and interact with that individual. With this attitude permeating our behaviour, we soon come to a realistic notion of two representatives of humanity encountering what is Christlike in each other.[37] This whole nexus of feeling and thinking should remain as a fundamental mood of the soul during any encounter with another human being, whether meaningful and significant, or fleeting and inconsequential; but at least the lowest rung in the ladder of social interaction, namely common courtesy, will have been mounted.

Our eyes, it is said, are the windows of our soul, and the abstract term "eye contact" is employed in common speech nowadays. Rudolf Steiner extended this notion in typical fashion:

> *Kind words spoken to us have a direct effect on us, just as colour affects our eyes directly. The love living in the other's soul is borne into your soul on the wings of the words. This is direct perception; there can be no question here of interpretation.*[38]

As the soul is the arena for the interplay between

sympathy and antipathy, our likes and dislikes in all their variety figure large in our everyday life. Reflection will show that whatever is present in our *antipathy* tends in the general direction of our faculty of *thinking*, whereas our *sympathy* inclines towards our faculty of *willing*.[39] As remarked earlier, it is uncommonly difficult to be entirely objective about anything, but the cold reserve of the cerebral melancholics, and the bland indifference and caution of the phlegmatics, generally ensure that nothing rash or impulsive, not to mention imprudent, is seriously contemplated. Such folk are not, of course, paragons of objective virtue, for the counter-balance swings in with a vengeance! They may be objective about the outer world, but they are thoroughly subjective about themselves and their own little worlds. They may not have illusions about their environment, but delusion may reign within.

It is reasonable to contend, therefore, that the more passive, reflective, "inner" individuals, the typical convergent thinkers, are those of melancholic or phlegmatic propensities. Melancholics are so innately self-involved that they are generally happy in their own company, and may resent interference and distraction. Phlegmatics don't like to be bothered about anything that does not coincide with their idiosyncratic interests, and by the same token will not be inclined to bother other people unnecessarily. In their own way, phlegmatics and melancholics are "closed in": melancholics pre-occupied with their own physical body with all its dullness and heaviness, and phlegmatics content to be left to stew in their own juices.

Conversely, it is to be expected that the more active, extraverted, energetic individuals, those who tend to think divergently – and they include so-called lateral thinkers – are sociable in nature, and tend towards "flowing over" into their environment in acts of will, mostly leaving their mark temporarily (sanguines) and rather more permanently (cholerics). In any case their qualities of creativity, including artistic creativity, enthusiasm, zeal and vision (with just a hint of the visionary, perhaps), are unquestionably Luciferic in character. Such characters find it difficult to be objective with regard to the outer world, because they are, so to speak, too "close" to it, too involved, too much wrapped up in it. They may survey whatever tasks need to be addressed, and plan accordingly in great and sufficient detail. But any such objectivity is all too often swept away by some grandiose, pretentious, or high-flown scheme or other that amounts to little more than castles in the air. So when the crash comes, in terms of shattered pride and self-esteem, or perhaps in monetary terms, objectivity-plus cuts in, and a few well-deserved lessons are learned.

Rudolf Steiner was always careful to point out that Lucifer and Ahriman work together, or at least appear to. In any case you may be sure that if you get a whiff of Luciferic enticement, Ahriman will be around to scent it too, and get you by the scruff of your neck! This is always a most profitable exercise set by the school of life; for it is said that in the final analysis experience is by far the best teacher – because it manages to teach us very thoroughly the lessons we don't want to learn! When it comes to politics, right wing parties are under the influence of Ahriman, whereas left wing parties are firmly in the clutches of Lucifer – simply follow their antics!

Ahriman versus Lucifer in human nature

Lucifer, as light-bearer, is responsible for our capacity for sense-perception and hence our waking consciousness by reason of our *astral body*. He it is who "fires us up" with fervour and enthusiasm, who aids us in our creative thinking, and everything associated with *enlightenment* or *illumination*. In a very real sense, he is the god of tomorrow, who imparts the qualities of hope, eagerness, anticipation and ardour. In addition, Lucifer rules in our passions: we have him to thank for our intensities of love and hate, our raptures, blisses, ecstasies and thrills, and all that we experience as euphoric. Needless to say, therefore, he is above all the god of *temptation*.

The dichotomous model of ourselves as being of Ahrimanic propensities (corporeal nature comprising physical and etheric bodies), and Luciferic influences (soul/spiritual nature comprising astral body and ego), is a basic one, and needs to be kept in mind. The event of the temptation of Eve in the Garden of Eden marks the point at which these Luciferic influences became prematurely mixed up in the soul-powers contained in our astral nature, namely thinking, feeling and willing. This legacy is of course with us still, for confusion of these soul-functions may be taken to be strongly characteristic of human nature and behaviour. We are very much awake in our thinking, but we are dreaming in our feeling life, and unconscious in the activation of our will impulses.

The danger in all this is of course the tendency for the astral forces, impulses and stimuli to gain precedence over the ego itself, when the reverse situation should obtain. We discuss elsewhere how the etheric body, sandwiched as it were between the physical body below and the astral body above, is well placed for influencing both. It is evident from observation and experience, however, that although co-operation with and power over the patient, long-suffering physical body is abundantly plain, influence of any significance over the astral body is not very apparent. This is because, as Rudolf Steiner explains, the etheric body as it were rebounds, seeking preponderance over the astral nature.[40]

It is at this interfacing plane in the human constitution that Lucifer and Ahriman actually confront each other: the astral forces, which are centrifugal in their mode of operation, strive to work their way more deeply into the etheric body, and the etheric forces with their centripetal dynamics attempt to gain ascendancy over the astral nature. In this scenario the etheric body suffers ascendancy by the older physical body in the lower nature, and in our higher nature the astral body is subject to the preponderance of the ego, both thereby bringing pressure to bear towards the central area of confrontation between Lucifer and Ahriman. We are, at all times and in all circumstances, striving to maintain a state of equilibrium between Ahriman, ensconced in our lower, corporeal nature, and Lucifer, equally snugly entrenched in our higher, soul-spiritual nature. This meditation given by Rudolf Steiner can be illuminating with reference to the four temperaments.

See thou, mine eye,
The Sun's pure rays
In crystal forms of Earth.

See thou, my heart,
The Sun's spirit-power
In Water's surging wave.

See thou, my soul,
The Sun's cosmic will
In quivering gleam of Air.

See thou, my spirit,
The Sun's indwelling God
In Fire's abounding love.[41]

Ahriman is by intention atomistic and fragmentary; that is to say, well and truly *reductionist* in goal and objective, and it must not be forgotten that he invented the "divide-and-conquer" strategy, and frequently succeeds in obtaining his aims and ends by this means. Rudolf Steiner was tireless in his warnings that Ahriman is already busy at preparing the way for his incarnation in the third millennium AD, thus *balancing out* Lucifer's incarnation in China in the third millennium BC.[42] The central point between the two is of course the Incarnation of the Christ in the body of Jesus of Nazareth at the baptism in Jordan. This gesture of equilibrium is expressed in "The Group", and from this we get the clear message that, as Christ maintains Lucifer and Ahriman in balance, so must we – and this with more than a hint of the notion of "Christ in me".

Lucifer and Ahriman are at their most dangerous to our evolutionary progress when we are not aware of them, when we are not alert to their wiles, for they are both constantly watching for opportunities to entrap us, and bend us to their purposes. In a very real sense, it is a battle for our consciousness, and in terms of the present state of conflict Ahriman is very well placed, at least in our Western-type culture. As mentioned elsewhere, Lucifer has to a certain extent already done his best and his worst as far as civilization is concerned, and Ahriman is already preparing for his incarnation in the third millennium.

Since Lucifer's incarnation in the third millennium BC, the most significant event in human and indeed cosmic history has been the incarnation of the exalted spiritual being known to us as the Christ, who has united his destiny with that of the Earth, and is, as it were, resident in the etheric environment of our planet itself. Without this intervention, the human race, and even the Earth itself, would have been doomed to extinction. This notion, needless to say, forms the basis of what we know as Christian religious beliefs and their formation and development over the past two millennia. With regard to Christian doctrine concerning the so-called second coming, Rudolf Steiner steadfastly maintained that it lies in humanity's evolutionary way forward for us to become capable of perceiving the Christ Being in the Earth's etheric envelope.[43] It need hardly be added that these events have to do more with cosmic history than the beliefs which form the justification for the organized Christian religion we know today.

"I am the Way, the Truth and the Life"

It has already been mentioned how the Christ being is seen to occupy a central point in many and various ways. Lucifer is still influential in the East, where so many religions tend towards traditional ritual and a kind of devaluing of the human ego. In the West it is Ahriman who rules, where the sense of ego is artificially enhanced by emphasis on personal survival after death, "being saved" and so on. Midway between the two appeared the Christ, symbolically as well as actually placed in terms of both geography and history. The westward sweep of our Indo-European civilization carried Christianity with it, so that Christendom developed in occidental countries rather than oriental ones.

By the same token, Lucifer's influence in the East has waned somewhat, with many oriental nations becoming more and more Ahrimanic in character. In the West, Ahriman's power has reached overwhelming proportions, and it is small wonder that so many westerners are turning to the East for spiritual sustenance. The main ingredient that attracts are the twin doctrines of reincarnation and karma, and there is ample evidence that these existed also in the West, but were crushed by Church doctrine over the centuries. Rudolf Steiner argued that these truths are in every respect compatible with a Christianity bereft of them, and asserted that their verity will be re-established by reason of historical necessity in the near future. Gradually and slowly, world balance in these regards is being brought about.

> *When the great impulse, the Christ Impulse, came upon the Earth, there resounded for the first time, clear and distinct, a new speech... Christ transformed the speech of the old initiates and said: "It is possible for all individuals to cultivate their own personality; it is possible that they should not obey the physical bond of blood relationship alone; but that they should look into their Ego, there to seek and find the Divine!" In that Impulse which we have called the Christ Impulse, lies the power which enables us, if we have united ourselves therewith, to establish a spiritual bond of universal kinship among all people, in spite of the individuality of the Ego.*[44]
>
> Rudolf Steiner
> *The Gospel of John* (Cassel course)

Chapter Five
Living with Lucifer and Ahriman

You must feel the whole weight of these words: to love the Truth; not to love lies for the sake of convention, for the sake of a pleasant social life. To be easygoing when it comes to lies is just as bad as loving them. In the immediate future the world will not progress through frivolous indifference where lies are concerned, but only if we freely and openly profess ourselves for the Truth.[45]

Rudolf Steiner
Polarities in the Evolution of Mankind

Nature versus sub-Nature

Since the dawn of early civilization about 100 centuries ago, our ancestors have experienced an extraordinary richness and variety of every kind in their religious and artistic life, as the relics of successive civilizations and cultures amply demonstrate, from Ancient India and since in the Persian, Egyptian, and Greco-Roman times. However, in modern times, that is to say, since the fifteenth century, it is safe to assert that a gradual deterioration has set in, and this coincided with the growth in individualism in the social sphere and the tremendous spurt in the advancement of material science and technology. All this is symptomatic of the steady progress of Ahriman, and of his influences becoming more and more evident since the Middle Ages. Moreover, in the last few centuries every aspect of our whole Western culture has been infiltrated by purely materialistic ideologies and philosophies, accompanied by a rapid decline of interest in religious faiths, particularly those of the organized churches.

The wisdom and extreme spirituality of Lucifer is

also in danger of decline, to be replaced by the sheer intellectual cleverness of materialistic science, the god of which is Ahriman. He is also the god of the underworld, of *sub-nature,* to which belongs everything mechanical, electrical and electronic in nature and construction. His speciality is lying and deviation from what is true and authentic. We have only to think of the whole realm of *graphics* and "virtual reality", which conjure up pictures of that which is unreal and unnatural. Ahriman has coerced Lucifer, by means of the agency of human powers of imagination and ingenuity, to serve his own purposes.

We see the world around us becoming increasingly *de-natured* by every possible means. The Earth and its resources have been ruthlessly exploited to serve Mammon in the shape of vested business and commercial interests, and we must be forgiven if despair, apathy and listlessness begins to permeate our own thinking, feeling and willing. Ahriman is merciless, implacable and seemingly invincible; and the blind indifference to his wiles, lies and sub-natural procedures is evident in such practices as organ transplants, in vitro fertilization and mechanistic medical treatments, immunization, vaccination and other prophylactic measures, which are operative in every hospital and surgery in the West. Ahriman is also the deity of death, and the growing interest in euthanasia, cryonic suspension and other macabre practices must be expected to increase even more.

As ever, Lucifer is stirring up enthusiasms for holistic approaches to medicine instead of atomistic; "green" attitudes to agriculture and nature conservation in general, anti-pollution measures of all kinds – all pro-life and anti-death in philosophy and practice. As always, the surest way to bring matters back into some kind of equilibrium is to conspire with Lucifer against Ahriman, and wrest from him what is his. In our increasingly mechanistic environment, and in a world where the short-term profit motive rules, and economic considerations are put before social considerations,[46] we need to introduce whatever Luciferic attributes we can muster. By calling upon as much optimism and enthusiasm for the task, however long and arduous, we are thereby combating Ahriman and keeping him at bay. This will almost certainly entail a kind of *willing-out-of-the-spirit* – and that is a very long and arduous task. Rudolf Steiner often quoted Goethe's statement to the effect that working out of love for the task is eminently expressive of freedom in action.

It is always helpful to bear in mind that they should be regarded as being somehow reciprocal in their operation: the Luciferic powers balancing out the Ahrimanic, and vice versa, as a matter of spiritual-scientific principle. That is to say, if Luciferic influences are seen to be at work in a particular area, we may be absolutely sure that those of an Ahrimanic nature are also present in some form or other, even if they are not directly or immediately detectable. Take, for instance, our choice of words when speaking or writing. If we require a word, as in writing a poem or other work of literary licence, to be of a multi-faceted nature, with many connotations and inferences, or even in the nature of *double entendres*, that is to say, in an artistic way, we would do well to call upon the powers of Lucifer, god of the arts and the artistic. If, however, we are writing a scientific treatise, and need to define our terms and express ourselves with great precision, with exactness of understanding in mind, then we summon Ahriman to our aid. Fixity in every sense is entirely appropriate in such circumstances, whereas when we are expressing ourselves through poetry and verse it is Lucifer, the god of freedom to whom we owe this precious possession, who should be invoked.

Everyday living with Lucifer and Ahriman

We have Lucifer to thank for all that is connected with Religion and Art and all things for which dedication to a cause and creative zeal for everything beautiful is involved. However, even with such an essentially Luciferic determinant as religion, Ahriman is lurking nearby to exact his share of the feast. Into the midst of all the euphoria and gladness of knowing that one's immortal soul has been saved, the hymns of praise and the fluttering of angels' wings in the astral nature of the whole of worship, Ahriman makes his presence felt. Congregations in the older, established churches are showered with commandments, precepts, teachings and preachings, even warnings and threats, concerning what has to be done to remain in God's favour. Liturgies and rituals, ceremonies and other prescribed programmes are religiously observed, all reeking of tradition and authority, and rigidly fixed beforehand. However, when Lucifer stirs even greater fires of religious ardour, we have the so-called charismatic, "free" churches, with no official hierarchy of priesthood nor set prayers, but with free congregation participation, and even mildly frenetic popular music. The rhetoric flows, everyone is an orator when inspiration strikes, and the atmosphere is positively aglow with celestial radiance.

The musical-poetical arts, which are open to imaginative interpretation of an individual nature, are super-Luciferic in constitution, whereas those of plastic-formative nature and more fixed in character, such as painting and sculpture, are tinged with Ahrimanic qualities. Music has progressed from the notion of "a concourse of sweet sounds" through its Romantic phase, which retained for the most part recognizable components of rhythm, harmony and melody, to a kind of spiky, cacophonous discord in both "serious" and popular music, both of which have developed the more intellectual, inartistic treatment in favour of the tunes every errand-boy could whistle only a short time ago, and sentimental songs to swoon to. Here again we can easily detect the "free" or Luciferic influences, and the Ahrimanic ones, though it seems that, with dead, electronic, heavy sound-projection, he seems to have won the day. But antagonists are always present – always. The chap who lived next door to a DJ who projected such sound to excess, in terms of both length of time and strength of decibels, became so inflamed with Luciferic fervour that, he, with all the vigour at his command, took his axe, stormed up the next-door's stairs and laid about – not the DJ, but his infernal noise machine. He got off the subsequent charge of assault on the apparatus with a small, yet decidedly Ahrimanic, fine.

The Stock Exchange is a temple to Mammon, but Lucifer is certainly more than welcome there. As belonging to the League of Bulls, ever ready to entice others to buy, buy, buy, so that they, having bought cheap, may sell later at a fat profit, he peddles in *greed*, and of course *hope.* As the only calamity left in Pandora's box after she had opened it, Hope remained available to humankind as a source of easement for all ills that had been released into the world. Ahriman is a patron of the Lodge of Bears, which also peddles in greed and hope, persuading punters to sell, sell, sell, so that they may buy cheap, and sell later at a fat profit. All the Bulls and Bears need is a cool head and good judgement – rare assets indeed! The other attribute they both deal in is that of *fear.* The Bulls fear that the market will fall, but at least not before that have taken their profits, whereas the Bears fear that it will rise, but at least not before they have had chance to buy cheap. The factor of hope included in Pandora's box of calamities is not by any means an unqualified gift from the gods strictly for employment on Earth.

Words, words, words

We cannot escape employing words, and here again ample opportunities for bending our twin tormentors to our will present themselves. Briefly, it is a matter of Luciferic picture versus Ahrimanic concept. Up above we have the *metaphor*, inflaming our imagination and inspiration, our fancy and phantasy, our vision and creativity. Down below we have the *definition*, fixed, rigid and final within its strict semantic limits. We can readily see the genuinely useful parts that both Lucifer and Ahriman play in our speech and writing, but as ever they have to be kept within limits. Incomprehensible verse masquerading as poetry is just as useless as jargon, unfamiliar idiom or sheer gobbledygook. Imaginative writing can and does give much pleasure and amusement, perhaps even more when set in liaison with its close cousin, the muse of music. Opera, operetta, and the modern musical are entertaining, and entirely Luciferic in nature and character. The words in themselves often express this:

> You must lie upon daisies and discourse in novel phrases
> of your complicated state of mind,
> The meaning doesn't matter if it's only idle chatter
> of a transcendental kind.
> And everyone will say,
> As you walk your mystic way,
> If this young man expresses himself in terms too deep
> for *me*,
> Why, what a singularly deep young man
> this deep young man must be!

Sir W S Gilbert: *Patience*, I

Ahriman, as mentioned elsewhere, is serious and sober, and there is not much mirth contained in the following extract from a computer manual:

> The encryption algorithm may be incompatible with the copy-protection techniques used by certain applications, and if you encrypt such a copy-protected programme, it may not run properly after decryption.

We may well ponder lingeringly on Ludvig Wittgenstein's maxim concerning words: "Don't ask for the meaning; ask for the use". We know that Ahriman is the Father of Lies. We also know that "terminological inexactitudes" are part of his stock-in-trade, as are the vocabularies of politicians, lawyers, estate agents and salespeople everywhere, not to mention copywriters for the printed and audio-visual media – and of course advertising agencies. The words themselves are always innocent; it is their users and the way they use them that have to be watched. For example, lottery and scratch card tickets are now referred to as "products", and the money thus gambled as "investments".

Rudolf Steiner once remarked that the time would come when the terms *Ahrimanic* and *Luciferic* would be employed in scientific circles in very much the same way as *negative* and *positive* are employed today. The spiritual beings thus referred to in collective terms must be taken as concrete realities, and on no account as abstractions. Moreover, it is most unwise – as well as wrong – to regard the Ahrimanic and Luciferic powers as somehow evil, destructive, or malign in absolute terms. Many people take the view that they should be shunned altogether, and even feared, but if they cannot exactly be welcomed as friends, at least they should be regarded as being possible allies as and when the circumstances and opportunities permit. According to these, we should feel free enough – *and confident enough* – to make use of Lucifer and Ahriman as allies as and when it suits us. In any case there is nothing we as human beings can do about their very real influences involving us, and it up to us to utilize them as far as possible for our own advancement on the road to perfection.

> *Thus we see how the progressive development of individuals is brought about by a kind of equilibrium, a kind of balancing of the two impulses. The story of the temptation, Christ's rejection of Lucifer and Ahriman portrayed in different ways by the evangelists is a sign that through the Christ Impulse, through the Mystery of Golgotha, people will be able to find the right path of development in the future. It is part of the true development of the Self and the astral body of every person that in this transformed Self and astral body individuals can receive the impressions of the parts played by Ahriman, Lucifer and Christ in human evolution; a correct development of the Self and the astral body will lead to this knowledge of the three impulses which determine the evolution of human beings. If we are to develop along the right lines we must overcome the egoity of the astral body in favour of the general interests of humankind and the world.*[47]
>
> Rudolf Steiner
> *Effects of Spiritual Development*

Chapter Six
The Age of the Consciousness Soul

We must ask ourselves what is the profoundest characteristic of precisely our epoch, of the evolution of the consciousness soul. It is that the human being must become acquainted in the most profound and the most intense way with all those forces which oppose the harmonising of humanity as a whole. For this reason a conscious knowledge of those Ahrimanic and Luciferic Powers working against the human being must be gradually spread.[48]

Rudolf Steiner
In the Changed Conditions of the Times

The twenty-first century and beyond

The coming centuries will witness a tremendous growth in the power of Ahriman in the evolution of the human race. The divine wisdom which lived in our ancestors, and which was available to their leaders for guidance of the various peoples was already falling away during the Age of the Intellectual Soul, represented in world history by the span between approximately the foundation of Rome in 747BC and around 1413AD. The power of *genuinely individual thinking* emerged at the time of the development of Greek philosophy and the Roman legal system from around the fifth century BC onwards. A period of comparative stagnation from the early centuries AD until about the fifteenth century, especially in northwestern Europe followed, when a great surge forward occurred in terms of political, social and economic affairs. This quickly developed throughout the Age of Reason and the Industrial Revolution to the Technical Revolution of modern times. The giant strides taken by modern materialistic science bears by very definition an unmistakably Ahrimanic character. The mastery of the physical-mineral kingdom by contemporary science and its attendant technology is virtually total, and this domain is firmly under the rule of Ahriman.

It is no coincidence that electricity emerged onto the scene of practical application at around the same time (1879) as Ahriman was given, in terms of cosmic and Earth history, a freer hand in terms of human history. Invisible and sinister when not properly under control, electrical technology formed the basis of electronic technology, and this kind of thing together with what has emerged as nuclear science was characterized by Rudolf Steiner as *sub-natural*, and belonging not to nature as dynamic and vibrant, but as purely mechanistic and dead. The ingenuity of the inventors and engineers in the development of electronic devices of all kinds, particularly in the fields of communication and audio-visual apparatus, is truly staggering. Their work has resulted in much good for humanity, but also – and inevitably so – much that is potentially highly harmful and destructive.

As always, whenever and in which field of operations Ahriman is discerned in his inspirational forces, Lucifer is close at hand to take advantage. This is particularly evident in the application of sub-natural techniques to television and associated gadgetry, which has provided an extraordinarily huge bonanza for Lucifer in that the *pictorial*, and hence by implication artistic, is necessarily and essentially involved. He it was who facilitated the introduction and development of all the arts in all their diversity and infinite variety. Music in its multiple forms, drama from serious works to ephemeral sit-coms and soap operas, competitive quiz shows and competitions involving sports and games, and entertainments of all kinds *which appeal to the human senses and emotions* in all their patterns, all bear the stamp of Luciferic influences taken to excess by the urge present in human nature for pleasure and self-indulgence. To have too much of even a good thing is not good in the long run; indeed it may be, and frequently is, evil. Of course, Ahriman claims a relatively small share in the shape of thought-provoking items such as documentaries, but even these are, quite deliberately, entertainingly tinged with Luciferic brilliance by their producers.

Earlier on it was mentioned that Ahriman is, at the present time, making supreme efforts to bring human consciousness under his control, and it would appear that television is one of his most powerful means of securing this. However, as Rudolf Steiner has stated again and again, it is rather a *Christ-consciousness* that humanity actually needs; and he maintained that the time is now here for the Christ Being to be perceived in the etheric realms associated with the Earth. An important consequence of such perception and subsequent understanding of this would be a raising into humanity's consciousness the realities of the truth that matter is complementary to – indeed a product of – what is spiritual in human beings and in Nature. Ahriman would have us believe, as orthodox materialistic science would have us believe, that we are creatures of body only, and not constituted as body, soul and spirit. The fourfold view of human nature can readily be reduced to a two-fold view; that is to say a corporeal nature comprising physical body and etheric body, and a separate soul-spiritual nature with which it is closely associated. The relationships of these principles to Ahriman and Lucifer respectively have been discussed elsewhere, as well as the Representative of Mankind as holding the two in balance.

The attainment of Christ-consciousness

It is Lucifer who incites us to *action:* he it is who inspires the conviction that we possess *the will to win*, which in order to be expressed must be followed up by actual *deeds*. However, in order for our actions to be meaningful we have to be in possession of *knowledge of Nature*, and since we live in the material world, this must include awareness of the substance of matter, its constitution and the laws by which it works. This knowledge must be acquired by means of our senses and their extension in the form of tools, instruments, and other apparatus, and brought to our consciousness. This knowledge of outer Nature is, so to speak, the gift of Ahriman. However, we have Lucifer to thank for the impulse for action, so that changes may be implemented in the outer world for optimal efficaciousness – and this, needless to say, for good or ill. So all the resourcefulness and imagination, ingenuity and inventiveness, initiative and energy, and determination to succeed bestowed by the Luciferic powers can be put to use in the manipulation by human beings of the knowledge of nature, and the laws of physics, chemistry, metallurgy and so on supplied by the Ahrimanic powers. Thus the scene is set for action, and humanity left free to choose whatever arena is necessary or desirable for the appropriate deeds to be done.

Living as we are in the Age of the Consciousness Soul, the element of *individuality* is dominant in our present culture, which signifies itself in all kinds of ways in which the ego expresses itself. Moreover, we know that our ego has a special relationship with our physical body, and hence is able to work with absolute directness through it. Sport is, as Steiner has asserted on many occasions, the religion of materialism, and it is small wonder that it is a modern craze. The growth in the areas of professional sports, athletics and organized games runs parallel to this, and the monetary element involved is another pointer to Ahrimanic influences. The frenetic pursuit of physical fitness, from ordinary jogging to regular work-outs at the local gym or fitness centre, are symptomatic of this cult of the purely physical – the *bodily.* Needless to say, all this propels active sportspeople. and even non-participant spectators, straight into the arms of Ahriman, who, as mentioned elsewhere, is mostly strongly influential in our corporeal nature as represented in our physical and etheric vehicles.

As we know, Lucifer and Ahriman always work in concert, and this is apparent in the increasing (Luciferic) interest in sports and games of a competitive nature, and the present enthusiasm for physical activities and exercises of all kinds. The feelings of euphoria, both those which arise from within the body by very reason of the activities themselves, and also those of a purely astral nature, such as enthusiasms expressed in team or personal loyalties for sports teams and individuals alike, indicate further the equalizing presence of Lucifer. Other practices which involve the ingestion or inhalation of hallucinogenic (tending to the Luciferic and illusion) and psychedelic (more towards the Ahrimanic and delusion), and similar drugs point clearly to experiences of an astral nature produced out of our physiological nature, our Ahrimanic nature. Alcohol directly affects the ego itself, and the consequences also fall into the realm of Luciferic experience.

Maintaining ego strength

If the ego is to maintain a balance between the opposing influences of Lucifer (above) and Ahriman (below), it must be *strong*. We should be able – indeed *must* be able – to stand firm within our own being, to actually *feel* that we are integrated within ourselves, and in command of our faculties, particularly in our power to think clearly and logically, and in our will. That is to say, we must possess sufficient determination to tackle the task before us to the very best of our ability, and complete it. Unfortunately, modern life does not provide much opportunity for people's ego strength to develop as it needs to – and just when genuine strength of character is demanded by it. Our whole system of education as provided by mainstream schools does not allow of this, for it all too often produces school leavers and higher education students who are woefully lacking in this personal quality. While at school they are virtually told what to think, and when they get home they are bombarded by radio and television news and other programmes which perpetuate the situation. Escape into drugs may seem an easy way out, but it is one that presents seriously escalating problems. All young persons need all the help they can get to withstand the tremendous pressures of various kinds exerted by the mass media.

It seems that only those schoolchildren who are naturally precocious are able to cope with the excessive demands made on them. Those who can't keep up the pace opt out of the system, and both over- and underachievers tend to suffer a state of "burn-out" soon after puberty. Pupils and students have little defence against the pressures, stresses and strains which crowd in on them from all sides. The result is a tendency to lapse into indolence and lethargy, love of ease and entertainment, and apathy concerning the diminishing number of job opportunities. The growing incidence of truancy, the increasing nervousness and anxiety which afflict examinees when the results are awaited, expressed as worry, fear and even dread to the point of suicide, all point in the same direction.

Even the ordinary vicissitudes of life prove too much for many people, as indicated by the increasing numbers of individuals seeking medical help because of panic attacks, depression, the need to escape from their predicament, and so on. The rapid changes in the political, social and economic life of the country leave people bewildered and anxious. They are continually told what to think, and even what to feel, by the appropriate "experts" and commentators, politicians, radio and television presenters, programme makers and entertainers alike; they grow up to be weak-willed, wavering in opinion and lacking in true powers of judgement. All these kinds of things result directly in lack of opportunities for the ego to develop properly.

The stresses and strains of modern life, the excessive importance placed on materialistic interests and ideologies, and the demise of everything that is spiritual in character, have had a scattering, weakening effect on everyone. People are finding it increasingly difficult to, so to speak, hold themselves together, to remain stable and in control, and give due consideration to everyday affairs. There is in ever-increasing tendency to "let go", simply because the ego is not strong enough to maintain the necessary firmness and resoluteness for true self-control. This letting go results in the inhibitions we all possess in terms of courtesy and common consideration for others being swept aside, and brute Luciferic selfishness to arise in their place.

The increasing number of ways in which egotism is made manifest in its many guises, is evident in "road rage" and similar aggressive behaviours; unwillingness to accept advice, fashion-consciousness and attention-seeking, arrogance and pride, the cultivation of status symbols and so on, are all becoming disturbingly obvious. Many people regard being self-assertive and drawing attention to oneself to be the mark of a strong ego, whereas the opposite is more likely to be the case. A true egotist possesses a weak ego, not a strong one; for it requires a very strong ego to act in genuinely unselfish and altruistic ways. Aggressors are usually bullies, and bullies are weak. Furthermore, attention seekers and possessors of status symbols act as they do in order to boost their ego and self-image, and advice is acceptable only from authority figures, "experts", and the ever-increasing numbers of professional counsellors. Astrologers are regarded as such, and command high fees. Readers of Sunday broadsheets, daily tabloids and magazines of all types get their advice free!

The individual who is able, even instinctively rather than consciously, to keep Lucifer and Ahriman in balance, is thereby exhibiting inner firmness, inner strength. Such a person is able to manipulate the powers and forces of each against the other in as effective a way as they are able. Take, for example, the "players" in a country's National Lottery, which is presented to the public as a "game" to be played. Ahriman usually sets the scene. In the current state of world economy, there are many without jobs or job security; many people on State benefit, and members of all socio-economic classes who do not feel secure financially who are, to say the least, disheartened if not downright depressed. The prevailing atmosphere in all deprived areas is one bordering on despair for their livelihood, and fear and even dread for the future. All such pessimistic feelings are thoroughly Ahrimanic in nature and character. The outlook is dark in every sense, with feelings and thoughts cramped, contracted and listless. The Christ in us can give us an understanding of how they feel within and suffer from the conditions imposed from without.

Desires, wishes, hopes and enthusiastic anticipation for better things are all wholly Luciferic. It matters not that such optimistic expectations of winning the jackpot are wildly unrealistic, with the chances of actually acquiring such a bonanza – and financial security – both equally remote in statistical terms. If such a near marvel does occur, and great riches won – alas! – the result is usually not as so fondly and eagerly imagined. Lucifer may have paid off, but there will be attendant troublesome problems that had never been expected, or even thought of – and all of an Ahrimanic nature. Resentment, envy, jealousy, covetousness, mistrust, suspicion, paranoia, even spite and grudge-bearing, will all be evoked – and such will be the price of success in terms of Luciferic temptation and enchantment. Unwittingly, punters are invoking Lucifer and Ahriman at the same time, whether the money involved is lost or won.

Whole nations are not exempt

Another example of Lucifer and Ahriman, ever the unforgiving and unabashed opportunists ready to work together when circumstances permit – *and always towards their own ends, of course* – is the present state of affairs in Europe. In the Balkans, Ahriman is doing his best to ensure that sheer, unabashed nationalism, even to the extent of ensuring "ethnic cleansing" bordering on genocide, takes place. As god of dissension, disharmony, discord and disunity; of hindrance, fragmentation and division, he is all too willing to keep the various ethnic groupings separate and distinct. The Luciferic counter-agencies are represented by impractical and ineffective United Nations "protectionism", the work of those praiseworthy, idealistic organizations such as the Red Cross, Mèdicins sans Frontieres, and the dozen or so charitable relief agencies from various countries.

As regards the so-called European Union, here strong Luciferic influences are seen to be at work, striving for unity, co-operation and concord. This may seem to be all very well as an ideal – and Lucifer loves ideals, especially the more unattainable ones – but the practical realities are proving to be stubbornly Ahrimanic in nature. For example, the issues surrounding a common currency, the contributions from the member states and the distribution of grant-aid monies, the various edicts and rules issued by unelected commissions and other bodies, intellectually conceived and bureaucratically administered, the so-called social chapter, and so on, are all sources of contention and dispute – and dare it even be mentioned – vested interests, from business opportunist business-people to the mafia.

Investigative journalism is revealing fraudulent practices which will bring more dissention, and *dis*unity. Through Ahrimanic newspapers the journalists' Luciferic aspirations are balanced by means of thorough, painstaking Ahrimanic research, revealing thereby in this case the Luciferic aspirations of those who gain their Ahrimanic ill-gotten monetary gains from graft, misrepresentation and downright lying and distortion of the truth. Remember, Lucifer and Ahriman help as well as hinder us in our divine discontent with what is happening at this time in history.

Nowadays, with society anything but stable, nothing is certain except uncertainty itself, and security of any sort is decreasing more and more rapidly. People are puzzled and bewildered at the recent and current changes that have shaken the hitherto solid foundations of social and economic life which have contributed enormously to the air of instability and volatility that is almost palpable. That society will continue to change there is little doubt; and people increasingly feel that they are not understood, that nobody cares about what the general public think. Yet it is urgent and vital that some degree of stability be fostered by means of a better understanding of ourselves and others. People are no longer able to cope with even minor vicissitudes of life, and the stresses and strains within society have resulted in ever-increasing numbers of sufferers seeking counselling or psychiatric help.

Rudolf Steiner stressed that we should do all in our power to cultivate our *ego sense,* one of our twelve senses. By this he meant not our own sense of self, *but the ego of another person*. This ego sense is experienced when we confront one of our fellow human beings, and is experienced for the most part unconsciously, though our conscious impression of the other person's individuality also contributes to this sense of ego. Ahriman is closely involved in this process, for it is one of his tasks to disunite and fragment in a reductionist manner that which is combined. The "unit of society", for so long thought to be the family, is no longer so: the basic unit of society is the *individual,* and this is everywhere evident in present times, with egotism and self-seeking becoming everywhere increasingly apparent. This is another argument in support of the urgent necessity for developing this ego-sense referred to earlier, because it will assist immensely in the development of our capacity to experience ourselves as belonging to the whole world which is increasingly developing alongside the ability to perceive the "I" or ego of other people, as Steiner pointed out.[49]

Lucifer and Ahriman alike, then, are good servants but bad masters, and they will gleefully exacerbate, intensify, magnify and strengthen virtues and vices alike, regardless of the consequences to whoever is sufficiently unaware, ignorant or wilful of these. Broken hearts, torn souls, crushed spirits – Lucifer cares not a fig. Ahriman urges us to disregard everything that cannot be validated by cold reason, icy intellectualism and frigid logic, all of which have their place in appropriate circumstances. At the same time he fosters ill-will, irresponsibility for the truth, insufficiently thought-out ideas, half-truths, and needless to say, lies of every kind. If human beings, out of their free will, lack of knowledge, proneness to persuasion, gullibility, naïvety, mental aberration or whatever *choose* to behave as they do, what business of anyone but their own? If they cannot differentiate between what is good or bad for them, how on earth are they going to learn – except by bitter experience? But it is on Earth that all experiences which result in further progress along the path of spiritual development have to be undergone. And what will come from experience of these are rewards for the spirit-filled ego in the shape of, for example, patience, longsuffering, compassion, steadfastness, altruism, fortitude, equanimity, self-sacrifice, tolerance and other desirable spiritual qualities which, when firmly incorporated into the individuality, are well beyond the reach of both Lucifer and Ahriman.

> *To the external aspect of Christian development the* inner *aspect will be joined more and more. What may be known through Imagination, Inspiration and Intuition about the higher worlds in connection with the Christ Mystery will increasingly permeate the thought, feeling, and will-life of humanity.*[50]
>
> Rudolf Steiner
> *An Outline of Occult Science*

Chapter Seven
Hope, Courage, Fear

For out of a rightly understood wisdom will a rightly understood goodness and virtue be born in the human heart. Let us strive after a real understanding of world evolution, let us seek after wisdom – and we shall find without fail that the child of wisdom will be love.[51]

Rudolf Steiner
The World of the Senses and the World of the Spirit

Where do we stand today?

In temporal terms, we are about one-quarter into the Age of the Consciousness Soul, which is due to run for another fifteen hundred years or so. Events in terms of preparation for the incarnation of Ahriman have intensified and accelerated. In terms of the three fields of human endeavour, namely Religion, Art and Science, Science is well in the lead. Religion is now moribund, for the human spirit has been denied as a clearly identifiable quality. Ministers of religion now talk in terms of psychology, but the soul has been annihilated by psychologists. Art, the other area thoroughly permeated with Luciferic influences, is barren with intellectualism, and thus also under attack from Ahriman.

Monistic materialism is now reigning supreme in every area of science – and this is the sphere of influence par excellence of Ahriman, as discussed elsewhere. Reductionist/atomistic ways of approaching Nature is the norm, and this, it will be recalled, is also an archetypal Ahrimanic attribute. The emphasis on individualism which has been growing steadily over the last few centuries, has taken a sudden spurt forward. Nationalism is everywhere rife in underdeveloped nations and countries, and on the individual level in so-called civilized societies this is also evidenced by the rapid growth of feminism, the destruction of the nuclear family, and the increasing consciousness of self evidenced by the escalating numbers of ways that egotism in society is expressing itself.

Having a strong ego is one thing, but the imposition of autocratic, self-centred behaviours of all kinds is another. If freedom of action be claimed as a right, then with it must go a commensurate degree of responsibility. Freedom of action on the part of others must be regarded as equally important, as must certain standards of Equality and Fraternity, the fostering of both of which also belongs to our evolution throughout the Age of the Consciousness Soul.[52] In very great measure Equality, Fraternity and Liberty are societal virtues strongly supported in Western democracies, as history shows. They also have strongly Luciferic qualities as witness the raising of expectations of the deprived masses, offering them hope and release from despair. At the same time Ahriman is seeking to exercise contrary influences and forces in the shape of conformity and uniformity, and maintaining affairs by bureaucratic methods, and the various European Union Commissions, by keeping everything in line – fixed, orderly and hedged in by myriads of rules and regulations – affords a good example of this.

The Fifth Post-Atlantean Epoch, or Age of the Consciousness Soul, will be marked as by historical necessity, anti-social behaviours of all kinds, not only by individuals and companies "to realize their full potential" and "do their own thing" in the form of Luciferic self-interest, but also by whole communities, nations and races, inspired by Ahriman and his divisive forces expressed in the currently rampant nationalism, "ethnic cleansing" and civil wars and disturbances in approximately thirty different areas of the world today (1995). Rudolf Steiner, a social scientist with a proven record of fulfilled prophecies, had this to say in 1919: "A chaotic economic life without direction; a life of rights become a mere striving for power; a spiritual life degraded to hollow phrases: this is the threefold character of social life we have had, and of which we must rid ourselves".[53] We have not been able to do this, and the affairs referred to are in a much more parlous state than they were immediately after World War I. As things stand today, they can only get even worse.[54] Steiner foresaw and warned of what was likely to happen, but he nevertheless maintained that the worsening social, political and economic conditions would result, eventually, after much pain, suffering and anguish, in a new social and personal awareness that would lead to stability and equilibrium throughout the civilized world.[55]

All fear and hope must be eliminated

As we have seen, fear is a thoroughly Ahrimanic trait, and hope is its Luciferic counterpart. With Rudyard Kipling's poem "If–" in mind, it is easy to relate fear to *disaster*, which we all fear, and hope to *triumph*, which we all aspire to in our endeavours:

> ...If you can wait and not be tired by waiting,
> Or being lied about, don't deal in lies,
> Or being hated, don't give way to hating,
> And yet don't look too good, nor talk too wise;
>
> If you can dream – and not make dreams your master;
> If you can think – and not make thoughts your aim;

If you can meet with Triumph and Disaster
And treat those two impostors just the same;
If you can bear to hear the truth you've spoken
Twisted by knaves to make a trap for fools,
Or watch the things you gave your life to, broken,
And stoop and build 'em up with worn-out tools...[56]

The meditative nature of the whole poem is plain, and reflective attention to it is richly rewarded. Triumph and Disaster are readily identifiable as imps of Lucifer and Ahriman respectively, and there are other clues in the poem, for example Kipling's emphasis on the Will as well as Thinking and Feeling, and his insights into spiritual matters, which included knowledge of reincarnation and karma. He was contemporaneous (1865-1936) with Rudolf Steiner, and was steeped in Indian culture.

Present help

As the central battlefield between these two opponents who, it must be emphasized, have no *conscious* evil intent towards humanity, we are not by any means left entirely on our own, without help or guidance. Rudolf Steiner gave some preliminary advice to those who have aspirations to follow the path of knowledge of the spiritual worlds which should be constantly kept in mind, stating the three areas of error to be avoided: exuberant violence of will; sentimental emotionalism, and cold, loveless struggle for wisdom.[57]

Since the instinctive wisdom our far ancestors possessed has fallen away, we have been left to our own devices. But means and methods of re-attaining such wisdom, *but in full consciousness*, are nevertheless available to us. The Western cultures have for the most part embraced Christianity as a source of certain aspects of this wisdom, but the emphasis was upon maintaining faith in the authority manifest in the scriptures in the Bible rather than direct attempts at attaining it. At the same time, if the guidance contained in these scriptures is religiously followed, considerable advancement is possible, and knowledge gained concerning those spiritual beings who have, in a certain but very definite sense, sacrificed their own progress to our own. These are, of course, Lucifer and Ahriman, otherwise the Devil as Tempter and Satan as the Evil One; and the Lord's Prayer can teach us much concerning these.[58]

The basic requirements to be observed by those aspiring to achieve knowledge of the spiritual worlds or divine wisdom as indicated by Rudolf Steiner[59] are readily discernible in the Christian scriptures. Briefly, these are:

(1) To pay heed to the advancement of bodily and spiritual health.
(2) To feel oneself co-ordinated as a link in the whole of life.
(3) To realise that one's thoughts and feelings are as important for the world as one's actions.
(4) To acquire the conviction that one's real being lies not in the outer world but in the inner world.
(5) Always to be steadfast in carrying out a resolution once taken.
(6) To be thankful for everything for which humanity is favoured.
(7) Unceasingly to regard life in the manner demanded by these conditions.

There can never be any incompatibilities between Christian doctrine rightly understood and the requirements for esoteric training or indeed spiritual science itself. What is of the greatest possible importance is that both paths lead eventually to an understanding and appreciation of the mission of Christ to the Earth and humanity.[60]

All this being so, it is reasonable to contend that individuals, whether progressing along the path of spiritual development by way of knowledge or that of observing the highest principles of the Christian faith, are all aiming to achieve the situation where they can truly say: *Not I, but the Christ in me*, in the meaning of Paul.(Galatians 2:20) We have seen all along that Christ, as the Representative of Man, in the sense of both Paul and Rudolf Steiner, as well as numerous mystics and divines, has as part of his task the keeping of Lucifer and Ahriman in balance on a cosmic scale. In order for us to be able to do likewise, it is essential that we recognize these opposing powers by dint of their characteristics. Now we know that the choleric and sanguine temperaments exhibit to a considerable extent the attributes of Lucifer, whereas the phlegmatic and melancholic temperaments those of Ahriman. From this it follows that we, insofar as we bear Christ within us in the Pauline sense and through our understanding of the temperaments, should strive to discern the Christ in people we meet and interact with. By reason of this, we should further endeavour to adjust our own behaviours with the end in view of enabling such individuals, as and when opportunities present themselves, better to understand themselves and their fellows.

This indication finds echoes in the second requirement for aspirants to spiritual enlightenment listed earlier, and supports arguments made elsewhere that we must strengthen our ego in the right way, the healthy way. The imp on either shoulder, which each one of us bears, can cease to be a concern for us in a negative way, for as a consequence of our knowledge of them we are able to harness their perfectly legitimate forces in ways that are altogether positive, and this not only for the furtherance on our own path to perfection, but also for that of our neighbours on theirs.

Looking forward to the Sixth Epoch, due to commence in about 1500 years' time, Rudolf Steiner contended, in a lecture given in Zurich on 9 October 1918, that early signs are already evident for the manner in which humanity is likely to develop. Spiritual science is in its germinal state at present, but the necessity for it to complement orthodox materialistic science in order for a fuller understanding of Nature and the universe to be reached is slowly gaining recognition. This will result in the widespread acceptance of the fact that human beings are primarily spiritual in nature, and only secondarily as material in constitution. From this will stem the conviction that within every human being resides a hidden divinity, which will lead in turn to a genuine conviction of the appropriateness of recognizing the universally human qualities in all races and nations of the world. That is to say, the factor of *kinship*, of all human beings being regarded so to speak as God's children, will become more and more firmly rooted.

Furthermore, there will be equally universal recognition of every individual's right to *religious freedom*. In effect, the established churches which represent organized religion will gradually be seen to be redundant, and already there are many indications of this coming about. Another important development will be the enhancement of the facility for attaining to spiritual insights and perception through thinking, by which the *reality of the supersensible worlds* may become clear to everyone. Thus should become established universal fellowship on the bodily level, freedom of religious life on the soul plane, and full recognition of spiritual science on the spiritual plane.

Ever-present help

Between Hope and Fear stands Courage, and again we are reminded of the Group. Courage is a thoroughly human characteristic, and is central to every endeavour, whether on the material or spiritual plane. This quality is certainly necessary in our keeping of hope and fear in proper proportion – until, that is, we no longer find them useful as crutches or as an excuse not to pursue the appropriate course of action. It is of course enormously difficult to strengthen our ego to this stage of control over our soul qualities which necessarily find their expression in Thinking, Feeling and Willing, yet this must be our constant aim. The following exhortation attributed to Dr Steiner is entirely relevant:

> *We must eradicate from the soul all fear and terror of what comes towards us out of the future. We must acquire serenity in all feelings and sensations about the future. We must look forward with absolute equanimity to all that may come, and we must think only that whatever comes is given to us by a world-direction full of wisdom. It is part of what we must learn in this age, namely to live out of pure trust, without any security in existence: trust in the ever-present help of the spiritual world. Truly, nothing else will do if our courage is not to fail us. Let us discipline our will, and let seek the awakening from within ourselves, every morning and every evening.*[61]

Notes and References

Theme quote:

Steiner R *Initiation, Eternity and the Passing Moment*, Anthroposophic Press, 1980, p 123

Chapter notes and references

1 Steiner R *The Four Temperaments*, Rudolf Steiner Publishing Co, 1944, p 6
2 Note: Lucifer (Luciferus) is the *light-bearer*, and not the Light itself, which is identifiable with the Christ (John 1: 8,9)
3 Steiner R *The Spiritual Guidance of Mankind*, Rudolf Steiner Publishing Co, 1946, p 84ff
4 à Kempis T *Of the Imitation of Christ* (XII, 2) Oxford University Press, 1947, p 19
5 Goethe W J von *Faust*, F Warne & Co, 1885, Part I, Scene III
6 Steiner R *The Effects of Spiritual Development*, Rudolf Steiner Press, 1978, p 59
7 *Von Seelenrätzeln*, Rudolf Steiner Verlag, 1990, (GA 21)
8 Childs G J *Understand Your Temperament*, Sophia Books, 1995, p 135
9 Steiner R *The Effects of Spiritual Development*, p 60
10 Childs G J *Steiner Education in Theory and Practice*, Floris Books, 1991, passim
11 Steiner R *The Effects of Spiritual Development*, p 45
12 ibid, p 44
13 Schwenk T *Sensitive Chaos*, Rudolf Steiner Press, 1965, p 65
14 Dickens C *A Christmas Carol*
15 Steiner R *The Effects of Spiritual Development*, p 46 and passim
16 *Knowledge of the Higher Worlds and Its Attainment*, G P Putnam's Sons, 1930, p 94
18 *Towards Imagination*, Anthroposophic Press, 1990, p 4f
19 Childs G J *Understand Your Temperament*, passim

20 Steiner R *Towards Imagination*, pp 27-35
21 Note: list of recommended books
Lucifer and Ahriman
The World of the Senses and the World of the Spirit
The Riddle of Humanity
22 Childs G *Understand Your Temperament*, passim
23 Steiner R *Anthroposophical Ethics*, Anthroposophical Publishing Co,1928,pp 60-62
24 Steiner R *The Effects of Spiritual Development*, p 45
25 Steiner R *The Riddle of Humanity*, Rudolf Steiner Press,1990, p 157
26 Steiner R *Theosophy*, Anthroposophic Press, 1946, p 60f
27 Steiner R *Theory of Knowledge Implicit in Goethe's World-Conception*, Anthroposophic Press, 1940, p 30 & Chap VIII, passim
28 Steiner R *Study of Man*, Rudolf Steiner Publishing Co, 1947, p 77
29 Childs G & S *Your Reincarnating Child*, Sophia Books, 1995, passim
30 Steiner R *Initiation, Eternity and the Passing Moment*, Anthroposophic Press, 1980, p 123
31 *The Destinies of Individuals and of Nations*, Rudolf Steiner Press, 1986, pp 77-78
32 *Anthroposophy and the Inner Life*, Rudolf Steiner Press,1994, p 130
33 The Group can be viewed at the Goetheanum, Dornach, Basel, Switzerland. See also:
Fant A, Wilkes J, Klingborg A, *Rudolf Steiner's Sculpture*, Rudolf Steiner Press, 1975, passim
Steiner R *Christ in Relation to Lucifer and Ahriman*, Anthroposophic Press, 1978, p 15
34 Note: The implication of ill-ness in other senses of badness is also present in this Hebrew word, although that for *bodily sickness* employed in the Old Testament is *chalah*.
35 *Verses and Meditations*, p 153
36 *Toward Imagination*, p 56f
37 *Life Between Death and Rebirth*, Anthroposophic Press,1975, p 78
38 *Toward Imagination*, p 54
39 *Education and Beyond*, Floris Books, forthcoming title, table

40 *World of the Senses and World of the Spirit*, p 44
41 *Verses and Meditations*, Rudolf Steiner Press, 1979, p141
42 *Lucifer and Ahriman*, p 10
43 Note: A comprehensive list of Dr Rudolf Steiner's Christology lectures and books is available from Rudolf Steiner Press, 51 Queen Caroline Street, London, W6 9QL
44 *The Gospel of John* (Cassel course) Rudolf Steiner Press, 1944, p 65
45 *Polarities in the Evolution of Mankind*, Rudolf Steiner Press, 1987, p 171
46 *World Economy*, Rudolf Steiner Press, 1949, passim
47 *Effects of Spiritual Development*, pp 137-138
48 *In the Changed Conditions of the Times*, Anthroposophic Press, 1941, p 85f
49 *The Riddle of Humanity*, p 199
50 *An Outline of Occult Science*, Anthroposophic Press, 1985, p 357
51 *The World of the Senses and the World of the Spirit*, Rudolf Steiner Press, reprinted Steiner Book Centre, 1979, p88
52 Steiner R *The Mission of Folk-Souls*, Anthroposophical Publishing Co, 1929, passim
Steiner R *The Threefold Commonwealth*, Anthroposophical Publishing Co, 1923, passim
Steiner R *From Symptom to Reality in Modern History*, Rudolf Steiner Press, 1976, p 44f
Barfield O *Romanticism Comes of Age*, Rudolf Steiner Press, 1966, pp 104-125
Childs G *Education and Beyond*, passim
53 Steiner R *Education as a Social Problem*, Anthroposophic Press, 1969, p 25
54 Childs G *Education and Beyond*, passim
55 Steiner R *How Anthroposophical Groups Prepare for the Sixth Epoch*, Anthroposophic Press, 1957
Steiner R *The Work of the Angels in Man's Astral Body*, Rudolf Steiner Press, 1980, passim
56 Kipling R *"Brother Square-Toes" – Rewards and Fairies*
57 Steiner R *Knowledge of the Higher Worlds*, G P Putman's Sons, 1923, and Rudolf Steiner Press, 1969, p 185
58 Steiner R *The Lord's Prayer*, Rudolf Steiner Press, 1942
Childs G *The Realities of Prayer*, Sophia Books, 1994, passim

59 Steiner R *Knowledge of the Higher Worlds and Its Attainment*, pp 93-106
60 Steiner R *Christ in Relation to Lucifer and Ahriman*, Anthroposophic Press, 1978, passim
61 Steiner R lecture, Bremen, 27 November 1910 (?). Various sources suggested, none of which is definitive.

Please note that these are but a few references to Steiner's six thousand or so lectures, and his written work. See note 43 for further information.

C# PROGRAMMING

EVOLUTION

SAMS 800 East 96th Street, Indianapolis, Indiana 46240

C# Programming Evolution

International Standard Book Number: 0-672-32602-7

Library of Congress Catalog Card Number: 2004091249

Printed in the United States of America

First Printing: April 2004

07 06 05 04 4 3 2 1

Trademarks

All terms mentioned in this book that are known to be trademarks or service marks have been appropriately capitalized. Sams Publishing cannot attest to the accuracy of this information. Use of a term in this book should not be regarded as affecting the validity of any trademark or service mark.

Warning and Disclaimer

Every effort has been made to make this book as complete and as accurate as possible, but no warranty or fitness is implied. The information provided is on an "as is" basis. The author and the publisher shall have neither liability nor responsibility to any person or entity with respect to any loss or damages arising from the information contained in this book or from the use of the CD or programs accompanying it.

Bulk Sales

Sams Publishing offers excellent discounts on this book when ordered in quantity for bulk purchases or special sales. For more information, please contact

U.S. Corporate and Government Sales
1-800-382-3419
corpsales@pearsontechgroup.com

For sales outside of the U.S., please contact

International Sales
1-317-428-3341
international@pearsontechgroup.com

Associate Publisher
Michael Stephens

Acquisitions Editor
Neil Rowe

Development Editor
Mark Renfrow

Managing Editor
Charlotte Clapp

Project Editor
Elizabeth Finney

Copy Editor
Kitty Jarrett

Indexer
Larry Sweazy

Proofreader
Linda Seifert

Technical Editor
Doug Holland

Publishing Coordinator
Cindy Teeters

Multimedia Developer
Dan Scherf

Book Designer
Gary Adair

Page Layout
Stacey Richwine-DeRome

Contents at a Glance

Table of Contents

About the Author

Kevin Hoffman started programming on a Commodore VIC-20 donated by his grandfather. Ever since then, he has been hopelessly addicted to programming. Instead of spending time outside, absorbing rays from that big yellow thing (he's not even sure what it's called), he spent most of his time as a kid and up through high school and college learning as many programming languages as he could get his hands on. At one time or another, he has written applications in ADA, Assembly, Scheme, Lisp, Perl, Java, Python, Tcl/Tk, C, C#, VB.NET, C++, Pascal, Delphi, Visual Basic, VAX/VMS Pascal, and BASIC, dozens of proprietary scripting languages, PL/SQL, and probably a few more that he can't remember. Oh, and he's even written a few programs for OS/2 and Mac OS X.

He started out working for a company that produces scientific instruments. He wrote code that interfaced PCs with data logging and gathering tools as well as real-time data analysis programs. From there he moved on to working technical support for Unix systems, PCs, SQL databases, and client/server applications. After that he made the infamous jump to a dot-com, where he wrote an extensive amount of Visual Basic, VBScript, and ASP code. After another job working with another n-Tier, COM-based ASP application, he moved to Houston, where he now endures the heat with his wife, dog, and two cats while working on ASP.NET and Web service applications, providing public records search Web sites and services.

Dedication

I would like to dedicate this book to Walter Kavanaugh MacAdam. When I was 10 years old, he gave me a Commodore VIC-20 and a wirebound BASIC programming guide. Sure, some kids might've wanted a BMX bike or something else, but he knew that's what I wanted more than anything else.

My uncle rescued the computer from the garbage, and my grandfather repaired it, hooking up a Commodore 64 disk drive and slowing it down to work properly on the VIC-20. I started teaching myself to program in BASIC and, with some help from Grandpa, managed to create my own text-based adventure game, complete with weapons and 12 rooms all painstakingly created with DATA statements. It was so efficient I still had 2KB left of memory when I was done. The world was my (albeit black-and-white) oyster.

Once I outgrew the VIC-20, my grandfather supplied me with a Compaq. It was a 486 Dx2/66 with 16MB of RAM. At the time, it was a powerhouse, and had plenty of horsepower for my new toy—Borland Turbo C.

Ahh, my C compiler. It was a good friend that served me well. I struggled with learning C. Strangely enough, that was the first advanced programming language I learned. Grandpa taught me patience and helped me learn how to teach myself what I needed to know.

Throughout my childhood, my grandfather supported me in learning everything I could get my hands on. If there was something related to learning that I needed, he made sure I had it. I might not have had all the advantages other people my age might have had, but one thing I never lacked was the ability to improve myself through learning.

After Grandpa gave me all the notes he'd taken while he was learning C, we both learned C++. Together, we wrote our first Win32 GUI front end. The GUI was a menu front end for his survey analysis program, aptly called Survey. It worked beautifully on Windows 3.1 and worked just fine on Windows 95.

This book is as much about the process of learning new technology as it is about the new technology itself. When I had to decide what sample application I wanted to use to illustrate all this cool technology and to teach people .NET, I couldn't think of a better example than Grandpa's Survey program.

I'm hoping that by using what he gave me (a world of opportunities), I'll be able to give some of that back to him by educating other people, something he valued above most else.

With that said, this book is for you, Grandpa.

Acknowledgments

First and foremost, I would like to thank my wife, Connie. She has somehow managed to put up with me coming home from my "day job," turning on my laptop, and working on this book shortly thereafter. I'm not sure how or why she tolerates it, but I'm certainly glad she does. In addition to putting up with my horrible schedule, she is the strongest source of support for everything I do.

This book couldn't be possible without the great people at Sams, including, but not limited to, Neil Rowe, Daniel Kent, Doug Holland, and Kitty Jarrett. I'm glad people like them are around to help edit and coax my random babbling into something coherent and pleasant for the reader.

I would like to thank Altaf and Jyoti for showing me how to live life instead of worry about it. Their simple advice has done me a world of good, including helping me relax while working on this book. Good friends like them are hard to find.

Lastly, I would also like to thank Agastya Kohli for invaluable help in coming up with the Hindi phrases for the globalization samples in this book.

We Want to Hear from You!

As the reader of this book, *you* are our most important critic and commentator. We value your opinion and want to know what we're doing right, what we could do better, what areas you'd like to see us publish in, and any other words of wisdom you're willing to pass our way.

As an associate publisher for Sams Publishing, I welcome your comments. You can email or write me directly to let me know what you did or didn't like about this book—as well as what we can do to make our books better.

Please note that I cannot help you with technical problems related to the topic of this book. We do have a User Services group, however, where I will forward specific technical questions related to the book.

When you write, please be sure to include this book's title and author as well as your name, email address, and phone number. I will carefully review your comments and share them with the author and editors who worked on the book.

Email: feedback@samspublishing.com

Mail: Michael Stephens
Associate Publisher
Sams Publishing
800 East 96th Street
Indianapolis, IN 46240 USA

For more information about this book or another Sams Publishing title, visit our Web site, at `www.samspublishing.com`. Type the ISBN (excluding hyphens) or the title of a book in the Search field to find the page you're looking for.

Introduction

How many times have you gone to Google and typed in some keywords for a problem that you need a solution for, only to find page after page of simple "Hello, World" examples? If you want to accomplish something by using Microsoft message queues, you'll undoubtedly find hundreds of examples on how to create a message that contains extremely simple data and put it in a queue. Or say you're looking for some good information on how to create an optimized data access layer. You'll certainly be able to find hundreds of examples on how to manually create a `SqlCommand` instance and invoke a stored procedure, probably from the Northwind database.

What if you're looking for information on how to integrate the data and functionality of a PocketPC application with a Windows Forms application? Likewise, what keywords do you give to Google if you're looking for best practices, design guidelines, and code samples for integrating a Windows Forms application with a Web service?

There are probably a few people out there who can pick up a book, read the examples in the book, and somehow manage to absorb and retain the material contained in that book. If those people really do exist, then I salute them and their supernatural learning abilities. We mere mortals learn by *application*.

Someone once told me that the more pathways there are to a particular bit of information in the brain, the longer it will be retained and the more quickly it can be recalled. This person probably knew a little something about programmers. The way I typically learn something new is by picking up a book. I start reading the book with the intention of making it through to the end. Invariably, somewhere around page 10, I put the book down and start tinkering. There are three different steps that have to take place for me to *really* learn the information I'm trying to absorb:

1. Read about the new technology until I get "lost."
2. Tinker with the technology until the haze of confusion wears off.
3. Apply the new technology in a form or method that wasn't shown to me by a book or an example. In other words, I make the technology my own.

There are a lot of excellent books on the market right now that cover some kind of .NET-related topic. You can find books solely on remoting, books that cover nothing but data access, and other books that cover nothing but low-level networking. While I certainly don't discount the value of a good book, a good book just isn't enough.

Most of us are, as I said, mere mortals. We can't simply scan from page 1 to page 600, look up, and declare to all those around us, "Excellent. I am now a .NET master." To complement the value of all the great books and the examples contained within them, we need to tinker. We need to get our hands dirty and poke around and play with the code. For some, just the act of manually typing in the code samples creates new pathways in the brain, making the material sink in even further.

After we've read the chapter that describes what we want to do and we've tinkered with it, run all the code samples, and maybe even changed a value or two, we're still not done. When we've tinkered to the point where we no longer get the glazed-over look in our eyes when someone discusses the topic at hand, we need to find a way to reapply the technology.

By *reapply*, what I mean is to take the sample that was given to us and use the technology behind it to accomplish something *else*. A (probably bad) habit I have is learning a new technology and then asking myself, "That's great, but how do I make a game out of that?" You might think I play far too many video games (and I do), but this is a way of forcing my mind to think of what I'm learning in a new context.

Think of it this way: Imagine that you've never used an XML document for anything other than to store the following XML document:

```
<?xml version="1.0" encoding="UTF-8"?>
<hello>
  <greeting>
    Hello World!
  </greeting>
</hello>
```

This is a terrific little document. You can write code to retrieve the inner text of the `<greeting>` element; you can probably write code that adds attributes and even write an XPath query against it. Finally, you decide to get fancy and use an XSL Transformation to create an HTML document that uses this source XML document.

So far, all you've managed to do is absorb (step one) and tinker (step two). You haven't done any kind of reapplication, customization, or improvement on your knowledge.

Now suppose that you create a new XML document:

```
<?xml version="1.0" encoding="UTF-8" ?>
<GameScores>
  <Score owner="Kevin Hoffman" game="Asteroids" value="2500000000" />
  <Score owner="Neil" game="Space Invaders" value="2" />
</GameScores>
```

On the one hand, you have your typical "Hello, World" XML document. On the other hand, you have an XML document that has a real-world purpose, one that you can probably relate to (even if you don't play these games). Do you think you're more likely to retain your XML skills by working with the sample provided to you in the book or by converting the sample provided in the book into an XML game score management system?

About This Book

This book is designed to take advantage of the learning methods I just described. I don't think that just attempting to absorb or memorize the information you find within a book is enough. To truly learn a technology, especially one you might not already be familiar with, you need to absorb it, tinker with it, and then customize and improve it to make it your own. Only after you've done all three will you really feel confident and comfortable with what you've learned.

This book accommodates that theory. Instead of cramming you full of "Hello, World" examples for remoting, database access, Web services, Windows Forms, and the Compact Framework, this book presents a real application. The application is by no means something that you should consider selling to the general public. However, it is a realistic model of an application that might be built in the real world.

This book starts you off by having you look at the application as it originally stands (and as it sits on the accompanying CD). It walks you through installing and configuring the application so that you can build and debug it on your own machine.

Once you do that, you'll take a look at how the sample application works. This will essentially be a business overview of the application features.

Then you'll move on to seeing the code (the "absorb" step in the process). After you've seen the code as it is, you'll spend some time tweaking it and changing values to see what happens (the "tinker" step). Finally, I'll challenge you to create some new features and enhance the application in a way that will be entirely your own (the "reapply" step).

The following sections briefly describe the chapters in this book that will lead you through this learning process.

Chapter 1, "Setting Up Your Development Environment"

Chapter 1 gets you up and running on the Survey Development Suite. Instead of just installing the application from an InstallShield Wizard or an MSI file, you'll be copying the files from a CD. Why do it the hard way? Because you're probably reading this book because you want to do more than just absorb the information. By putting the information to use right away, you'll see what a fairly big Visual Studio .NET solution looks like and what you need to do to get a development workstation running on that solution.

Chapter 2, "Using the Survey Development Suite"

When you have the code installed and you've run some "smoke tests" to make sure that it's working, you're good to go. Chapter 2 takes you through the business side of the Survey Development Suite, showing you what the application does and why. You might be wondering why a chapter like this is in a book on coding. The truth of the matter is that very few of us have the luxury of being pure programmers. Very often we participate in design meetings and consult with business people on features and requirements analysis. Chapter 2 gives you some good information on the set of requirements that drive the functionality and the code you'll see throughout the rest of the book.

In addition, in this chapter you get a really good overview of all three of the applications in the Survey Development Suite. The goal here isn't to learn how the Survey Development Suite is put together but to figure out how you can *reapply* that information to your situation and projects you want or have to build. Your code is only as good as your design.

Chapter 3, "Exploring the Code of the Survey Development Suite"

Having looked at the business side of what the Survey Development Suite does and how people will be using it, in Chapter 3 you start taking a look at some code. This chapter examines the architecture of the Visual Studio .NET solution and the application itself. It takes a look at the code that drives most of the major pieces of the Survey Development Suite applications.

Chapter 4, "Experimenting with the Code for the Survey Development Suite"

The first three chapters of the book all deal with the absorption part of the learning process. By this point, I will probably have fed you so much dry, context-less information that you'll be itching to get at the code. Thankfully, that's just what you do in Chapter 4.

This chapter begins the "tinker" phase of the learning process. You're going to be poking around the Survey Development Suite applications, making changes here and there and seeing what the effects are and why. I strongly recommend that you follow along with this chapter with Visual Studio .NET open and warmed up on a nearby computer. In each of the three chapters that focus on an individual application in the Survey Development Suite, you'll be working on tinkering and with improving the code in the application.

Chapter 5, "Customizing Survey Repository"

Chapter 5 examines, in plenty of depth, the Survey Repository application. This application serves as the back end for the Survey Development Suite you'll be working on throughout this book.

Chapter 6, "Customizing Survey Development Studio"

Survey Development Studio is a Windows Forms application that interfaces with the Survey Repository. Chapter 6 covers tinkering with the code that makes this application run; you'll be getting down into the guts of the application and seeing what makes it tick.

Chapter 7, "Customizing PocketSurvey"

PocketSurvey is an application built on the Compact Framework that provides a facility for administering opinion surveys to people at remote locations, such as shopping malls, where mobility is a concern.

Chapter 8, "Improving the Code of the Survey Development Suite"

The past few chapters all reinforce the "tinkering" method of learning and retaining new information. Chapter 8 is a transition chapter. Instead of just modifying a line of code here and there, in Chapter 8 you make some fundamental changes to the code to make it run faster, make it more efficient, and make it more maintainable.

Chapter 9, "Extending the Survey Development Suite"

At this point you should have a pretty good grasp not only on the Survey Development Suite that comes with the book, but also on all the various skills and technologies used to implement the three applications in the suite. By this point you've seen the code displayed in the book, you've tweaked it and tinkered with it, and you've even enhanced some of it. Chapter 9 challenges you (and provides some help and examples) to take the code to the next step and customize it and make it your own.

What You Need for This Book

The first thing you need for this book is the desire to learn. If you don't want to learn any of the material in this book, the book won't do you any good.

Second, you need to have some familiarity with the C# language and the .NET Framework in general. While some of the things you'll be doing might be considered easy, to understand a lot of the code changes, you need a fairly decent knowledge of the .NET Framework. If you've never seen C# before and never used the .NET Framework before, then you probably want to pick up a different introductory book. On the other hand, if you have had a little bit of exposure or you consider yourself an expert, this book will definitely come in handy.

Technology-wise, you need a copy of SQL Server 2000 Personal Edition or Enterprise Edition or a free trial of any of the editions. All the code in this book was compiled on the .NET Framework version 1.1, using Visual Studio .NET 2003. While you don't need an iPAQ or another PocketPC device to use the mobile application (an emulator is available through Visual Studio .NET), it does come in handy to have an actual device to play with. Also, they're cool and you could probably use an excuse to buy one.

Setting Up Your Development Environment

1

CHAPTER

When people learn new technologies and techniques, there are generally a few different ways they do so. One way is to start from scratch: You learn the technology and then try to implement it in a complete and practical way. Another way to learn is by example: Someone shows you how that technology works in a real-world example.

Unfortunately, there are a few problems with these methods. By starting from scratch, you might have the technological knowledge, but you don't have any knowledge of the practical application of that knowledge; you don't know how you should be implementing things. The second method gives you the "how" of the practical implementation, but because the solution given to you is traditionally a complete solution that has already undergone multiple revisions, there is nothing for you to do but look at the code. This book aims to be different by not giving you a complete application and not patronizing you with "Hello, World" examples.

In this chapter, you're going to be getting your environment ready to work with the application that comes with this book. You'll be going through the following:

- Installing the SQL Server 2000 database backup
- Installing the Visual Studio .NET 2003 solution
- Verifying that that Web service is working properly
- Verifying that the Windows Forms application is working
- Verifying that the Pocket PC application is working

Getting Started with Your Development Environment

This book does things a little differently from other books. It starts with a mostly complete application. Throughout the book you'll modify, enhance, refactor, and add on to the initial application. This will not only show you the technology behind what you're doing, but it will show you how things work internally. You'll get to see how the application is affected by your changes and, most importantly, you should be able to learn why you make the decisions you make.

So, to get started and prepare for the rest of the book, you need to get your workstation set up to not only run the application you'll be working on but to modify the source code, recompile, redeploy, and examine the consequences. The rest of this chapter walks you through installing the SQL database that provides the back end for most of the application, as well as all the various pieces of the Visual Studio .NET solution. When each piece is installed, you'll run a few quick tests to make sure that it is up and running properly.

By the end of this chapter, you should have a pretty good idea of what kind of application you've built and what you're going to do to that application throughout the rest of the book, and you should have a functioning development workstation that is ready for you to start coding.

Before you get into installing and configuring anything, you need to make sure that the machine you've chosen to do your development and experimentation on meets the following requirements:

- **Operating system**—Windows 2000/XP Professional or better
- **Framework SDK**—.NET Framework SDK version 1.1
- **IDE**—Visual Studio .NET 2003
- **Database**—Microsoft SQL Server 2000 (any edition)
- **Mobile device**—A Pocket PC device or Visual Studio .NET 2003's emulator

The operating system is something you can't change: ASP.NET does not run on Windows 98 or Windows Me. You can download the latest version of the .NET Framework SDK from Microsoft's Web site. Visual Studio .NET 2003 is available in student editions, and you can find affordable copies if you buy a single-language version (for example, only C# or only Visual Basic .NET). You can download trial editions of SQL Server 2000, and you can also find 120-day trial copies of SQL 2000 in the backs of various books on the subject (for example, *MCAD/MCSE/MCDBA Self-Paced Training Kit: Microsoft SQL Server 2000 Database Design and Implementation, Exam 70-229*, from Microsoft).

STEP-BY-STEP GUIDE: Installing and Configuring the SQL Database

Included on the CD that accompanies this book is a backup of a SQL 2000 database called `dbbackup`. When you extract this file, you can put it anywhere you like. You'll find this backup file on the CD in the `MSSQL\DBBackup` directory.

Before doing this, however, you need to make sure that your SQL 2000 installation is working properly. Follow these steps:

1. You can do this by opening Enterprise Manager and running a few quick queries against the Northwind database. You can quickly issue the following two SQL statements to SQL Query Analyzer; they should give you some valid results if Northwind is installed and running properly:

   ```
   SELECT * FROM Categories
   SELECT * FROM [Order Details]
   ```

2. When you're satisfied that things are as they should be, you can move on to restoring the backup that is included on the CD.
3. Using Enterprise Manager, create a new database called `SurveyRepository`.
4. Accept all the default options; you can always modify the settings later, as needed.
5. Click OK to complete the operation. The SQL database is created.
6. Right-click the new database and choose `All Tasks, Restore Database`. The Restore Database dialog appears, as shown in Figure 1.1.

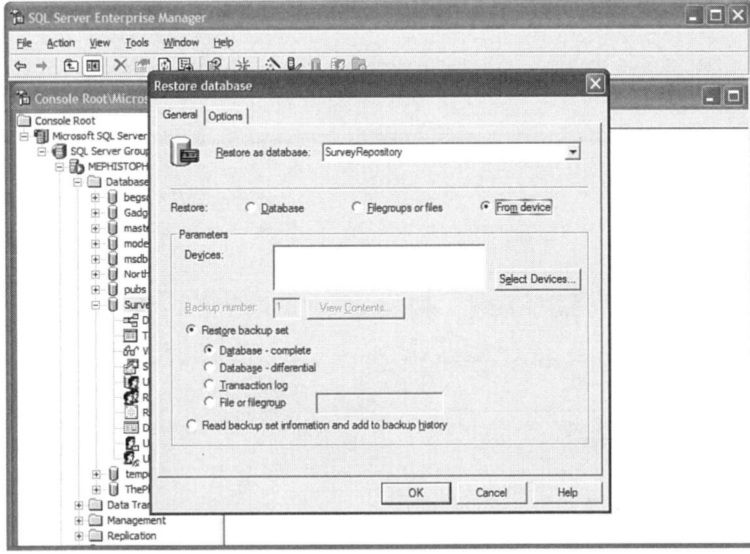

FIGURE 1.1
The Restore Database dialog.

In the Restore Database dialog, select From Device and then click the Select Devices button. The Choose Restore Devices dialog appears, as shown in Figure 1.2.

7. From the Choose Restore Devices dialog, browse to the location of the backup file on the CD-ROM by clicking the Add button.
8. Click OK and accept the dialogs until you return to the Restore Database dialog (see Figure 1.3). Make sure that Restore Backup Set is selected and that the Database – Complete option is also selected.

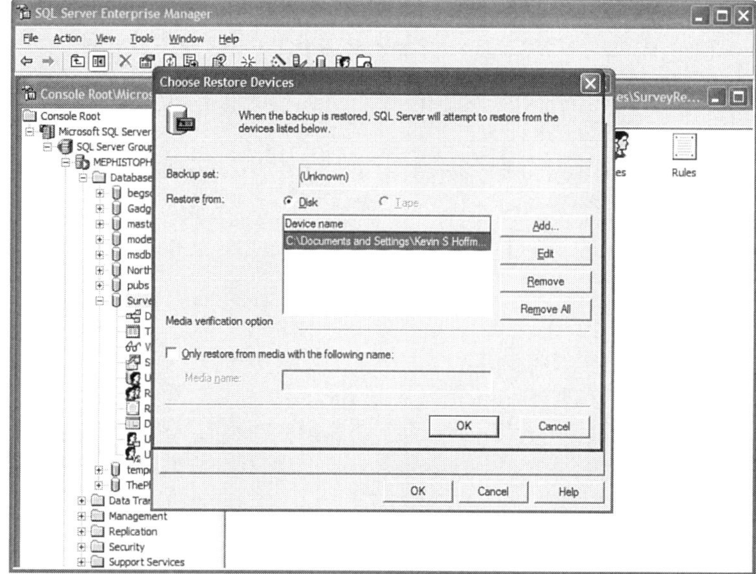

FIGURE 1.2

The Choose Restore Devices database restore dialog.

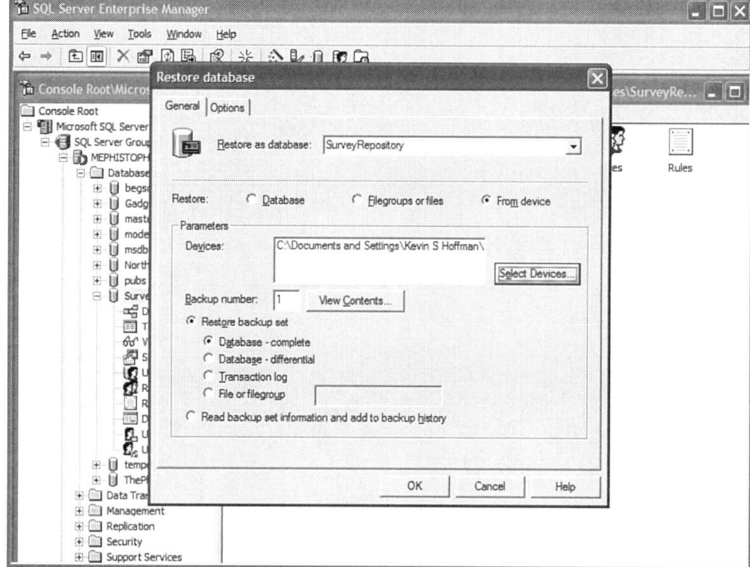

FIGURE 1.3

The Restore Database dialog with a file-based device selected.

9. When you're ready to restore the database, click OK, and you receive a message indicating that the database was successfully restored.

At this point you have nothing but a database. When you write code against a database, you need to provide some means for authenticating the application against the SQL database—either Windows or SQL. In the case of the sample application that we'll be talking about throughout this book, I decided to go with pure SQL authentication for various reasons.

10. To complete the installation of the database, create a user that the application will use to log in and that will have sufficient access to the database.

To create a new user specifically for the new database, expand the `Security` folder underneath the tree node for your server and right-click the `Logins` node.

> **SECURITY TIP**
>
> When creating users for applications to use in connecting to the database, make sure you don't use blank passwords. Also, avoid using the stock `sa` user at all costs. Ideally, you want to create users that have the fewest database privileges needed to get the job done.

11. After selecting New Login, you are presented with a dialog that prompts you to create a new login.

12. Select SQL Server Authentication and supply a username and a password. For the default code that comes with the book, the user is `survey`, with the password `survey`. Depending on the situation, your restored copy of the database might already contain a database user called survey. (In this case, you can skip the user creation steps and move on to setting permissions.) Obviously, in a commercial application, the choice of password would be a bit more secure.

13. Click the Database Access tab of the SQL Server Login Properties dialog box for the new login and then click the check box next to the `SurveyRepository` database.

14. In the Permit in Database Role list view on the Database Access tab, check db_owner. When you're done, click OK. You are prompted to enter the password a second time. At this point, you should be ready to run a couple tests to make sure the `SurveyRepository` database is installed and ready for you to start developing against.

STEP-BY-STEP GUIDE: Verifying the SQL Database

Just two more things to do, and you can get on to installing the code. There are two verification steps you need to take before you can consider the database ready:

1. First, run a test query within SQL Query Analyzer to make sure that the database is working properly and that the newly created user is also working. After you've verified the database with Query Analyzer, you need to verify that .NET can connect to the database (using the user you created) and can get some results from a simple query. When you've gotten some results from Query Analyzer, you know that the database is working properly.

   To test your SQL connectivity, open SQL Query Analyzer. From there, select the `SurveyRepository` database and run the following sample query:

   ```
   SELECT * FROM SVY_Users
   ```

   You should see some results. Even if you see zero rows, the following columns should appear in your result set: `UserId`, `Username`, `Password`, and `FullName`. Now you can create a new user for yourself that you can use to log in to the Survey Repository application later in the book. To do that, issue the following statement to SQL Query Analyzer:

   ```
   DECLARE @userid int
   exec SVY_Create_User 'test2', 'test', 'Test User', @userId
   ```

   SQL Query Analyzer should then respond with `(1 row(s) affected)`. Obviously if you don't like the username `test2` or the password `test`, you can feel free to change them.

2. Check to see whether .NET can access the database. You need to always keep Code Access Security in the back of your mind as you build applications. Depending on how an application was installed, it might not have the capability to make network connections, read files from the disk, and so on. At this point you need to create a new console application in Visual Studio .NET and enter the following code to test the new database:

   ```
   using System;
   using System.Data.SqlClient;
   using System.Data;
   ```

```
namespace SQLTester
{
 class Class1
 {
  [STAThread]
  static void Main(string[] args)
  {
    SqlConnection conn = new SqlConnection(
     @"server=mephistopholes\dev; user id=survey;
➥password=survey; initial catalog=SurveyRepository;");
    conn.Open();
    SqlCommand cmd = conn.CreateCommand();
    cmd.CommandText = "SELECT * FROM SVY_Users";
    cmd.CommandType = CommandType.Text;
    SqlDataAdapter da = new SqlDataAdapter( cmd );
    DataSet ds = new DataSet();
    da.Fill(ds);
    foreach (DataRow user in ds.Tables[0].Rows)
    {
      Console.WriteLine( "User: {0}/{1}, Full Name: {2}",
        user["UserId"],
        user["Password"],
        user["FullName"] );
    }
    cmd.Dispose();
    conn.Close();
  }
 }
}
```

You should change the SQL connection string to something that matches your configuration. In my case, I run two instances of SQL Server on one machine, so I need to specify the instance by including a backslash and the name of the instance after the server name. If you're installing both the code and the SQL database on the same machine, you can specify `localhost` as the server name.

When you compile this and run it in a console window, you should see the following output:

```
User: 1/Kevin, Full Name: Kevin Hoffman
```

This output indicates that there is one user in the database.

If you get a security error at this point, select Start, Settings, Control Panel, Administrative Tools and run the .NET Framework 1.1 Configuration tool to modify the security defaults for your machine.

Troubleshooting the Database Installation

If you have gotten through all the preceding instructions, yet your database still doesn't work, you can examine the following list of symptoms and possible causes and solutions:

- **I can't restore the backup of the SQL database**—Double-check the version number of your SQL Server database. The backup file is a binary file that was created by SQL 2000 and should only be imported by SQL 2000 servers. If you are running SQL 2000 and the backup file fails to restore properly, you can try creating the database through a script file. On the CD in the `MSSQL` directory, you will find a file with the extension `.sql`. This is a text file that contains a script that you can run through SQL Query Analyzer to create the database and all the objects within the database. To run this script, you simply copy the contents of the script file into SQL Query Analyzer and click the Execute button. Within a short period of time, the database and all the database objects should be created.
- **The sample query didn't work on the Northwind database**—If you ran the sample query against the Northwind database, and it returned an error, or if your Northwind database is simply missing, you may have trouble with your SQL Server installation. Continue on with the restoration of the SQL backup from CD and see if that works. If it works, you should be fine. If it fails to restore, I suggest that you reinstall SQL Server 2000, making sure to install all the documentation and sample databases.
- **The sample query didn't work on the `SurveyRepository` database**—You've managed to restore the `SurveyRepository` database and everything looks fine, but for some reason you get an error when you try to run the sample query. If the error you are getting indicates that there are missing or invalid database objects, you should try the restore operation again. If the restore operation fails, you should delete the database you created and follow the instructions for executing the `.sql` script file detailed in the first point in this list.
- **I can't establish a connection to SQL Server via the sample .NET code provided**—The first thing you should do is make sure that your connection string properly reflects the machine on which you installed the SQL database. The format for the database connection string is as follows:

```
"server=(servername);user id=(user);password=(password);
initial catalog=(database name);"
```

Make sure that the connection string you're using conforms to this format. Also, make sure that the project you created still has a reference to `System.Data`. If SQL Server is not on the same physical machine as the test client application you wrote, you need to troubleshoot your network. Make sure that your machine can see the other machine on your network and that it can establish a connection on the SQL Server machine's network ports. If there is a firewall between your client computer and the SQL Server machine, this might be interfering with communications. You can temporarily retry the connection with the firewall down to verify that the firewall is the issue. If it is, you can check SQL Books Online for the right port numbers to open on your firewall.

STEP-BY-STEP GUIDE: Installing the Survey Development Suite Code

When you have the database running and you've tested it to make sure that .NET can access the SQL Server database, you need to install the Visual Studio .NET 2003 solution.

Remember that when you add a Web project (either a Web application or a Web services application) to a solution, the location of all the files for that project is, by default, in the IIS Web application tree. Therefore, you have to take two steps in order to install and configure the development environment: you have to install the Web application and install the Visual Studio .NET solution.

Here's how you install the Web application:

1. Double-click the file `SurveySuite_Inetpub.zip`, which is in the `SurveyV1` directory on the CD that accompanies this book. WinZip (or whatever archiving program you have installed) appears. If you don't have WinZip, you can look for the uncompressed version of this directory tree that is also available on the CD.
2. Make sure that you don't have any of the individual files highlighted and then click Extract in WinZip.
3. Make sure that the Use Folder Names option is checked and click Extract again after specifying the WWW root directory. In my case, this directory is `c:\inetpub\wwwroot`. You can find out what your IIS virtual root is by opening up the Internet Information Services management console and getting the properties for your default Web site.

4. Make sure that your new directory is an actual Web application. To do this, open IIS Manager, right-click the new directory, and click the Create button next to the Application box. You can also accomplish this by setting it up from the Web Sharing tab in the folder properties dialog box.
5. Open the `AssemblyInfo.cs` file that comes with the `RepositoryV1` Web project.
6. Edit the value for the `Survey.snk` strong-name key pair file to a value that indicates the true location on your hard drive. This file comes with the solution on the CD that accompanies this book and is required to build the application.

Here's how you install the Visual Studio .NET solution:

1. Double-click the file `SurveySuite_VSNetSolution.zip`. WinZip (or whatever archiving program you have installed) appears.
2. Make sure you have the Use Folder Names option checked and then click Extract for the final time. You can choose to use whatever folder you like. I find that it makes things easier if the code I'm working on is within the `My Documents\Visual Studio Projects` folder tree. After you click Extract, it might take a minute or two for all the files to be extracted, depending on the speed of your machine and hard drive.
3. For each of the projects that you installed, go into the `AssemblyInfo.cs` file and change the location of the strong-name key pair file to the appropriate directory on your hard drive. This might be tedious, but when it's done, you won't have to modify the code again.

Now that you have all the starter code for the book installed and you've got the database installed and verified, you just have a few more things to test before you can start getting your hands dirty.

STEP-BY-STEP GUIDE: Verifying the Web Application

The sample Web application is actually a Web service application. Therefore, it doesn't have any user interface. However, IIS allows you to browse the list of methods available for a given service by browsing to the `.asmx` file associated with the service. Here's what you do:

1. Make sure that the `Web.config` file in the `RepositoryV1` project properly reflects the SQL information that you supplied when you

set up the SQL database earlier. You will find this information in the DefaultDSN configuration setting in the `appSettings` node.

2. Make sure that the local machine's `ASPNET` account has sufficient permission to access the `RepositoryV1` application directory.

3. If you installed the Web application by following the preceding directions, browse to `http://localhost/RepositoryV1/login.asmx`. The Web service for the sample application is actually two different services: one for authentication and one for the actual interaction between the client and the back-end data.

4. Click on the `LoginUser` method. The simple test wrapper that appears asks you for the username and password.

5. Enter the username and password of the user that you viewed in the SQL test application. If all goes well, and things are running properly, Internet Explorer should display some XML that looks very similar to this:

```
<?xml version="1.0" encoding="utf-8" ?>
<string xmlns="http://www.samspublishing.com">
748912bd-6d07-4b5c-a33b-498ba6288bce
</string>
```

Chapter 3, "Exploring the Code of the Survey Development Suite," covers what that result means and how the application uses it. For now, it's proof enough that the Web service is functioning properly and you've installed it properly.

Troubleshooting the Web Application Installation

If you've managed to get this far and you are still having trouble getting the Web application to work properly, you can take a look at the following list of common problems and solutions to getting Web applications to work properly. If, after taking a look at this list, you're still having trouble, you can always contact Sams for help:

- **I get an error when I try to access `login.asmx`**—Make sure you have done the following things to ensure that the Web application is running properly:

    1. Make sure that the `RepositoryV1` directory is actually an application.

    2. Make sure that the `ASPNET` account has been given Read, Execute, and List permissions on the `RepositoryV1` directory.

3. Make sure that IIS is actually running and that Default Web Site is set to Started. You can verify this from the IIS management console. To quickly load the console, you can select Start, Run and then enter `\winnt\system32\inertsrv\iis.msc`. (Obviously, if your Windows installation is not in the `winnt` directory, you should use a different location.)

4. Make sure that anonymous access has been enabled to the `RepositoryV1` application. This is also a configurable property in the IIS Control Panel.

- **I get an error from ASP.NET itself, complaining about DLL versions**—If you get a version error from ASP.NET when it tries to load `Login.asmx`, you might have a problem with the .NET Framework itself. First, make sure that you have installed.NET Framework version 1.1 and that you have rebooted at least once since that installation. Check the `RepositoryV1\bin` directory for DLLs. You should see several DLLs, including these:

```
SAMS.Survey.Core.MonitorServices.dll
SAMS.Survey.Core.RelationalDb.dll
SAMS.Survey.Repository.dll
SAMS.Survey.RepositoryV1.dll
SAMS.Survey.SecurityServices.dll
```

  If you don't see all these DLLs, you might want to consider reinstalling the application from the zip file. Make sure you have the Use Folder Names option checked so that all the files will extract to the appropriate directories.

- **I can get `Login.asmx` to load, but when I try to run a test method, I get database errors**—You should check the `Web.config` file. In the `<appSettings>` tag is an `<add key="DefaultDSN" value="..."/>` tag. In that tag, make sure that the connection string is *exactly* the same as the connection string you used when you ran the sample .NET Framework–SQL connectivity application from the Step-by-Step Guide "Verifying the SQL Database." If you never got the SQL connectivity application running, return to that Step-by-Step Guide and also take a look at the section "Troubleshooting the Database Installation."

STEP-BY-STEP GUIDE: Verifying the Windows Application

Throughout the rest of the book, you're going to be examining, modifying, and adding code to the solution you just installed. In addition to making sure the Windows application works, you need to make sure that your development environment for that application is working as well. Follow these steps:

1. Open Visual Studio .NET.
2. Choose Open Solution and browse to the `SurveyV1` solution file in the directory where you installed it. For me, that file is in `My Documents\Visual Studio Projects`. The entire solution should open, and you should be able to see a few class libraries, the Web application, the Windows application, and the Pocket PC application.
3. Right-click the Survey Development Studio Windows application and select Debug, Start New Instance. In most cases, you can choose Debug, Start (or press F5) from the main Visual Studio .NET toolbar. However, because there is a Compact Framework application in the solution, when you do a normal debug, Visual Studio .NET automatically tries to deploy to whatever device you've chosen. To avoid having to constantly deploy to the emulator just to run your Windows application, you can explicitly choose to start a new instance of the Windows application.

   When the application starts, you are greeted with the main form, as shown in Figure 1.4.
4. To make sure that the Windows application is configured properly and is set up to communicate with the Web service, click the Repository menu item and then click Log In. The application prompts you for a username and password.
5. After you enter a username and password, the application attempts to authenticate against the login Web service. If it is successful, the status bar of the main form looks as shown in Figure 1.5.

FIGURE 1.4

The main form for the Survey Development Studio.

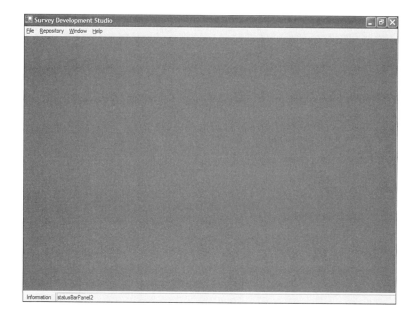

FIGURE 1.5

The status bar of the Survey Development Studio application after a login.

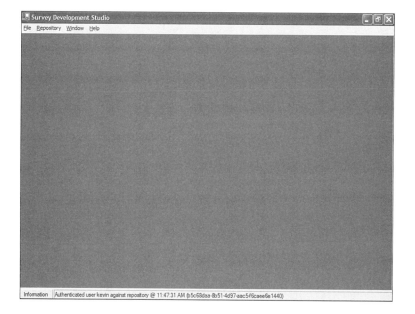

If there is an error, you might want to check the previous steps for verifying the database and the Web application. The application as it ships doesn't set the URL for the Web service, so it assumes the host `localhost`. If you aren't using `localhost`, you need to modify the code to use a different URL.

Troubleshooting the Windows Forms Application Installation

If you get to this point and you still cannot get Survey Development Studio (the Windows Forms application) to work properly, if at all, take a look at the following list of problems and solutions:

- **I get cryptographic failures when I try to sign an assembly during the build process. Visual Studio .NET 2003 indicates that the `Survey.snk` file is missing or cannot be loaded**—If you're experiencing this problem, then more than likely, the installation of the Visual Studio .NET project did not complete properly. First, you should check to make sure that the `Survey.snk` file is actually on your hard drive in the `SurveyV1` directory created when you extracted the files from the zip archive. If it isn't there, you should re-extract the files, making sure that the Use Folder Names check box is selected. If the key file is there, and you're still getting error messages, you need to check your `SharedAssemblyInfo.cs` files. Every project in the solution, except for the `RepositoryV1` project. contains one of these files. The `RepositoryV1` project has an `AssemblyInfo.cs` file. In each of these files, there is an attribute that looks like this: `[AssemblyKeyFile(@"...")]`. Make surep that the text inside the quotes is the actual physical location of the `Survey.snk` file on your hard disk. You need to make this change to *all* the `AssemblyInfo.cs` files in the solution.

- **I get an error that looks like a network error from the Web service after the application seems to lock up for a while**—Is the Web service installed on *`localhost`*, or did you install the Web application on a different machine than you used to install the Visual Studio .NET 2003 project? If the Web application is on a different machine, you need to specify that in the Windows Forms code for the Survey Development Studio application. If you need to change the URL at which the client application accesses the Web service, you should find the `RepositoryClient.cs` file in the `SurveyStudio` project and change the `RepositoryClient` method so that it looks like this:

```
static RepositoryClient()
{
  loggedIn = false;
  loginService = new repositoryLogin.Login();
  loginService.Url = "http://yourserver/RepositoryV1/Login.asmx";
  repositoryService = new
    repositoryMain.RepositoryService();
  repositoryService.Url = "http://yourserver/RepositoryV1/
  ➥RepositoryService.asmx";
  singletonInstance = new RepositoryClient();
}
```

If the Web service is local to the client, go back to the steps in the section "Troubleshooting the Web Application Installation" to verify that the Login service is up and running properly.

Hopefully, the problem you're experiencing is listed here, and the solution will help you get your application working. Because of the explorative nature of this book, you really should have your entire application development environment working before you move on. Therefore, I highly recommend that you not continue with this chapter until your Survey Development Studio application is working well enough to be able to log in to the Survey Repository Web service.

STEP-BY-STEP GUIDE: Verifying the Pocket PC Application

Unlike the first release of Visual Studio .NET, the Compact Framework is a built-in part of the environment in the 2003 version of Visual Studio .NET. With the .NET Framework 1.0, the Compact Framework was an additional download. This means that you no longer have to do anything special to get the Compact Framework installed. To test the Pocket PC application, follow these steps:

1. Right-click the `PocketSurvey` project file in the `SurveyV1` solution that you already have open and choose Debug, Start New Instance.
2. Sit back and relax a minute while Visual Studio .NET not only compiles the application but deploys it to the mobile destination. For now, you can choose the emulator as your target. I wouldn't recommend using an actual Pocket PC device for testing until you think your application is ready for a production release. After a minute or two, the emulator appears. Don't do anything when it comes up with the calibration screen. Visual Studio .NET starts copying the .NET Framework onto the emulator.
3. Keep watching until the PocketSurvey application appears in the emulator, as shown in Figure 1.6. (Note that a different survey may appear for you.)

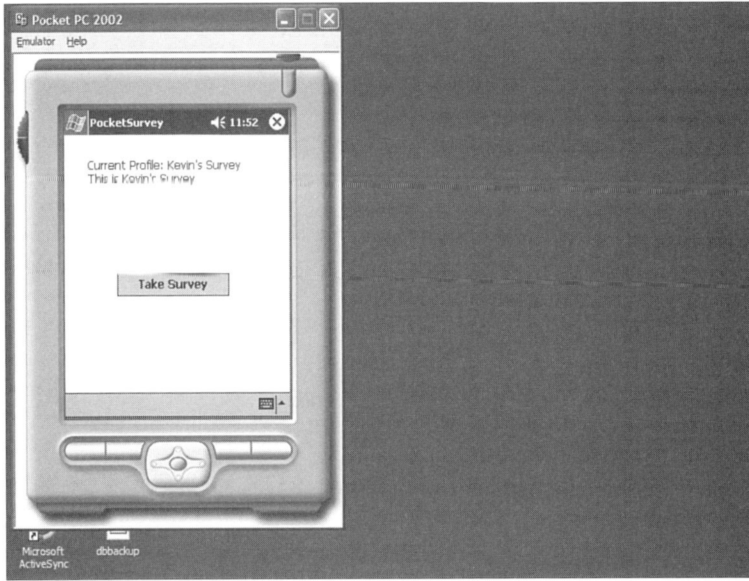

FIGURE 1.6
The PocketSurvey main form in Visual Studio .NET 2003's Pocket PC emulator.

Troubleshooting the Pocket PC Application Installation

If you weren't able to complete the tasks in the preceding section to verify the Pocket PC solution, then you might want to take a look at the following common problem and possible solution to see if your problem can be solved by following some of the advice listed. If you still have problems after that, you can contact Sams:

- **I get errors indicating that the emulator could not be found or started**—If this is the case, then one of two things has likely occurred. The first is that your Visual Studio .NET 2003 installation is incomplete or you chose to have certain things not installed. In that case, you might need to reinstall Visual Studio .NET 2003, being careful not to leave out any important components. Another issue, which is more rare, occurs when you have Smart Device Extensions (SDE) installed. If you did any Compact Framework development with version 1.0 of the .NET Framework and then you installed Visual Studio .NET 2003, you might still have SDE (the predecessor of the Compact Framework) installed. This can cause conflicts not only in building applications but in the use of Pocket PC emulators. Make sure you uninstall SDE before you try and do any work with the Compact Framework.

The Sample Application: The Survey Development Suite

Now that you've spent time and effort installing the application on which you're going to be spending the rest of the book working, let's talk about what the application is all about.

Survey is an application that my grandfather wrote back in the good old days of shareware and 2400-baud dial-up bulletin boards. The Internet was still something that most people used for publishing scientific papers and, of course, FTPing the latest images from the NASA archives.

Survey's original version allowed users to create survey profiles, which essentially contained definitions of questions and the survey itself. In addition, it allowed the data entry of survey responses. As responses were entered into the application, they were tabulated and analyzed so that the users could see the analysis of the survey results. The original version of the Survey application was a DOS application written in QuickBasic that has an ANSI-colored menu interface that prompted users for data and displayed data in a friendly white-on-blue screen. An update was made to the application that wrapped all the QuickBasic modules in a C++-driven Windows 32-bit application that provided a new graphical front-end menu.

The updated version of Survey that I've created for this book—which I've called the Survey Development Suite—allows the same basic functionality as the original Survey, but it also allows for quite a bit more. I wanted to create an application suite that demonstrates some of the most powerful features of the .NET Framework and illustrates what I think the future of enterprise applications looks like.

The version of Survey that we're working with is a suite of interrelated applications that forms a larger, enterprise-scale application that I call the Survey Development Suite.

Figure 1.7 illustrates the architecture of the new version of Survey, updated to take full advantage of the .NET Framework.

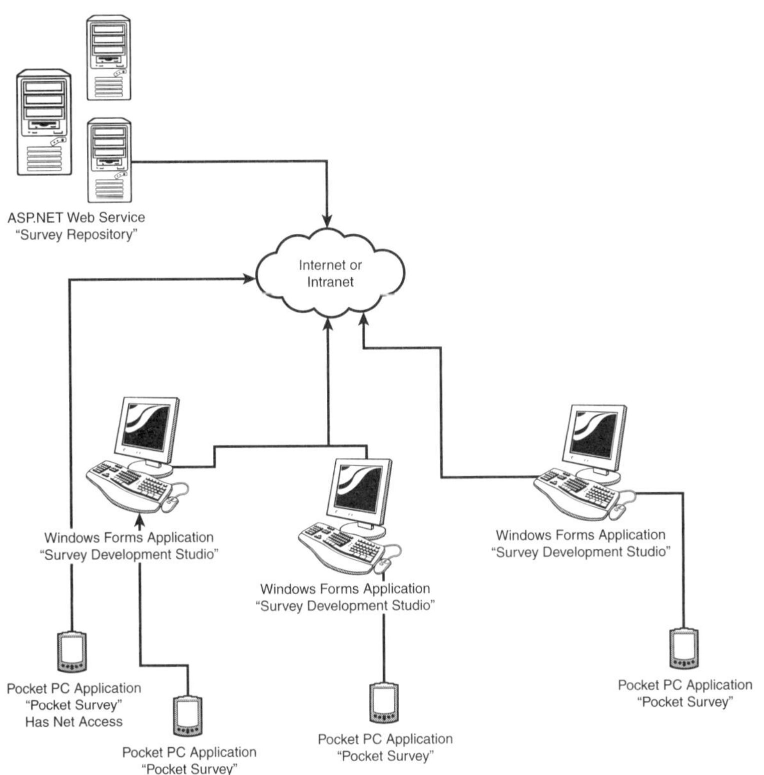

FIGURE 1.7
The Survey Development Suite architecture.

We will talk about the code and implementation of all this in the coming chapters. The following three applications together form the Survey Development Suite:

- **Survey Repository**—Survey Repository is the Web service application that is responsible for acting as a warehouse or vault for survey profiles and runs. We'll talk more in later chapters about what exactly those are. It should suffice for now to think of Survey Repository as a kind of Visual SourceSafe application that is designed specifically to handle survey-type data.

- **Survey Development Studio**—Survey Development Studio is a Windows Forms application that is the core development environment for creating surveys. It not only allows the user to create profiles of surveys, but it allows people performing data entry to enter the results of surveys that have already been administered. Survey Development Studio can work offline with XML files, or it can work in connected mode, checking those XML files in and out of the Survey Repository as a warehouse or vault for survey data.

- **PocketSurvey**—PocketSurvey is probably one of the most interesting aspects of this application suite. Have you ever been in a shopping mall, trying to get something done, only to be accosted by a clipboard-toting surveyor looking to find out what your opinion is on the latest product or trend? One thing that both the survey administrator and respondent appreciate is being able to get it over with quickly. PocketSurvey allows for the respondent to simply use an iPAQ or another Pocket PC device, tap the screen a few times, and be done with it. The results are stored on the portable device and can easily be transferred to the main computer, running Survey Development Studio, for analysis or for submittal to Survey Repository.

As you can see, each of these applications has a finite purpose and might seem somewhat uninteresting on its own. However, as a whole, this next-generation enterprise application can exhibit some incredibly powerful features that, just a few years ago, we would've thought either impossible or too difficult to be practical for inclusion in a development project.

Moving On

The .NET Framework not only gives programmers a uniform framework on which to build managed code, but it gives us the capability to push the envelope further than ever before, to create new and exciting applications that have a degree of interaction and connectivity that would be impossible or impractical to create without it.

The rest of this book looks at the code that's on the CD that accompanies this book. You'll analyze how this code works and why, and then you'll move on to making tweaks and changes to it to see what happens. Then you'll start adding features and refactoring the existing application to incorporate some new designs.

I strongly urge you to keep your laptop or your development machine nearby while you are reading this book. What you will learn with the help of this book you will learn by reading, by experimenting, by tweaking, and by enhancing and customizing. You will certainly get quite a bit of information by reading the book, but I think you will retain far more of it by following along with the code and trying things out on your own. In fact, before you continue to the next chapter, you might be well served by poking around the code and examining it for yourself; see what you can make sense of and what you can't. If you have questions about the code, they should be answered in the upcoming chapters.

Using the Survey Development Suite

CHAPTER 2

As mentioned in Chapter 1, "Setting Up Your Development Environment," this book walks you through doing everything from modifying existing code, to redesigning the application, to adding code of your own to create new features.

We will be looking at a lot of code throughout the rest of the book, and it will help you understand the changes and additions you're making if you have a good grasp of how the sample application, the Survey Development Suite, is supposed to work. This chapter gives you a good idea of how to do the following things with the Survey Development Suite:

- Create survey profiles
- Conduct survey runs
- Add response sheets
- Use Survey Repository
- Conduct surveys using the Pocket PC

This chapter walks you through a few use case scenarios for the application. It shows you how to create a survey, how to conduct a survey run, and how to interact with the Survey Repository Web service.

Survey Profiles

Before we talk about creating a survey profile, we should at the very least cover what a survey profile is. Without the aid of computers, when people conduct surveys, they typically have a printout that contains a list of questions and possible choices. The surveyor approaches a potential respondent and gets a list of that person's responses. At some point after all the results have been obtained, the results are all analyzed and tabulated, and charts and graphs are created.

A good rule of thumb when designing an application is to start out by modeling all the different entities that the application deals with. After that is accomplished, you might have a better idea of what kind of database you need, what the GUI might look like, and so on.

In the case of the Survey Development Suite, the following is a list of the entities we are going to be dealing with:

- Respondents
- Questions
- Responses
- Surveyors
- Response options (lists of available responses)

Given this list of entities that the Survey Development Suite needs to model, I decided to come up with two distinct concepts. The first concept is the survey profile. The survey profile is the list of all the questions and their potential responses (if the question is multiple choice), as well as any other information pertinent to the survey itself, such as a title and description.

The second concept is the survey run. A run consists of a list of response sheets. A response sheet is the collection of responses given by the respondent and optional information about the respondent himself or herself.

You might be asking, "Why did you create the idea behind a run? Couldn't we get along with just gathering the responses and then analyzing them?" The answer is that quite often when surveys are conducted, the same set of questions may be administered to many different sets of respondents at many different times. For example, assume that a company is taking a consumer opinion poll about the flavor of a new chocolate bar. It sets up shop in a shopping mall and queries passersby until it has enough of a result set to perform a good analysis. This result set is what we're referring to as a *run*, and it is defined as a logical unit or collection of response sheets. The reason for the run is that in the future, the company may want to administer the same survey to a new set of potential respondents. By keeping the runs separate, the company can perform two different sets of analysis and compare the results between each run in some meaningful way. Perhaps during the summer, people really didn't like the chocolate bar, but during the winter everyone seemed to love it. By looking at the two different runs, the people conducting the survey can draw more meaningful, context-influenced conclusions about the survey.

STEP-BY-STEP GUIDE: Creating a Survey Profile

Now that you know a little bit about the problem domain that the Survey Development Suite attempts to solve and you've learned what a survey profile and a survey run are, let's get to work and see the application in action.

We'll be getting into the code shortly, and we'll get fairly technical in short order. However, before we look at the code that drives the application, you need to see how the application looks, feels, and works in a real situation. This will help you interpret the code you'll be looking at in the next few chapters. The following steps show you how to create a new survey profile:

1. If you're in the Visual Studio .NET 2003 environment, right-click the `SurveyStudio` project file and select Debug, Start New Instance. The main form appears.

2. Select File, New, Survey Profile. At this point the form for a new survey profile should appear. Keep in mind that nothing has been saved. At this point you're working with disk files, and you're not dealing with a database or a back-end Web service.

3. Create a survey profile based on the Yummy Chocolate Bar Company, which is interested in finding information about people's candy preferences. The company also wants to know what age groups prefer its chocolate bar and which age groups don't so it can better target its advertising campaigns.

   Figure 2.1 is a screenshot of the form that prompts for the basic information about a survey profile (note that it doesn't have any questions yet).

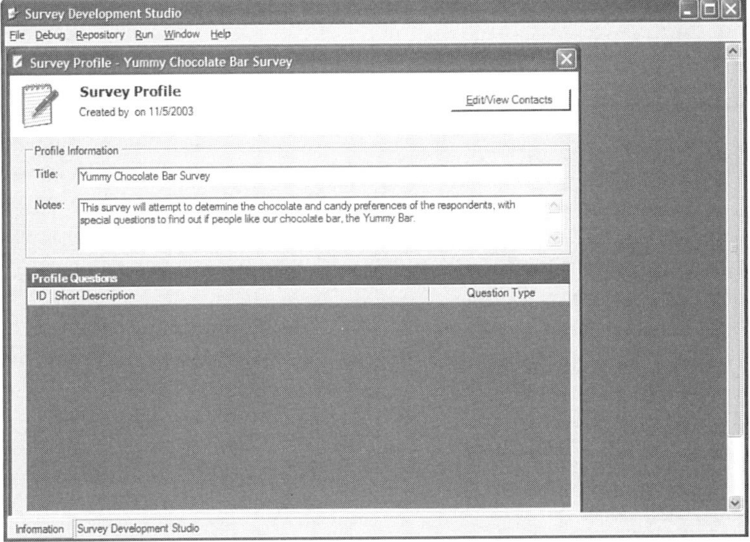

FIGURE 2.1

The Create Profile window in the Survey Development Studio application.

4. If you're like me and a caution bordering on phobia of lost files causes you to save compulsively, you can now press Ctrl+S to save the survey profile to disk. You are prompted for a filename (for example, `YummyChocolate.svp`). Hereafter you won't be prompted for a filename, and Ctrl+S will save changes to that file.

5. Create the first (and only, in this case) demographic question. Click the Add Question button at the bottom of the form. You are presented with a question editor dialog.

6. In the question input dialog, fill in some simple information, such as the question ("What is your age?") and some notes. Choose the question type Choice List, Single Answer.

7. Click the ellipsis (...) button to create a new list of responses. Note that the way this application works, you can share response lists among multiple questions, making it easier to create surveys that have the same response lists to multiple questions.

   Figure 2.2 shows what it looks like to create this first question.

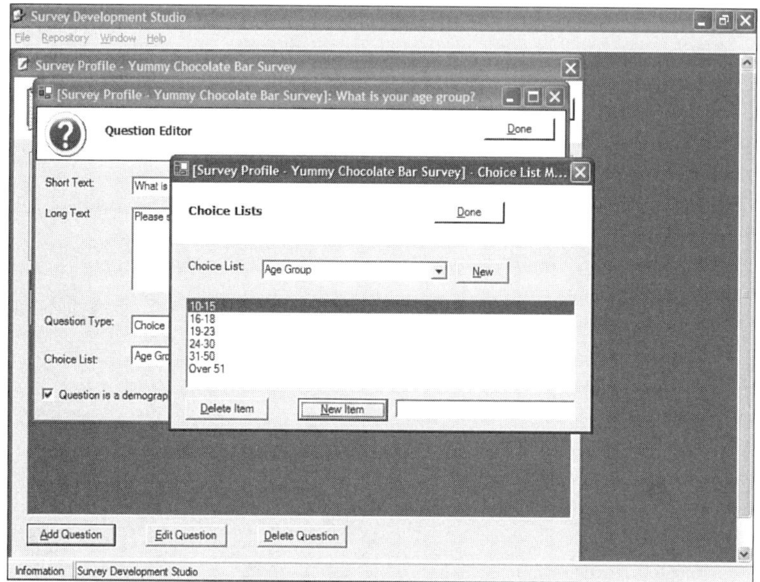

FIGURE 2.2
The choice list editor dialog and question editor.

There will be several questions for this sample survey. You can find the actual survey profile file on the companion disk for this book in the `SampleSurveys` folder. As shown in Figure 2.3, you need to create a second kind of choice list to contain the list of possible favorite candy types.

8. Add a few more questions to make sure that you have coverage of the different kinds of questions you can ask the respondents. For example, add a question that asks the respondent to rank his or her favorite candy types in numeric order, as well as to check off all the different kinds of candy that he or she eats, without regard to which ones he or she likes the most. There is also another question for how often the respondent eats candy. All these questions should give the fictitious Yummy Chocolate Bar Company some good information about where to place its marketing budget and what products it should be developing.

9. When you're all done building the sample survey profile, the profile editor should look something like the one shown in Figure 2.4.

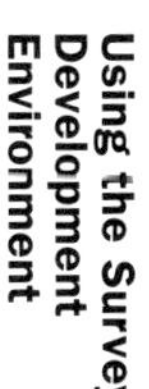

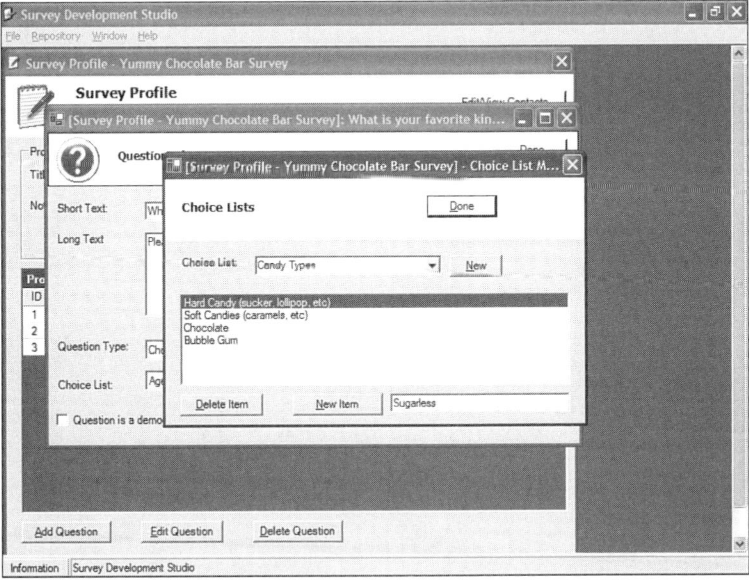

FIGURE 2.4

The survey profile editor with questions entered.

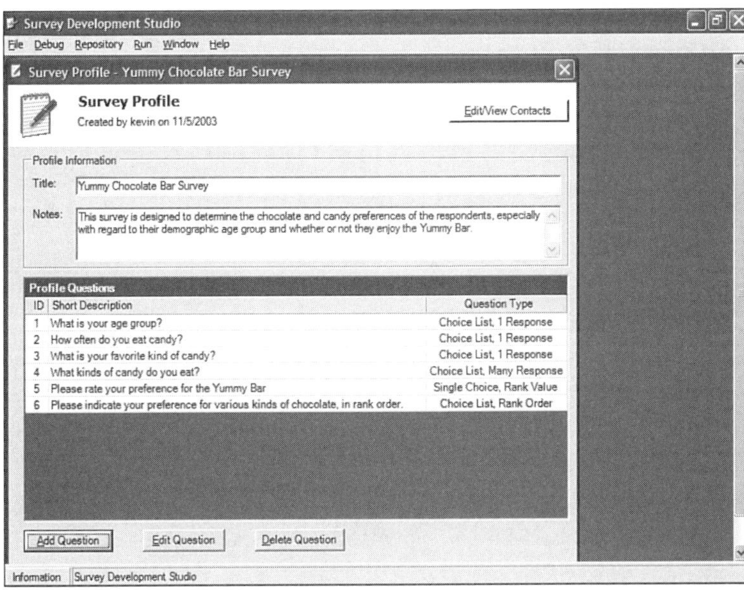

FIGURE 2.3

The survey profile editor dialog with question and choice list editor.

10. Now that you have a working survey profile, save the profile to disk. After that, you can move on to actually conducting the survey in an organized fashion.

Survey Runs

Before we take a look at how the application facilitates completing a run of responses, we need to know how a survey run might be conducted in the real world—or at least within the problem domain of the application developed for this book.

With a profile in hand, an organization conducting the survey will more than likely produce some kind of printout of the survey. To conduct a run, various surveyors will go out to the target location (or make phone calls, or in some other way make contact with the potential respondents) and conduct the survey. A response sheet is generated for each respondent; it contains the respondent's answers as well as any optional contact information the person left with the surveyor.

When enough information has been collected to build a wide enough set for good statistical analysis, the people conducting the survey consider the run complete, and all the response sheets are gathered together and analyzed as a unit.

STEP-BY-STEP GUIDE: Creating a New Run

Now that you know what a run is, you can create one with the sample application. Follow these steps:

1. Open the Survey Development Studio program (if you're in Visual Studio .NET, right-click the `SurveyStudio` project and choose Debug, Start New Instance. Keep in mind that a run is tied specifically to a single survey profile. Later on you'll see that runs can even be tied to different versions of the same profile if you're using Survey Repository to store all your information.
2. Because a run is associated with a profile, you need to open a profile. To do this, choose File, Open Profile, From Disk. An open file dialog box appears.
3. Navigate to the profile you created earlier (or the one you copied from the book's CD) and open the `YummyChocolate.svp` file.
4. When the survey profile is onscreen and available for editing, select Run, New Run. The New Run dialog box appears. It prompts you for some basic information about the run, such as the name of the person who was responsible for administering the run, a description of the run, and some additional notes. Figure 2.5 shows the New Run dialog.

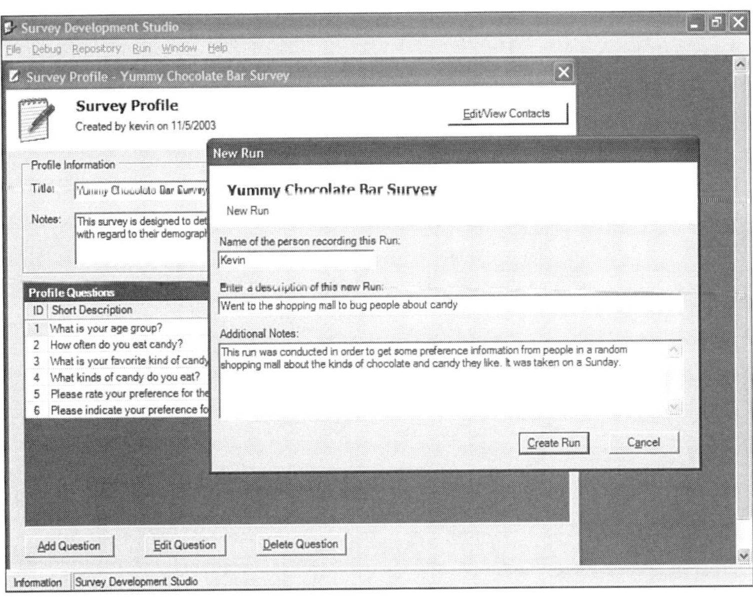

FIGURE 2.5

The New Run dialog.

5. After you supply the basic information about the run you're going to conduct and click the Create Run button, you're taken to the main form of the run editor. This editor contains a tabbed dialog with two tabs: Response Sheets and Respondents. The Respondents tab is a read-only tab. It displays a summary of all the respondents that have participated in the current run. Keep in mind that you can't add respondents manually: You add each one by creating a new response sheet.

STEP-BY-STEP GUIDE: Adding a Response Sheet

1. To add a response sheet to the run editor, simply click the New Sheet button at the bottom of the run editor. The response sheet editor appears. This form lets you provide information about the sheet. Remember that a response sheet is a collection of one single person's responses to the survey profile. For example, if you walk up to someone named Joe Shopper and ask him each of the questions on the survey, the set of his answers constitutes a single response sheet.
2. If you uncheck the Anonymous Respondent check box and click the blue link for the respondent's name, you are prompted with the Respondent Editor dialog (see Figure 2.6).

STEP-BY-STEP GUIDE: **Adding a Response Sheet**

FIGURE 2.6

The Respondent Editor dialog.

3. Next you need to record the person's responses. This is a common task that will probably be performed often by data entry clerks or temporary staff hired to enter and tabulate the results. Therefore, the user interface is not as pretty as it could be—there is plenty of room for improvement here.

4. Click the line in the data grid that corresponds to the response you're recording, and you are prompted for the information on the response sheet (as shown in Figure 2.7). In cases where more than one value is recorded, such as a ranked list or unranked check boxes, list the items (indexed starting at 1) in a comma-separated list.

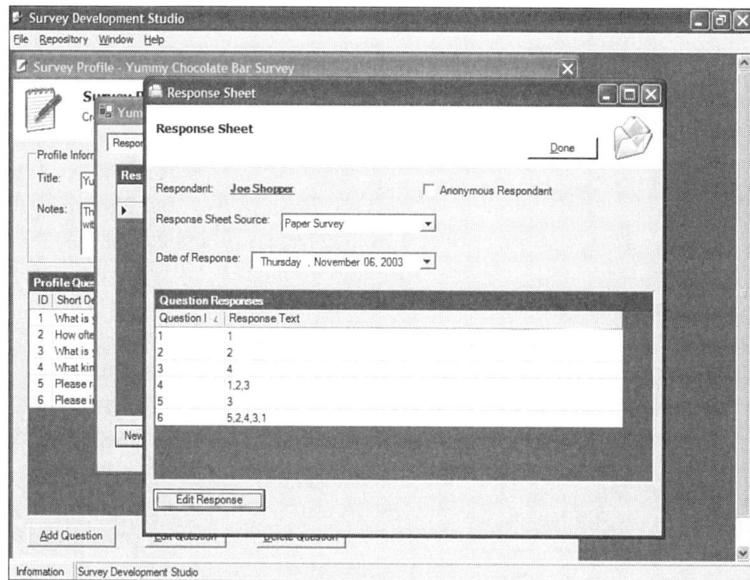

FIGURE 2.7

The Response Sheet dialog.

5. When you've finished adding all the person's responses, you're done with this particular response sheet and you can go back to the main run editor.
6. When you are returned to the run editor, select the Respondents tab, and you see the respondent you entered for the new sheet.

Organizing Surveys and Results by Using Survey Repository

Before we get into a tour of the parts of the Survey Repository application, it might help if you know exactly what Survey Repository is and what problem it solves.

I've always thought that most problems are best described through examples. Take the fictitious candy company Yummy Chocolate Bar Company. It creates a survey profile that it wants to administer to people in a shopping mall. Everything seems to be working fine, and the company prints out the paper surveys to distribute to the people who will be canvassing the shopping mall.

Meanwhile, someone adds a question to the original profile and changes one of the response sets because the survey the company plans on conducting via a telemarketing firm will be slightly different from the one given to mall shoppers.

When the people administering the survey in the shopping mall return to record the results, the results they are recording no longer match the survey profile. As a result, they modify the profile again. When the phone survey is complete, the results those surveyors attempt to record no longer match *their* version of the survey profile.

Obviously, this is a slightly exaggerated example. However, the problem is real. Without some way of organizing and versioning the survey profiles, there is no way that you can reliably associate a run with a profile. Without a solid guarantee that when a run is completed, the survey profile against which the run was performed is intact, the results are meaningless.

Think of it as the consistency property of a transaction from the ACID (atomicity, consistency, isolation, and durability) principle. Assume that you've written a database query that selects a row from the database and performs a complex calculation, and then the row is updated. If the row is updated *while* you are performing the complex calculation, neither of the two updates will have any meaning—the data is considered out of sync.

The solution to this problem is to provide a central repository for not only the survey profiles but for the runs themselves. The repository provides a place to store profiles as well as multiple revisions of the same profile. For example, if someone needed to change the response list on a question for a survey, he or she could create a new revision.

When a run is created from a Survey Repository–managed survey, the run is linked to that profile's revision. This means that the result sets are strongly bound to a specific revision (you can think of it as an instance, if you like) of a survey profile. This makes the people doing the statistical analysis happy as they don't have to worry about skewed or incorrect results that occur because the profile and the run become out of sync.

STEP-BY-STEP GUIDE: Adding a Profile to Survey Repository

The following list of steps guides you through the process of adding a profile to Survey Repository by using the Survey Development Studio:

1. To add a profile to Survey Repository, all you have to do is check your current profile into Survey Repository. On the first check-in, the profile is created in Survey Repository as the first revision of that profile. Each time you check in an existing, managed profile, you are prompted for a revision comment in which you can describe the reason for the additional revision.

2. When you create a profile, the revision comment is set to Created, and you are prompted for the short and long descriptions of the profile that will appear in Survey Repository. Figure 2.8 shows this dialog in action.

   After the profile has been created, it is stored in the database. We'll take a look at what kind of footprint a profile leaves in the database in Chapter 3, "Exploring the Code of the Survey Development Suite."

Each revision of the profile is stored separately, allowing managers of survey teams to organize completely separate profiles and revisions of the same profile to guarantee statistical consistency among all the results.

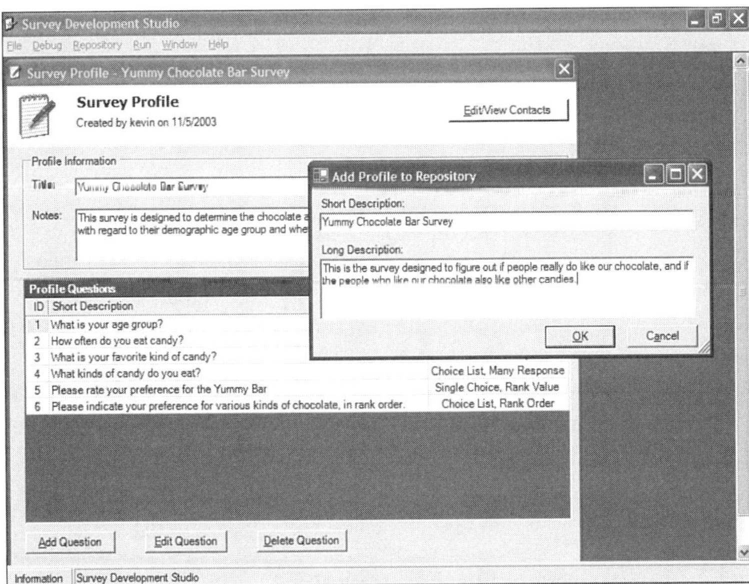

FIGURE 2.8

The Add Profile to Repository dialog, with input supplied.

STEP-BY-STEP GUIDE: **Adding a Run to Survey Repository**

As I said earlier in this chapter, a run is not complete unless it is associated with a survey profile. Therefore, you can't work with a run until you have at least opened a profile. In order to add a run to Survey Repository, the profile you have opened must be what is called a *managed* profile—that is, a profile that is controlled by Survey Repository. (You'll find a more technical explanation of a managed profile later on in the book, but this should suffice for now.)

With a managed profile open, you can open a run that was performed against that profile or create a new run. One important concept about managing runs is that you can't make changes to a run once it is in Survey Repository. If you need to add response sheets, you need to create a new run against that particular revision of the survey profile. This is to ensure that a run is a complete unit of work and not a gradually changing set of data. People taking surveys need to complete the entire set of results (which they can do against a disk file until they're ready to place it in Survey Repository) before submitting the run to the Survey Repository Web service. To add a run to Survey Repository, follow these steps:

1. Open a survey profile from Survey Repository.
2. Open a run from Survey Repository or from disk to get the run editor open.

3. Select Run, Add to Repository. You are prompted to choose a profile and a revision of that profile against which the current run was performed. If you choose a survey that doesn't match the survey data that is contained in the run, you receive an error message (see Figure 2.9).

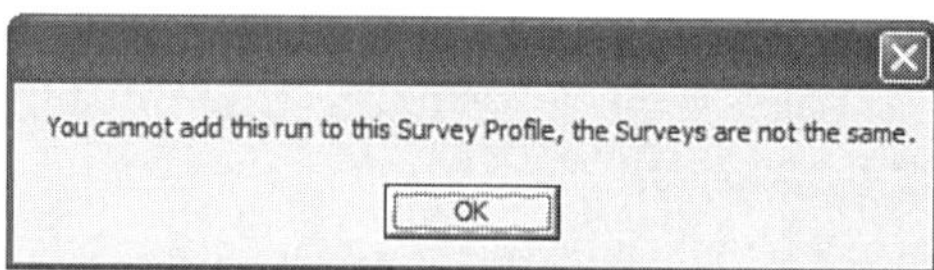

FIGURE 2.9
An error message indicating a survey profile mismatch when trying to add a run to Survey Repository.

This keeps the data consistent and prevents you from accidentally attaching a run to the wrong survey.

STEP-BY-STEP GUIDE: Modifying an Existing Survey Repository–Managed Profile

As with a run, when you're working with a survey profile that is being managed by Survey Repository, you can't just open it, make changes, and save your changes as you could with a disk file. This is the procedure for changing a managed survey profile:

1. Check out the profile.
2. Make your changes.
3. Check your work back in to Survey Repository.

This leaves the original revision of the profile intact and creates an additional revision of the profile that contains your changes. In this way, Survey Repository acts very much like a source control system that has been specialized for survey-related data.

STEP-BY-STEP GUIDE: Conducting Surveys on a Pocket PC

A Pocket PC is a handy device in many situations. It offers users enhanced portability and powerful processing power with a small form factor. However, there are some downsides, including the small form factor. You can fit very little information on the small screen of a Pocket PC.

A common misconception is that you can simply take a standard Windows application and perform some calculated shrinking on the forms, and that application will be able to run on a Pocket PC. In truth, applications that run on a Pocket PC need to be designed to run under the limitations of the mobile operating system, with the limitations as well as benefits of a mobile device being a core part of the design of any mobile application.

Our mobile application allows people performing survey runs to get rid of the paper and clipboard. They can approach a person they would like to survey and hand the person the stylus, and that person can then complete the survey at his or her leisure, with privacy and complete anonymity if desired. The following set of steps walks you through the process of conducting a survey on the Pocket PC:

1. In order for the PocketSurvey application to work, you need to copy a survey profile into the `\Program Files\PocketSurvey` directory on the mobile device. When the device is used, it will continually add response sheets to a file on the mobile device. The Visual Studio .NET 2003 solution that comes on the CD that accompanies this book is configured to have a sample survey deploy with the application so you can debug it on the emulator.

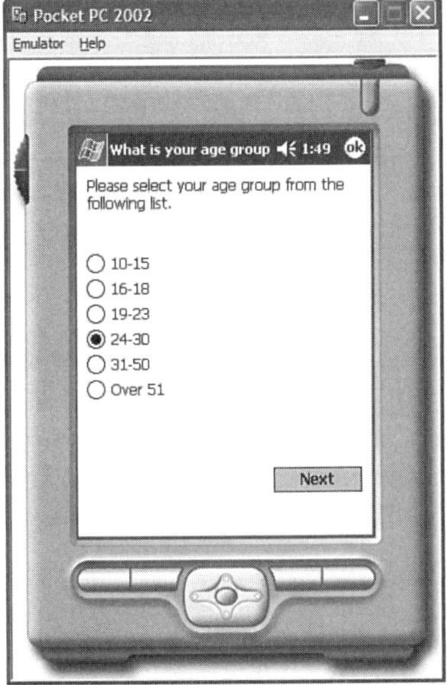

FIGURE 2.10
The sample survey on a Pocket PC device.

The information contained on the mobile device is not to be considered a complete run. Take the shopping mall example again. In order to conduct the survey, the survey administrators have people stationed in front of each of the anchor stores in the mall. This means that there could be as many as 10 or 20 different mobile devices accumulating response sheets for the same run.

2. To facilitate the combination of all these sheets into a single run from within Survey Development Studio, the Survey Development Studio application has a function called Import Sheets. This lets you open a file that is stored in the `\Program Files\PocketSurvey` directory on the mobile device and import not only the response sheets but the respondents from that device. When all the mobile devices participating in the run have had their sheets imported, you can then put the run into Survey Repository for safe keeping. When the run is in Survey Repository, the back-end database administration can take care of backing up the vital data.

Adapting the Survey Repository Application to Different Uses

Throughout this book, you will see a lot of code that performs fairly advanced tasks. You'll see database code, Web service code, Windows Forms code, Pocket PC code, and much more. One of the keys to learning is being able to adapt something you already have to a new purpose. For this book, you have a collection of code.

This book certainly doesn't assume that everyone reading it will be in need of a suite of software that is designed to administer customer opinion surveys. Instead, the real use of this book will be in giving you enough information to adapt the solution provided to the industry for which you are creating an application.

The following sections list some possible adaptations of this software to different markets. Don't take this list as a complete list. There will be many more uses that none of us involved in creating the book ever thought of. We will all have achieved our goal if you find a use for the knowledge you gained in this book to adapt the code to your own needs.

Inventory Management

Picture this situation: You work for a large company and you need to take inventory for several large warehouses. You have a team of 10 people who can help you with this task. The trick is to coordinate the results of all 10 people into a single unit that can be analyzed and possibly extracted into a stock management software package.

One way you could solve this problem is to have each person go out and take inventory by hand and then have someone tabulate all the results, add everything together, and hand-enter the inventory information into a desktop application. Unfortunately, this has a few bad side effects, such as a high probability of error and extensive manual labor for at least one poor soul stuck in front of the application for days.

On the other hand, you could adapt the Survey Development Suite to manage your company's inventory for you. You've already seen what a profile and a run are. Think about replacing the concept of a profile with a definition of a physical location that needs to have inventory taken. Each time a run was taken for the location, it could be added to the repository and stored with a specific date. This way, the application would know the results of each inventory each time inventory was taken. By using the Import Sheets feature in the Survey Development Studio, you could aggregate the results from multiple Pocket PC devices into a single, cohesive run (or inventory batch, or whatever you wanted to call that particular control unit).

Now you would have an application that would allow people to go out into the warehouses and storage facilities and take physical inventory of items by using a Pocket PC. When those Pocket PCs were synchronized with the controlling desktop, the results could be aggregated into a single run. That run could then be checked in to the repository and stored in an XML format in the SQL server.

To take this application to the next level, you could write an export process that grabs the XML that represents an individual run, parses it, and then inserts it into whatever application the company uses for physical inventory tracking. By comparing the results of two different inventory batches (or runs), you could examine trends and make forecasting decisions based on average rate of decay of inventory. All this would be possible with just a few modifications to the PocketSurvey program and some cosmetic changes to the Survey Development Studio and Survey Repository applications.

As I said previously, the real aim of this book and the sample applications isn't to teach you how to build a survey administration program. It is to teach you how to create an enterprise-class, connected, agile application that you can adapt to your own needs.

Quality Control

Quality control is certainly an area that a lot of companies spend a lot of time, effort, and money on. Quality control applies to virtually anything that needs to be verified as functioning properly—anything from a software application to a meter on the side of a building, all the way to a temperature sensor on a vat of liquid in the middle of a manufacturing plant.

To apply the Survey Development Suite to a problem like this, you would need to make very few changes to the application suite. The following paragraphs describe a sample usage scenario.

A supervisor or technician of some kind could use the adapted Survey Development Studio to come up with several profiles. Rather than these being survey questionnaire profiles, they could be testing profiles. Each profile would be a series of questions that, when answered completely, would return a profile of the quality level of whatever is being measured.

The results of quality control tests or surveys could then be placed in the repository for storage. Because Survey Repository already supports things such as storing the user who checked in a run and when the run was checked in, an audit trail would already be in place to log the quality control activities.

A custom tool could then be created to read the quality control survey results from the repository and create reports. Thresholds could be established, and when the results of the quality control surveys fell below the threshold values, warnings could be sent to the appropriate people so they could correct the situation.

In a live situation, this could be immensely useful. Someone who doesn't necessarily know what the values of specific meters mean could go out and read those values. The values would then be stored in the handheld device. As soon as the values stored in the handheld device were uploaded to the repository, a background process could reanalyze the data, looking for values outside the safety limits. If such values were detected, the system could then page or email an administrator or some other person who is capable of dealing with the situation. For situations where values outside the threshold could cause dangerous or fatal conditions, an adapted application like this might be extremely useful.

Market Research

Market research is an application of the Survey Development Suite that probably wouldn't require many code changes, if any at all. People interested in market trends would devise various survey profiles using Survey Development Studio. These profiles would ask questions in such a way that the results could be analyzed to reveal various trends or facts about particular demographic areas or potential markets.

After the profiles were created, people could go out and obtain opinion data, using the PocketSurvey application. The way the application is architected, a single run could take place across multiple handheld devices. This would allow you to deploy dozens of people to multiple locations in order to obtain consumer opinion data. When all those people had reported back with their handheld devices, the information on the devices could be aggregated into a single run.

The run could then be placed into the Survey Repository application, where it would be time indexed and stamped with the particular user who added the run. This run could then be analyzed using a third-party tool or a tool created by the original developers. The analysis could be generic, or it could be tailored specifically to extracting market trends from consumer opinion data.

Election Exit Polling

Thousands of people turn on the TV on election night to see who is winning. Before the polls start reporting their results, people want to know who is in the lead. This is usually determined with exit polls. People position themselves at strategic voting centers and ask people who they voted for as they leave the polls. The results are then somehow communicated to a central location, where the statistics are calculated. TV viewers can then see an estimate or a projection of what might be the final results.

You could easily adapt Survey Development Suite to automate this scenario. As people leave the polls, surveyors could approach them, Pocket PC in hand, and administer a specially designed survey, asking them how they voted on the various questions. Instead of waiting for the Pocket PC to synchronize with a desktop computer, people would need the results immediately so that a real-time estimate could be generated.

For the real-time analysis of ongoing results, you could modify the PocketSurvey program to transmit each response sheet to a Web service over the Internet. The only requirement would then be that the Pocket PC devices used by the surveyors have some kind of Internet access. If you added the response sheets in real-time, using a Web service, the results of the exit polls could be analyzed and broadcast.

Each exit poll could be a different survey profile. As response sheets were recorded by each surveyor, they would be added to a run. The response sheets could then be uploaded to the survey repository via the Internet and Web services. The results of the runs could then be extracted from the survey repository and analyzed by a tool specifically designed to produce exit poll results in a graphic format for display on a Web site or even broadcast on the nightly news.

Traffic Analysis

One possible use for the Survey Development Suite could be in determining traffic patterns and possibly determining solutions to complex traffic problems.

Assume that you have someone in the field using a Pocket PC. Instead of the Pocket PC administering a standard survey, it is administering a custom data entry form that requests data about traffic patterns, car counts, light durations, and so forth.

The person in the field could then submit the information from the handheld device to Survey Repository. Using a custom-developed tool, analysts could then obtain the data from the repository, aggregate it, and then come up with solutions to traffic bottlenecks or even do things such as determine the efficiency of a particular speed limit.

Education and Test Administration

Let's examine the problem domain for a moment. Most of us remember what it was like being in high school. We probably have nightmarish memories of the teacher's grade book—the voluminous tome that he or she carried around, held together with a giant rubber band, with dozens of unintelligible notes sticking out of it from all angles. After you took a test, the teacher collected all the tests and graded them. The teacher then placed all the grades in the magical grade book. Within that book, the teacher would then somehow arrive at a grade that you may or may not have been pleased with.

Now that we've suffered a flashback of our high school days, how can the Survey Development Suite be applied to this problem domain to create a unique and interesting solution? Take the following paragraphs as a use case for this particular adaptation.

The teacher could arrive at the classroom and gleefully hand out a difficult exam to the students. Everyone could take the test and then all turn in their papers. Later that night, the teacher would grade papers at home. As she graded each paper, the teacher would record the grades in a Pocket PC. When the Pocket PC was synchronized the next time, the grades for all the students would be transmitted to the school's central repository of grades, safe from student tampering.

An even more applicable use case might be this: The teacher could arrive in the classroom and tell the students the URL for an exam. The students would then take the exam on the school's intranet. The students would sequentially go through a series of questions defined by the teacher, and their responses would be recorded, keyed to their student ID numbers.

When all the students in that class had submitted their exams, the results of that exam would then be placed into an exam repository.

One really intriguing possibility here is that a *run* could be a set of grades that the teacher supplies by manually grading the tests. This would be necessary because (unfortunately) not all school tests are multiple choice. Some require essays and illustrated math formulas and so on.

For cases in which the responses to the test could be supplied with combinations of essay answers, multiple choice, ranked numeric answers, and more, each student's responses are treated as a response sheet. The teacher could use the adapted version of Survey Development Studio to create a profile (a quiz or a test). An instance of this profile would then be administered to all the students for a particular class (for example, fourth-period math or second-period English). When all the students for that class were done, the combination of the result sheets for that test would be compiled into a run and locked up in the repository for safe keeping and reporting later. This way, if the teacher taught three math classes, and she wanted to administer the same test to each of the three classes, she could create a run for each period taking the test and be able to keep them all separate. Survey Repository already allows you to label the runs you create, so the teacher could create a run called "first-period geometry" and another run called "second-period geometry."

Legal Depositions and Jury Interviewing

Another possible area to which Survey Development Suite could be adapted is the area of legal depositions and interviewing jury members. When someone gives a statement or answers questions from a lawyer, there is generally a need to have that statement recorded. If you were to modify the Pocket PC application so that a person's legal statement would become the equivalent of a run, you could do quite a bit more. The survey profile could actually be the definition of a particular case that an attorney was working on. Each time someone provided a legal statement, the attorney could then enter that into the application and store it as a response sheet. All the response sheets could then be collected into runs. Custom analysis tools could be used to detect inaccuracies and possible issues with statements when multiple-choice or numeric questions were asked (for example, asking 10 different people the same yes/no question to discern a pattern).

Because writing down someone's lengthy statement is often difficult, even when using a laptop or a dictation machine, you could take advantage of the Pocket PC's built-in microphone and audio recorder. You could then attach the recorded audio of a person's statement and bundle that with the response sheet. Then the audio files could be transcribed at a later time. Having a central repository of interviewee statements could be immensely useful to anyone working in a legal capacity.

I'm not a legal expert by any stretch of the imagination. However, I think it might be useful to discern patterns in the responses of potential jurors to certain questions. For example, say a lawyer asks jurors several multiple-choice and numeric-response questions. Instead of using those values to disqualify one or more jurors, the lawyer could use those responses to determine patterns in opinions and feelings among the jurors.

You could set up custom application around Survey Repository, to allow multiple attorneys working on the same case access to the store of case data. If you got a little more ambitious, you could modify the Pocket PC application to allow even more data entry to record investigative data and other facts that might be pertinent to the case. With some polish and some effort, it could provide a total workflow solution for investigative legal work.

Law Enforcement: Activity Logs and Witness Statements

There are some more potential legal-related uses for an application with the same architecture as Survey Development Suite. In essence, any application in which sets of data are obtained one or more times for a given set of meta-data is one that will fit the application style of Survey Development Suite.

One of those kinds of data has to do with law enforcement officials. Throughout the day, a police officer or detective obtains lots of information. You could provide a useful service by modifying the PocketSurvey application in such a way that it used a response sheet for information obtained from a person encountered throughout the workday of a police officer or detective.

With information such as witness statements stored in response sheets, you could create runs from the daily logs of law enforcement officials. These logs could then be secured safely within the repository.

In addition to storing things such as witness statements, the handheld device could allow people to store activity logs such as locations visited and times, observations, and so on. All this information could also be stored in the repository.

When all the important information was in the repository, it could be reviewed by detectives or other officials who might want to see the information recorded. By keeping a digital record of all the information encountered throughout a day, you could increase the reliability of the information.

In addition to increasing the reliability of information gathered, you could increase its accessibility. Rather than having to flip through a notebook of hand-written information, you could build full-text indexes on the information stored in the repository. This would allow you to find all the information related to a specific person, location, or case.

Again, the point here is not that there are hundreds of wonderful ways that you can adapt the Survey Development Suite to meet your needs. The point is that given the technology, architecture, and model used by the applications in this book, you can reuse information and reapply it elsewhere, hopefully to solve a problem for yourself or for your company.

Moving On

This chapter discusses how to use the PocketSurvey application and how the application's intended audience might use it. While you might not have done any actual coding in this chapter, you have actually been fairly productive. It is extremely hard to improve and enhance an application that you yourself don't know how to use. If you've had to work on an application you aren't familiar with, you know the truth in that. Hopefully, this chapter has given you some background on the applications you'll be working on for the rest of the book and you're eager to get coding.

Exploring the Code of the Survey Development Suite

CHAPTER 3

At this point you're probably pretty eager to get into the code. We've covered the basics of what the Survey Development Suite does and how it can be used. We haven't covered how the application actually accomplishes all the things we've seen it doing. This chapter covers the following:

- Infrastructure services
- Error handling
- Survey Repository
- Survey Development Studio
- PocketSurvey

Before taking a look at the application itself, we'll take a look at some of the core code that provides the basic foundation on which all the other code in the application is written.

The Survey Development Suite is divided into three parts: Survey Repository, which functions as a Web service back end, Survey Development Studio, which is a Windows Forms application, and PocketSurvey, which is a Pocket PC application for conducting surveys in a mobile situation. Each of these three parts is a separate, fully functioning application that also communicates with other pieces of the software suite. In this regard, we consider the collection of the three applications to be a single, enterprise-class application suite.

This chapter walks you through the process used to design the various pieces of the application and takes you on a tour of some of the most interesting highlights of the code that makes this application possible.

To make things as easy to grasp as possible, we'll start at the back end, with Survey Repository, and then we'll cover the Survey Development Studio Windows application. We'll finish up with coverage of the Pocket PC application.

This chapter takes a step-by-step approach to examining the code of the Survey Development Suite. People learn new technologies and techniques in very different ways. Some people prefer to be instructed without knowing anything about the new technology. Other people prefer to dive head-first into the code, gather a list of questions about the code, and then get more information. If the latter applies to you, you might want to open the Visual Studio .NET project that is on this book's CD and explore all the various projects within it. Spend an hour or so looking at the code and figuring out how everything fits together. When you're done, come back to this chapter and read it through from start to finish to fill in any gaps in your understanding of the code.

Survey Repository

As you know, Survey Repository is a Web service that provides a warehousing facility for survey profiles and survey runs. It is made up of two separate Web services (`.asmx` files): a login service and the repository service itself. This separation allows us to communicate with the login service via SSL and to keep the repository service communications clear for performance reasons.

Take a look at the architectural diagram in Figure 3.1.

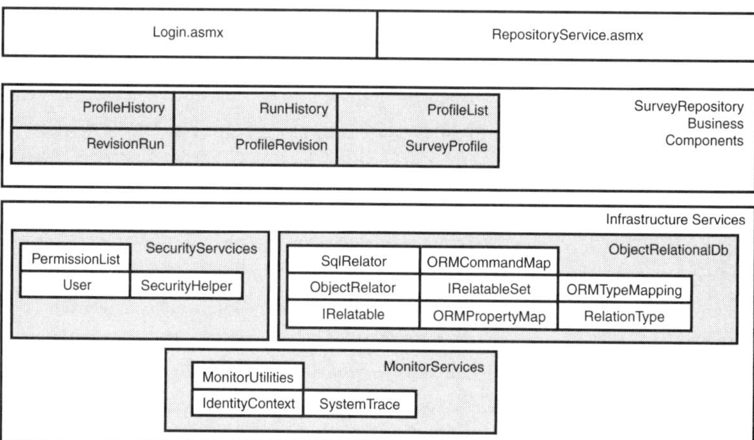

FIGURE 3.1
The logical structure of the Survey Repository Web service.

At the top level are the two service files `Login.asmx` and `RepositoryService.asmx`. These are the entry points into the Web service provided by Survey Repository. When these entry points are used, they in turn invoke any number of business classes represented by the second large box in Figure 3.1. These business components are used as an interface to the Object-Relational Mapping (ORM) mapper, which is contained in the lowest level, the infrastructure services.

Infrastructure Services

Whenever I sit down to come up with a design for a new Web site, one of the first things I do is come up with a list of all the services that the pages are going to need. Invariably, I come up with the same set of services every time, as virtually every data-driven Web application requires the same things:

- Security
- Tracing, monitoring, and instrumentation
- Data access
- Application-specific services

If you build applications with an architecture-first model, you will find that not only will your applications be quicker and easier to code but you may be able to reuse a lot of your infrastructure code for the next application.

For example, the data access services that I used for this application are an evolution of various data abstraction methods that I have been using for over two years. Each time I get to reuse the code, I find room for enhancements and improvements.

CODE TOUR: The `SecurityServices` Project

The `SecurityServices` project should be available within the `SurveyV1` solution. The purpose of this library is to abstract access to the security system used by the application. When you do this, you are in a better position to grow or change the security model in the future without affecting the entire application.

`SecurityServices` provides the classes listed in Table 3.1 (as well as some additional code that you'll see when we take a closer look).

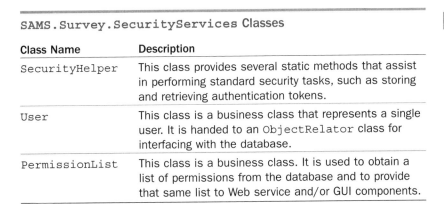

TABLE 3.1 `SAMS.Survey.SecurityServices` Classes

Class Name	Description
`SecurityHelper`	This class provides several static methods that assist in performing standard security tasks, such as storing and retrieving authentication tokens.
`User`	This class is a business class that represents a single user. It is handed to an `ObjectRelator` class for interfacing with the database.
`PermissionList`	This class is a business class. It is used to obtain a list of permissions from the database and to provide that same list to Web service and/or GUI components.

CODE TOUR: The `SecurityHelper` Class

When designing a class that abstracts security tasks, you need to take the time to figure out exactly what tasks you will need to have performed and where those tasks should be performed.

CODE TOUR: The `SecurityHelper` Class

The following are two of the most interesting methods of the `SecurityHelper` class:

- **`SetIdentityContext`**—This method stores user information in the `CallContext` class, making it available to subsequent method calls.
- **`GetUserIdFromToken`**—This method takes a string that contains an authentication token and returns the corresponding user ID, if there is one.

For the moment, let's focus on the last method, `GetUserIdFromToken`. In order to understand what this method does, you need to understand how the security system works for the Web service.

I needed a way to make sure that the password and username information remained secure, but I didn't want to incur the overhead of using SSL for every single transaction with the Web service. Knowing this, I couldn't very well pass the username and password with each and every request.

I didn't want to enable session state because that could lead down a road from which I couldn't return: mostly because if someone left his or her Survey Development Studio application running overnight and then clicked somewhere the next morning, the request would fail with unpredictable results due to that user's session having expired.

Although I could have used Microsoft Web Services Enhancements 2.0 to get access to some of the most robust security features that can be used within Web services, I didn't feel the need to use it. I wanted a very simple solution. The target audience for this application is a network site managed by a company that is involved in producing and conducting opinion surveys. For the most part, it didn't need all the extras included in Web Services Enhancements 2.0.

The solution I ended up with was the concept of tokens. You may have seen this concept if you have looked at some of the early prototypes for the Favorites Service that was produced by Microsoft. It was a sample application produced for Cold Rooster Consulting. You can find the documentation and a working demo of this sample at `www.coldrooster.com`.

A *token*, in our daily lives, is some piece of proof or evidence. In New York or Boston, a token might be proof that you are allowed to get onto the subway system. A token in the sense of a Web service is a piece of evidence that verifies that a given user is allowed to access the Web service.

The way a token works is fairly simple, as illustrated in Figure 3.2.

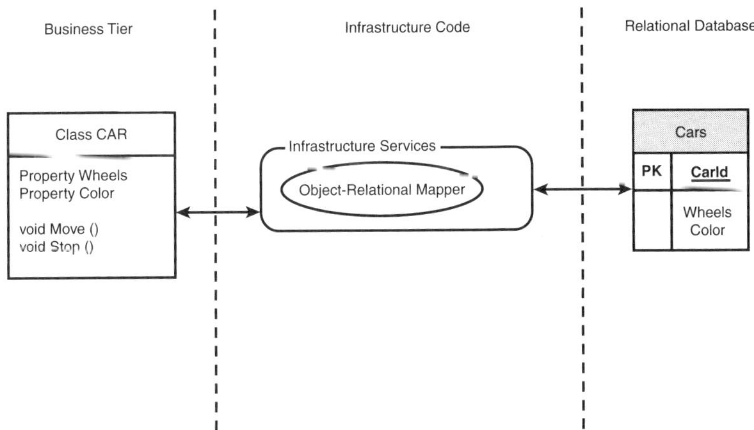

FIGURE 3.2

The login and token assignment process.

As you can see in Figure 3.2, the client application first makes contact with the login Web service by providing a set of credentials that includes a username and password. If this were a more complex application, a client might be required to provide a CD or license key to prove that the client application itself is legitimate. After the credentials have been validated, a token (in this case, a GUID) is returned to the client. The client is then able to pass that token to the repository Web service to gain access to the various methods exposed by that service. If a call to that service doesn't contain a valid security token, the client performing the action receives an error.

Behind the scenes, a lot is going on. First, when a set of credentials is received by `Login.asmx` (you will see the code for this later in this chapter), a call is made to the database to validate the username and password combination. If it is valid, a token (or GUID) is generated. That generated GUID is then stored in the ASP.NET application cache for some period (this application defaults to one hour), along with information on which user that GUID belongs to.

When a request comes in to the repository Web service, a check is made against the ASP.NET application cache for the supplied token GUID. If the token exists in the cache, the call is allowed to proceed as normal. Otherwise, the call is rejected. Listing 3.1 shows the code that obtains the valid user ID by looking up the authentication token in the ASP.NET application cache.

LISTING 3.1 SurveyV1\SecurityServices\SecurityHelper.cs
The `GetUserIdFromToken` and `SetIdentityContext` Methods

```
public static int GetUserIdFromToken( string userToken )
{
  System.Web.Caching.Cache cache = System.Web.HttpContext.Current.Cache;
  if (cache != null)
  {
     string securityKey = "Security-" + userToken;
     if (cache[securityKey] == null)
    return -1;
     PermissionList pl = (PermissionList)cache[securityKey];
     return pl.UserId;
  }
  else
  {
    return -1;
  }
}
public static void SetIdentityContext( int userId )
{
  IdentityContext ic = new IdentityContext();
  ic.UserKey = userId.ToString();

  // if we ever need to have more information about the user contained in the method
  // execution chain, we can just add it to the identity context.
  ic.DisplayName = userId.ToString();

  CallContext.SetData("SAMS_SURVEY_IDENTITY", ic );
}
```


You can see in Listing 3.1 that the key index used for the application cache contains the prefix `Security`. This is not completely necessary because GUIDs are guaranteed to be completely unique and never overlap any other code using the same cache. However, if someone is using an administrative tool to look at the contents of the application cache and that person sees hundreds of seemingly random GUIDs lying around, he or she might not know what they're for. With the method used in Listing 3.1, anyone examining the cache should immediately know the purpose of the GUIDs.

Also worth noting is that we're not simply storing the user's ID in the cache. We're actually storing the list of that user's permissions. Whenever a user is authenticated against the system, a call is made that obtains all of the user's security privileges. Those privileges are then placed in the cache, to be associated with the authentication token. This enables every single method of any Web service within this AppDomain class to be able to know what a given user can and cannot do, without making additional database calls.

Call Contexts

In Listing 3.1, you might have noticed the `SetIdentityContext` method. This method creates an instance of the `IdentityContext` class and then places it in the call context with the following statement:

```
CallContext.SetData("SAMS_SURVEY_IDENTITY", ic );
```

In order to get access to the `CallContext` class, you need to reference the `System.Runtime.Remoting.Messaging` namespace, which contains the code that makes call contexts work.

What is a call context? You can think of it as a stack that sits on top of a chain of execution. The first time you invoke a method within the .NET Framework, a call context is created. This context is attached to, and available from, every subsequent method call made after the context is created. This allows the remoting infrastructure to pass additional information between process boundaries. However, it has a handy side effect of working on nonremote method execution as well.

After you place data in a call context, the data becomes available to every method called thereafter, as well as to methods called by those methods, and so on throughout a deep level of recursion.

To place data in a call context, you use the `SetData` method. This allows you to place an object of any data type into a named slot that is represented by a string. In the case of the code in Listing 3.1, the named slot is `"SAMS_SURVEY_IDENTITY"`, but you are free to use any name you like. The only caveat is that you need to make sure there is a good chance that the name is unique. If your application is making use of another API that utilizes call contexts, the last thing you want to do is place your data in a slot expected by the API.

To retrieve data from the call context, you use the `GetData` method. This method returns an instance of an object of varying data type. It is up to you, the programmer, to know ahead of time the type of data that you placed in the call context.

Although using a call context can be handy, it can also have some serious drawbacks. The main drawback of call contexts is that their data is propagated each time a method is invoked. The more methods that are invoked, the more times data must be passed along the stack. If you rely too heavily on call contexts, you might end up degrading the performance of your applications.

A good rule of thumb to use with call contexts is to use them only when you know that the information needs to be available to any method, and the information you are passing along the stack has a very small memory footprint, such as a single integer or a short string.

CODE TOUR: The `User` Class

The `User` class is a business object that serves as a container for user-related information. In addition to holding information about a given user, it provides various methods that are applicable to users, such as `Validate`, `Create`, `Update`, and `Delete`. This class makes use of the ORM tools contained within the data access layer (you will be seeing those later in this chapter). Listing 3.2 contains the `User` class. Before you see the code for the `User` class, take a look at Tables 3.2 and 3.3, which list the properties and methods of the class.

TABLE 3.2 `User` Class Methods

Method	Description
`Validate`	This method is used to determine the validity of the current username and password combination. If the user is valid, a value greater than zero is returned.
`Create`	This method uses the values in the `FullName`, `UserName`, and `Password` properties to create a new user.
`Delete`	This method deletes the user indicated by the current value of the `UserId` property.
`Update`	This method updates the current user indicated by the `UserId` property with the values contained in the `FullName`, `UserName`, and `Password` properties.
`Load`	This method loads a specific user indicated by the `UserId` property. The results of the load operation populate the `UserName`, `FullName`, and `Password` properties.

TABLE 3.3

User Class Properties

Property	Description
UserId	Indicates the current value of the user's ID.
FullName	Gets or sets the user's full name.
UserName	Gets or sets the login name of the user.
Password	Gets or sets the user's password.

LISTING 3.2 SurveyV1\SecurityServices\User.cs
The User Class

```
using System;
using System.Data;

using SAMS.Survey.Core.MonitorServices;
using SAMS.Survey.Core.ObjectRelationalDb;

namespace SAMS.Survey.SecurityServices
{
  public class User : IRelatable
  {
    private int userId;
    private string fullName;
    private string userName;
    private string password;

    public User()
    {
    }

    public int Validate()
    {
    SqlRelator sr = new SqlRelator();
    sr.Relate( this, "Validate" );
    return this.UserId;
    }
```

LISTING 3.2 SurveyV1\SecurityServices\User.cs
The User Class
(continued)

```
        public void Create()
        {
        SqlRelator sr = new SqlRelator();
        sr.Relate( this, RelationType.Insert );
        }

        public void Delete()
        {
        SqlRelator sr = new SqlRelator();
        sr.Relate( this, RelationType.Delete );
        }

        public void Update()
        {
        SqlRelator sr = new SqlRelator();
        sr.Relate( this, RelationType.Update );
        }
    }
}
```


Note that I've stripped from Listing 3.2 the code that contains the public property definitions for the private members, as it is just straightforward `get` and `set` accessors.

A few things about the `User` class should stand out right away when you look at Listing 3.2. The first is that it implements a marker interface called `IRelatable`. This interface tells the ORM mapper that the class is eligible for interfacing with the database through an ORM. It is actually nothing more than an empty marker. While we could use an abstract base class or even a custom code attribute to perform such marking, the interface allows us to implement our own hierarchy if we chose while still maintaining the hierarchy. Also, testing for the implementation of an interface on a class instance is much faster than using reflection to query the list of custom attributes on a class.

The other thing that stands out in Listing 3.2 is that the class makes no use of stored procedures. In fact, it has absolutely no built-in knowledge of how to persist itself. As I'll discuss later in this chapter, this is a key point in true object-ORM. Instead of invoking stored procedures directly, the object simply tells the object relator "relate me to the database, using this mapping." The mapping is indicated by the `RelationType` enumeration.

CODE TOUR: The `PermissionList` Class

Just like `User`, `PermissionList` is a business class that makes use of the ORM mapper to communicate with the database. Its specific purpose is to retrieve the list of permissions associated with a given user.

Listing 3.3 contains the `PermissionList` class definition.

LISTING 3.3 `SurveyV1\SecurityServices\PermissionList.cs`
The `PermissionList` Class

```
using System;
using System.Data;
using System.Reflection;

using SAMS.Survey.Core.MonitorServices;
using SAMS.Survey.Core.ObjectRelationalDb;
using Microsoft.ApplicationBlocks.ExceptionManagement;

namespace SAMS.Survey.SecurityServices
{
[Serializable()]
public class PermissionList : MarshalByRefObject, IRelatableSet
{
  private DataSet internalData;
  private int userId;

  public PermissionList()
  {
    internalData = new DataSet();
  }

  public DataSet ResultSet
  {
    get
    {
```

LISTING 3.3 SurveyV1\SecurityServices\PermissionList.cs
The PermissionList Class
(continued)

```
    return internalData;
    }
    set
    {
    internalData = value;
    }
  }

  public int UserId
  {
    get
    {
    return userId;
    }
    set
    {
    userId = value;
    }
  }

  public void FetchPermissions( int userId )
  {
    this.userId = userId;
    SqlRelator sr = new SqlRelator();
    sr.Relate( this, RelationType.Select );
    SystemTrace.TraceVerbose("Selected user {0} permissions, Tables returned: {1}",
      userId, internalData.Tables.Count);
  }

  public bool HasPermission( int permissionId, int accessMode )
  {
    SystemTrace.MethodStart( MethodBase.GetCurrentMethod() );
    if (internalData.Tables.Count == 0)
    {
       ExceptionManager.Publish(
        new InvalidOperationException(
          "Cannot check for unfetched permissions.") );
```

LISTING 3.3 SurveyV1\SecurityServices\PermissionList.cs
The PermissionList Class
(continued)

```
    }
    else
    {
    DataTable perms = internalData.Tables[0];
    DataRow[] permission =
          perms.Select("PermissionId=" + permissionId.ToString());
    if ((permission.Length ==0) || (permission == null))
    {
       SystemTrace.TraceVerbose(
             "Permission check failed due to missing " +
             "permission {0}, total rows available : {1}",
          permissionId, perms.Rows.Count);
       return false;
    }
    else
    {
       return SecurityHelper.CheckAccess(
             (int)permission[0]["Access"],
              accessMode );
    }
     }
     return false;
  }
 }
}
```

There is some code in the PermissionList class that you haven't yet seen. Some of the methods belong to the SystemTrace class that we'll be discussing in the next section of this chapter. Those methods are all about tracing and making the job of debugging the application easier.

The FetchPermissions method works fairly simply. It relates the current instance of PermissionList to the database, using the Select ORM. This obtains all the permissions that the current user (indicated by the UserId property) has.

The HasPermission method is a bit more complex than FetchPermissions. It uses the internalData object, which is a data set, to look up all the permissions available to the user. If one of those permissions is the permission indicated by the argument, then the user has that permission.

There is a catch, however. Our system not only supports the notion of a yes/no type of permission, but it also supports the notion of access modes. For example, it is possible for a user to have a permission called `Survey Profiles`, but that user may only have the `Read` access mode. This person then has read-only access to the profiles contained within the repository. However, another person might have the same permission, but with a higher access level. With this system in place, administrators have the ability to fine-tune what each user can perform. Because our system is designed for role-based security, it is easy to manage as well as flexible.

The `MonitorServices` Project

The `MonitorServices` project is a project that contains classes that provide for unified tracing, easier debugging, and general monitoring-related utilities, such as an `IdentityContext` class. We will take a closer look at the `MonitorServices` project later in this chapter, when we take a tour of the unified tracing system in the application.

The `ObjectRelationalDb` Project

The `ObjectRelationalDb` project contains, as I'm sure you guessed, all the classes required to create ORM and to use these mappings to perform database operations in a seamless, transparent way that makes writing business objects a snap. We'll discuss this project in more detail in the code tour "A Look at the ORM Schema," after some discussion on the concepts surrounding ORM.

Data Access with ORM

In the following sections, we'll take a look at accessing data using an object-relational model. We'll compare this model to the standard procedural model for data access and talk about the benefits and drawbacks of using ORM.

What Is ORM?

When most programmers think about data access, they think about stored procedures, parameters, and SQL statements. They think about how to write code that wraps around a stored procedure or around SQL statements so that the tedium of accessing the database is taken away, leaving the programmers free to think about the overall business model of the application.

One particular train of thought on the subject of data access deals with the idea of ORM. This concept, as illustrated in Figure 3.3, deals with the mapping of information contained in the world of classes, instances, and objects to information contained in the world of a relational database, consisting of tables, columns, and rows.

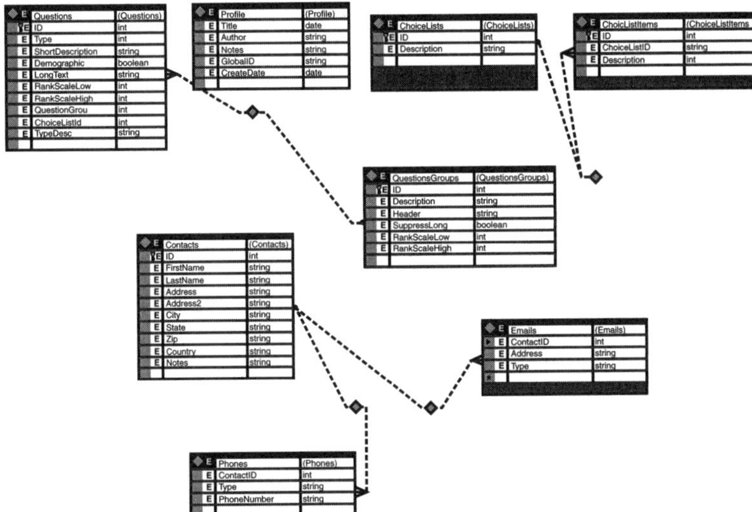

FIGURE 3.3
The `SurveyProfile` typed data set.

In its purest form, ORM implies that class instances are mapped to rows within database tables. Columns within those tables are mapped to public fields or properties on the class instance. When more than one row of data results from a query operation, the set of rows is then mapped into a collection of objects, and each object in the collection is an object that maps directly to one and only one row within the table.

As with all good programming theories, with ORM there is often a balance between the pure theory behind the solution and the practicality of implementing the solution. Often, implementations of ORM make certain sacrifices in pure OOP design in order to achieve some gains in performance, usability, or flexibility.

For example, an implementation from Microsoft that is part of a technical preview of a suite of tools called `ObjectSpaces` does an excellent job of mapping class instances to tables, columns, and rows. However, it only works with SQL Server Yukon (take a look at `http://msdn.microsoft.com/library/default.asp?url=/library/en-us/dnsql90/html/sql_ovyukondev.asp` for an overview of Yukon and its impact on developers) and doesn't currently support stored procedures. This is one of the tradeoffs made in order to place an implementation as close to the pure theory of ORM as possible. Microsoft may indeed add stored procedure support for its `ObjectSpaces` library in the future; in this case, you'll be well versed in the concepts involved, having looked at the code contained in this section of the book.

Why Use ORM?

If there are inherent performance concerns with building a system that implements the pure vision of ORM, why should we bother using it? It has quite a few benefits, as described in the following sections.

Provider Agnostic

In a true implementation of ORM, it should be possible to create business objects that have absolutely no embedded information about how to persist themselves, other than the fact that they can be persisted. For example, a non-ORM business object might have a `Delete` method. This `Delete` method might create an instance of a `Command` object, invoke the command, and then return some result. The problem with this is that if the database information changes, the `Delete` method could become completely invalid. If you decouple the business object from the means by which that object is persisted to some data source, the business objects can be freely versioned without worrying about the database. In addition, the database information can be changed easily without negatively affecting the entire collection of business objects in the application.

Declarative Persistence

Another of the incredible benefits of using an ORM model is that you can simply declare the mapping. Instead of writing 20 lines of code to create a set of command parameters, instantiate a connection, open the connection, and so on, you can simply declare, through some means, sufficient information to automatically map instance data to relational data. Some implementations use proprietary data formats (for example, J2EE's Container-Managed Persistence [CMP] uses meta-data files that are contained in `.jar` archives), and others use standard XML data to list the mapping information (for example, our implementation, Microsoft's `ObjectSpaces` implementation).

Code Simplicity

A side effect of storing all the persistence information in some meta-data mapping (XML, `.jar` file, and so on) is that the code required to actually perform a persistence operation is minimal. In general, the pattern is to create an instance of the mapper (or whatever tool you're using). When you have an instance of a mapper, you simply pass to the mapper the instance of the object you want to persist, along with some helper information, and the operation is performed for you.

If you're an architect building a framework on which a team of junior programmers will be building an application, this kind of scenario can be a lifesaver. The simpler it is for your programmers to write fundamental, core code for the application, the less chance there is of bugs creeping up.

Scalability

If ORM is implemented properly, you can actually change everything about your back-end database without ever having to recompile your business or data-tier objects. You might be thinking, "I never change columns or tables after I release a product." That might be true, but you're in the minority. The reality is that things change. You might upgrade your database server from Oracle 8 to Oracle 9, from SQL 7 to SQL 2000. This upgrade might cause some subtle change that breaks one of your stored procedure invocations. If all you have to do is modify an XML file or just recompile the assembly that contains the affected object, your life will be a lot easier.

The implementation of ORM that I've gone with for this book is a little bit different than the pure concept of what ORM is. Instead of mapping instance fields to table columns, I've decided to map instance fields to stored procedure parameters. This supports my ORM implementation as the code looks like any other ORM implementation, and I can still use stored procedures to give the application the most performance and flexibility possible.

ORM Versus CMP

Aside from being different acronyms, what exactly do ORM and CMP mean, and what is the difference between the two? ORM is pretty much exactly what it sounds like: You have an instance of an object, and the database access is performed by relating individual pieces of that object to the database in some fashion. Some implementations, such as the one used in this book, relate public class members to stored procedure parameters. Other implementations, such as Microsoft's `ObjectSpaces`, relate individual objects and their public members to SQL statements that are then executed on the database.

CMP differs from ORM in some minor ways. The concept of CMP involves an object instance and a container. The container is an abstraction of the underlying physical data storage medium. This container could be an abstraction of a relational database, but it could also be an abstraction of an XML file, a folder containing multiple files on disk, a Microsoft message queue, or even a Web service.

The two concepts ORM and CMP both have the same core idea: that the business or data object that is being persisted or related has no direct link to the underlying storage medium. The object instance doesn't know if it is going to be stored in a database, stored in a file on disk, or transmitted via SOAP to a Web service. Both CMP and ORM rely on this concept as a foundational aspect of their respective design patterns.

Where the two ideas begin to diverge is in the concept of how communication with the data source takes place. The traditional ORM model maps a single instance of an object to stored procedure parameters or to a SQL statement that is then executed. With CMP, the "container" model is more prevalent; an object instance is placed into a container, and that's all that the programmer ever sees. The act of inserting an object into a container triggers some functionality on the container that will determine what kind of persistence operation to perform. The data contained on the object combined with meta-data stored somewhere provides information about how to complete the persistence operation.

In reality, there are almost no pure implementations of either ORM or CMP. The Java implementation of CMP requires that the meta-data for persistence operations be stored in a `.jar` file on the server. Microsoft's `ObjectSpaces` uses attributes and meta-data to convert an object instance into a SQL statement that can then be executed against the database server. The implementation of ORM in this book uses XML meta-data stored embedded in assemblies; this meta-data is used to relate public member data to stored procedure parameters to interact with the database.

CODE TOUR: A Look at the ORM Schema

I've experimented with quite a few different variations on CMP and ORM. A previous version of CMP that I used had the mapping data stored in an XML file on disk. This file was opened upon application startup and was used to build an in-memory cache of mapping data. This cache was then used to dynamically create stored procedures, as needed by the application.

The problem I found with this approach is that the single XML file could get extremely large, especially when I had dozens of different assemblies all using this file for their own persistence information.

To make things easier to organize, I experimented with using one XML file per assembly. This made things easier to read, but I ended up with a stack of XML files sitting in my Web application's root directory.

I didn't feel comfortable with the plain-text files sitting in the application directory. The version I've implemented for this book actually embeds the ORM XML file directly in the assembly as a resource. This resource is then read via reflection and used to create the appropriate stored procedure whenever the ORM mapper is invoked.

Listing 3.4 contains a sample of an ORM that exists in the Survey Development Suite.

LISTING 3.4 `SurveyV1\SecurityServices\ORM.xml`
The `SecurityServices` Assembly's `ORM.xml` File

```
<relationalmapping>
  <type fullname="SAMS.Survey.SecurityServices.User">
    <commandmap storedproc="SVY_Validate_User" multiple="false" type="Validate">
      <propertymap member="UserName"
                   dbtype="Varchar"
                   dbsize="8" parameter="@UserName"
                   direction="Input"></propertymap>
      <propertymap member="Password"
                   dbtype="Varchar"
                   dbsize="8" parameter="@Password"
                   direction="Input"></propertymap>
      <propertymap member="UserId" dbtype="Int"
                   dbsize="4" parameter="@UserId"
                   direction="Output"></propertymap>
      <propertymap member="FullName" dbtype="Varchar"
                   dbsize="40" parameter="@FullName"
                   direction="Output"></propertymap>
    </commandmap>
  </type>
</relationalmapping>
```

The first important element here is the `type` element. This element is the root of a single ORM. It begins the mapping from the instance of a .NET Framework type to multiple stored procedures.

For each type, there can be an unlimited number of stored procedures to invoke. By default, the system has an enumeration for the four CRUD (create, retrieve, update, delete) operations: `Select`, `Insert`, `Update`, and `Delete`. I've named them `Select`, `Insert`, `Update`, and `Delete` because these names closely resemble the SQL statements that represent the kinds of operation they perform.

The mapping between a .NET Framework type (which can be any type that implements either `IRelatable` or any interface that inherits from it) and a stored procedure is defined by the `<commandmap>` element. The `type` attribute on the `<commandmap>` element indicates the kind of relational operation. It can be something custom, as in the preceding `Validate` command mapping, or it can be one of the pre-recognized keywords, such as `Select` or `Update`.

Beneath the `<commandmap>` element is the `<propertymap>` element. This element declares a mapping between a particular field on the given type and a parameter on the stored procedure. The ORM system developed for this book supports both input and output parameters, but the property or field on the object instance must be public; otherwise, the attempt to reflect data from that property will fail and cause undesirable results when communicating with the database.

CODE TOUR: The `ObjectRelator` Class

The `ObjectRelator` class is an abstract class that provides the basic framework for building your own `ObjectRelator` class. It defines two methods:

```
public virtual void Relate( IRelatable relatee,
RelationType relationType )
public virtual void Relate( IRelatable relatee, string relationKey )
```

These two overloads provide the basis for all ORM in the entire system. Any class that wishes to be an `ObjectRelator` class must implement these two methods. The methods allow us to relate an instance object to the database either using one of the four CRUD operations or through some custom-defined operation that corresponds to the `type` attribute on the `<commandMap>` element in the `ORM.xml` embedded resource.

The abstract base class `ObjectRelator` is key to implementing a provider-agnostic implementation of ORM.

CODE TOUR:
The SqlRelator Class

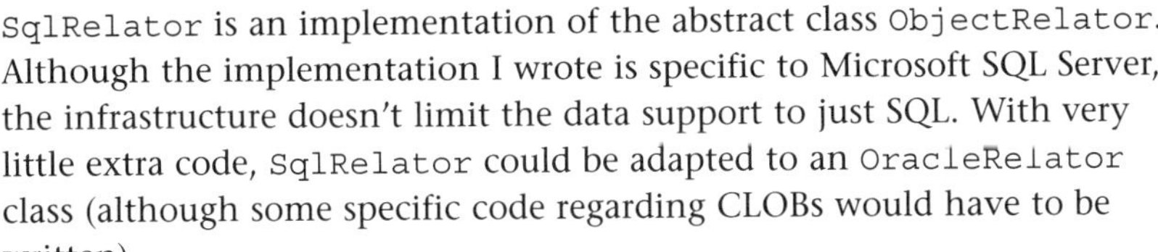

SqlRelator is an implementation of the abstract class ObjectRelator. Although the implementation I wrote is specific to Microsoft SQL Server, the infrastructure doesn't limit the data support to just SQL. With very little extra code, SqlRelator could be adapted to an OracleRelator class (although some specific code regarding CLOBs would have to be written).

The code for SqlRelator is arguably some of the most complex code in the entire Survey Development Suite, mostly because of its heavy reliance on reflection. If you haven't used reflection before or aren't all that familiar with it, you might want to take a moment to brush up on the basics of reflection with the tutorials at http://samples.gotdotnet.com/quickstart/howto/doc/GetTypes.aspx, or you can consult the MSDN documentation at http://msdn.microsoft.com/library/default.asp?url=/library/en-us/cpguide/html/cpconReflectionOverview.asp.

Listing 3.5 shows a protected helper method that is provided by the ObjectRelator class. This method is responsible for fetching a type map from the embedded ORM.xml file in a given type's assembly.

LISTING 3.5 SurveyV1\ObjectRelationalDb\ObjectRelator.cs
The FetchTypeMap Method

```
private ORMTypeMapping FetchTypeMap( IRelatable relatee )
{
  SystemTrace.MethodStart( MethodBase.GetCurrentMethod() );
  Type t = relatee.GetType();
  Assembly sourceAssembly = t.Assembly;
  string resourceName = t.Namespace + ".ORM.xml";

  XmlDocument xDoc = new XmlDocument();
  StreamReader xmlRaw = new StreamReader(
    sourceAssembly.GetManifestResourceStream( resourceName ) );
  xDoc.Load( xmlRaw );

  string query = "//type[@fullname='" + t.FullName + "']";
  XmlNode typeMapNode = xDoc.DocumentElement.SelectSingleNode( query );
  if (typeMapNode != null )
  {
```

LISTING 3.5 SurveyV1\ObjectRelationalDb\ObjectRelator.cs
The FetchTypeMap Method
(continued)

```
    ORMTypeMapping typeMap = new
     ORMTypeMapping( typeMapNode );
    return typeMap;
  }
  else
  {
    SystemTrace.TraceError("Failed to load type map for {0}", t.FullName);
    ExceptionManager.Publish(new
     NullReferenceException("Unable to fetch type map for " + t.FullName));
  }
  return null;
}
```


There are a couple interesting tricks going on here with reflection. Listing 3.5 all hinges on the basic fact that any given type within the .NET Framework knows from which assembly it was loaded. We use that information to get a handle on that assembly. With that, we can obtain resource streams from that assembly. The particular resource stream we're looking for is the `ORM.xml` file that is (we're hoping) embedded in the assembly.

When we have an `XmlDocument` instance, created from the `ORM.xml` file that we loaded from the assembly, we can look for a type mapping that matches the name of the type passed to this function. Finally, when we have the `XmlElement` element that contains the entire type mapping, we pass that as a constructor argument to the `ORMTypeMapping` class and return the newly constructed instance to the `Relate` method, which is shown in Listing 3.6.

LISTING 3.6 SurveyV1\ObjectRelationalDb\SqlRelator.cs
SqlRelator's Relate Method

```
public override void Relate( IRelatable relatee, string relationKey )
{
  SystemTrace.MethodStart( MethodBase.GetCurrentMethod() );
  ORMTypeMapping typeMap = FetchTypeMap( relatee );
  ORMCommandMap cmdMap = typeMap.GetMapByName( relationKey );
  SqlCommand cmd = BuildCommandFromTypeMap( relatee, typeMap , relationKey );
  conn.Open();
  if (cmdMap.ReturnsMultiple)
```

LISTING 3.6 SurveyV1\ObjectRelationalDb\SqlRelator.cs
SqlRelator's Relate Method
(continued)

```
  {
    SqlDataAdapter da = new SqlDataAdapter( cmd );
    IRelatableSet relateSet = (IRelatableSet)relatee;
    da.Fill( relateSet.ResultSet );
  }
  else
  {
    cmd.ExecuteNonQuery();
  }
  AssignOutputValuesToObject( cmd, relatee, typeMap, relationKey );
  conn.Close();
}
```

This method should be fairly easy to follow. The first thing it does is try to retrieve a type mapping for the object it is trying to relate via the `FetchTypeMap` method. When the map has been retrieved, we can then use the `BuildCommandFromTypeMap` method to create an instance of the `SqlCommand` class from the ORM data.

Listing 3.7 shows the remainder of the methods for the `SqlRelator` implementation.

LISTING 3.7 SurveyV1\ObjectRelationalDb\SqlRelator.cs
The AssignOutputValuesToObject Method and Other Helper Methods

```
private void AssignOutputValuesToObject( SqlCommand cmd,
        IRelatable relatee,
        ORMTypeMapping typeMap,
        string relationKey )
{
  SystemTrace.MethodStart( MethodBase.GetCurrentMethod() );
  ORMCommandMap ocm = typeMap.GetMapByName( relationKey );
  foreach (object ob in ocm.PropertyMaps)
  {
    ORMPropertyMap propMap = (ORMPropertyMap)ob;
    if (( propMap.DataDirection == ParameterDirection.Output) ||
    ( propMap.DataDirection == ParameterDirection.InputOutput ) )
    {
```

LISTING 3.7 SurveyV1\ObjectRelationalDb\SqlRelator.cs
The AssignOutputValuesToObject Method and Other Helper Methods (continued)

```
      PropertyInfo prop;
      Type t = relatee.GetType();
      prop = t.GetProperty( propMap.MemberName );
      if (prop != null)
      {
        if ( cmd.Parameters[ propMap.Parameter ].Value != DBNull.Value)
    {
      prop.SetValue( relatee, cmd.Parameters[ propMap.Parameter ].Value, null );
    }
      }
      else
      {
    ExceptionManager.Publish(
         new NullReferenceException(
          "Missing member " + t.FullName + "." + propMap.MemberName) );
      }
  }
 }
}

private SqlCommand BuildCommandFromTypeMap( IRelatable relatee, ORMTypeMapping typeMap,
➥ string relationKey )
{
  SystemTrace.MethodStart( MethodBase.GetCurrentMethod() );
  ORMCommandMap ocm = typeMap.GetMapByName( relationKey );
  if (ocm != null)
  {
    SqlCommand cmd = new SqlCommand( ocm.StoredProcedure, conn );
    cmd.CommandType = CommandType.StoredProcedure;
    foreach (object ob in ocm.PropertyMaps)
    {
      ORMPropertyMap propMap = (ORMPropertyMap)ob;
      SqlParameter newParam = CreateParameterFromPropertyMap( propMap );
      if ((newParam.Direction == ParameterDirection.Input) ||
      (newParam.Direction == ParameterDirection.InputOutput) )
      {
        SetParameterValue( newParam, relatee, propMap.MemberName );
      }
      cmd.Parameters.Add( newParam );
    }
```

LISTING 3.7 SurveyV1\ObjectRelationalDb\SqlRelator.cs
The AssignOutputValuesToObject Method and Other Helper Methods (continued)

```
    return cmd;
  }
  else
  {
    ExceptionManager.Publish(
     new NullReferenceException(
      "No such command mapping: " + typeMap.FullName + ":" + relationKey) );
  }
  return null;
}

private SqlParameter CreateParameterFromPropertyMap( ORMPropertyMap propMap )
{
  SystemTrace.MethodStart( MethodBase.GetCurrentMethod() );
  SqlParameter param = new SqlParameter();
  param.ParameterName = propMap.Parameter;
  param.SqlDbType = propMap.SqlDataType;
  param.Direction = propMap.DataDirection;
  if (propMap.Size != -1)
    param.Size = propMap.Size;
  return param;
}

private void SetParameterValue( SqlParameter param, IRelatable relatee, string member )
{
  SystemTrace.MethodStart( MethodBase.GetCurrentMethod() );
  PropertyInfo propInfo;
  Type t = relatee.GetType();
  propInfo = t.GetProperty( member );
  if (propInfo != null )
  {
    param.Value = propInfo.GetValue( relatee, null );
  }
  else
  {
    SystemTrace.TraceError("Read failed on member {0} on type {1}",
      member, t.FullName);
  }
}
```

In the first method in Listing 3.7, we see some code that maps the output parameters from a SQL stored procedure onto object instance properties. This enables us to place values that will be used as input to a stored procedure on an object instance, and we can store output and return values from the stored procedure on the same object instance. For example, to validate a user, we might want to pass the username and password, invoke the stored procedure, and then have a user ID on the same object instance populated when the stored procedure has completed.

The `BuildCommandFromTypeMap` method is a helper method that takes as input an `ORMTypeMapping` instance, a string indicating the type of relation being performed, and a reference to a relatable object (that is, an object implementing `IRelatable`). Similarly, the `CreateParameterFromPropertyMap` method helps out by taking an `ORMPropertyMap` instance and returning a complete and instantiated `SqlParameter` instance.

`SetParameterValue` makes use of the `PropertyInfo` reflection class in order to set the value for a specific parameter on a given `IRelatable` instance.

The `PropertyInfo` Class and Reflection

The ability for the Survey Repository application to relate live, in-memory instances of objects to the database hinges on the fact that the .NET Framework allows you not only to write code that inspect data types at runtime but to write code that can examine various members of an object at runtime.

Most of this work would not be possible without the use of the `PropertyInfo` class. The reflection process uses this class to obtain information about a particular class member. Not only can it query information about a class member, but it can be used to get and set the value of that member. This allows code to dynamically query and set properties at runtime. This dynamic query and set behavior allows the `ObjectRelator` class (and of course the `SqlRelator` class) to transfer information back and forth between the database and a class instance. Table 3.4 illustrates some of the properties of the `PropertyInfo` class.

TABLE 3.4

PropertyInfo Class Properties

Property	Description
Attributes	Gets the list of attributes for the current property. The list is of type PropertyAttributes.
CanRead	Indicates whether the property can be read.
CanWrite	Indicates whether the property can be written to.
DeclaringType	Acts as the Type object for the class that declares this member. This can be used to walk up object hierarchies with reflection.
MemberType	Gets the type of the current property as a MemberType instance. Types of members include constructors, properties, fields, and methods. This always indicates a property on a PropertyInfo object.
Name	Specifies the name of the property.
PropertyType	Gets the data type of the property.

Table 3.5 lists some of the methods on the PropertyInfo class.

TABLE 3.5

PropertyInfo Class Methods

Method	Description
GetAccessors	Returns an array of MethodInfo objects that indicate the get and set accessors for the current property.
GetCustomAttributes	Returns an array of objects that represent the custom attributes defined on the current property.
GetGetMethod	Returns a MethodInfo object for the get accessor for this property.
GetIndexParameters	Returns an array of index parameters for the property (if they exist)
GetSetMethod	Returns a MethodInfo object for the set accessor for this property.
GetValue	Gets the real value of the property as it exists on a given instance of an object that defines this property.
IsDefined	Indicates whether an attribute is defined on the current property.
SetValue	Sets the value of the property on an object instance. This method takes an instance and a value as arguments.

As you can see, the `PropertyInfo` class provides a wealth of power and functionality for dealing with live, runtime information about a data type, its members, and the values of those members as they exist on object instances.

Error Handling

Survey Repository makes use of the Microsoft application block for exception management (you can find reference material at `http://msdn.microsoft.com/library/default.asp?url=/library/en-us/dnbda/html/emab-rm.asp`). This is one of the published recommended practices from Microsoft. Microsoft also has application building blocks for other common tasks, including data access.

Even though the Microsoft application block is part of the solution that comes on this book's CD, the solution is still pointing to the `Program Files` directory for the application block. In other words, you need to have the Microsoft application block for the .NET Framework installed on your PC before you compile the application.

I chose to use the Microsoft application block because with it, the method of throwing exceptions becomes completely decoupled from the method of storing the information contained in those exceptions. For example, if you were to write a standard `try/catch` block without the aid of an application block, it might look something like this:

```
try
{
   // perform some code that might fail
}
catch (Exception ex)
{
    // do something with the exception
}
```

Although this might look elegant at first glance, it can become a maintenance nightmare. What happens if you want to store exceptions in a database? What do you do if you want to email the contents of certain high-priority failures (such as database failures) to a system administrator? Another possibility might even be to publish the contents of an exception to a system administrator's cellular phone via SMS messaging.

We can use the Microsoft application block for publishing exceptions, as in the following example:

```
try
{
    // perform some code that might fail
}
catch (Exception ex)
{
    ExceptionManager.Publish( ex );
}
```

In this example, we simply call `ExceptionManager.Publish`. What information gets published and to where it gets published is all contained within the `Web.config` file (or an `app.config` or a `machine.config` file). The big savings here is in maintenance. Let's say you've written 10,000 lines of code for a Web application back end. You then decide that instead of writing all your trapped exceptions to the Windows event log, you want to write them to a database and email certain types of trapped exceptions to a system administrator. Instead of having to sift through all 10,000 lines of code and paste new code into every single location, all you have to do is modify the application's XML configuration file to add a new exception publisher.

Survey Repository, as it comes on the CD that accompanies this book, doesn't make use of custom publishers. Out of the box, it actually doesn't set any of the application block's configuration parameters. Later on we'll tweak various settings with the application to see how they affect things.

CODE TOUR: Unified Tracing with the `SystemTrace` Class

Unified tracing is a concept that, until recently, most programmers didn't recognize the need for. If you're writing a Windows Forms application or a console application, you are probably familiar with the `System.Diagnostics.Trace` class. This class is used to write trace messages. You can store trace messages in text files if you like, or you can simply watch those messages appear in the output window while Visual Studio .NET is debugging the application.

Those of you who have built and debugged ASP.NET applications know that there is a `Trace` class available to ASP.NET pages. The problem is that this class is not the same as the `Trace` class available to Windows applications, class libraries, and console applications.

In the MonitorServices project, there is a class called SystemTrace. This class creates a wrapper around the common task of writing messages to a trace log. This wrapper not only writes messages to the trace log provided by System.Diagnostics.Trace, but it writes trace messages to a System.Web.TraceContext class instance. This is the class that makes possible all the additional information you can see at the bottom of ASP.NET pages when tracing page output is enabled.

Aside from a few overloads, all the code for SystemTrace eventually boils down to the code in Listing 3.8.

LISTING 3.8 SurveyV1\MonitorServices\SystemTrace.cs
The Trace Method on the SystemTrace Class

```
 [Conditional("TRACE")]
public static void Trace( TraceLevel messageLevel,
                          string message,
                          params Object[] paramData )
{
  if (messageLevel <= traceSwitch.Level)
  {
    message = ( message == null ? string.Empty : message );
    message = MonitorUtilities.SafeFormat( message, paramData );
    try
    {
      IdentityContext ic = (IdentityContext)CallContext.GetData("SAMS_SURVEY_IDENTITY");
      string userId = (ic == null ? "--No User Context--" : ic.UserKey );
      string userMessage = MonitorUtilities.SafeFormat("[{0}]{1}", userId, message );

      System.Diagnostics.Trace.WriteLine( userMessage );
      System.Web.HttpContext webContext = System.Web.HttpContext.Current;

      if (webContext != null )
      {
    if ( messageLevel == TraceLevel.Error )
    {
      webContext.Trace.Warn( userMessage );
    }
    else
      webContext.Trace.Write( userMessage );
      }
```

LISTING 3.8 `SurveyV1\MonitorServices\SystemTrace.cs`
The `Trace` Method on the `SystemTrace` Class
(continued)

```
        }
        catch
        {
            // exceptions that occur during tracing should be absorbed to
            // avoid creating an infinite loop trying to trace an error
            // that occurs during tracing.
        }
    }
}
```


Despite the small amount of code in Listing 3.8, there is actually a fair bit of technology being employed here. The first thing you might notice is the use of `TraceLevel`. It is an enumeration that is defined by the .NET Framework that can be controlled by XML tags in an application's configuration file through the use of trace switches.

A *trace switch* is aNET;trace switches> piece of functionality that the .NET Framework provides to all applications. To define a trace switch, you simply create a small subsection of an application's configuration file, such as the following:

```
<system.diagnostics>
  <switches>
    <add name="SystemTrace" value="4"></add>
  </switches>
</system.diagnostics>
```

This code looks fairly simple. In the `system.diagnostics` section, you make use of the `switches` section. Within the `switches` section, a standard name/value pair collection is defined. In this case, you define a key called `SystemTrace` and a value. The key is arbitrary and completely up to the programmer. You can define multiple switches within a single application for multiple purposes if you like, or you can do as I've done here and create a single, central value that indicates the trace value. The trace value itself can be any of four different values, each corresponding to one of the `TraceLevel` enumeration values, which are listed in Table 3.6.

TABLE 3.6 `TraceLevel` Enumeration Values

Enumeration	Value	Description
`Off`	0	No tracing should be used.
`Error`	1	Only errors should be traced.
`Warning`	2	Warnings and errors should be included in the trace log.
`Info`	3	Warnings, errors, and informational messages should be included in the trace log.
`Verbose`	4	Warnings, errors, informational messages, and verbose trace messages such as debug print statements should be traced. This enumeration value essentially indicates that everything should be included in the trace log.

Another piece of the code that might stand out is the use of a class called `IdentityContext`. I wrote this class as part of the `MonitorServices` project. It is a serializable class that implements the `ILogicalThreadAffinitive` interface. Its sole purpose is to simply store information while being passed along inside the call context.

If you're not familiar with call contexts, you might want to check out some samples that deal with remoting. In essence, you can think of a call context as a portable stack. The items in the stack are popped off each time a method is invoked, making those items available to the method body. When another method is called, that same stack is passed to the called method. In other words, by placing information in a call context, you guarantee that information will be available to all subsequent method calls, regardless of how nested those method calls are, or where those calls go, even across remoting and process boundaries.

The use of call contexts does have some drawbacks. Information passed in a stack to each method call can be fairly expensive. To keep your application performing optimally and still take advantage of call contexts, the data you pass along on a context should be as small as possible.

In the case of the Survey Repository application, we are passing an `IdentityContext` instance on the call context. This class simply contains the authorization token supplied by the user and the user's real name. By passing this on the call context, we can assure that anywhere in the back end of the application, our code knows who is invoking that code. If something goes wrong and we need to trace information about an exception, we can also trace information about which user invoked the method that had a problem. This becomes an invaluable troubleshooting tool.

In Listing 3.8, once the code has built a suitable string to be traced, making use of an `IdentityContext` instance, if one is available, it performs the actual trace. This trace is performed by writing to the `System.Diagnostics.Trace` class as well as the `System.Web.TraceContext` class. By sending the text to both of those classes, we can be sure that all our trace messages will show up in anything that makes use of a trace writer, as well as on the output of an ASP.NET page if tracing is enabled.

Without unified tracing, the tracing details on the ASP.NET page output are limited to only those events that take place within the code-behind class itself. By using unified tracing, code in the back end, as low as the database layer itself, can write information that will appear on the output of the ASP.NET page trace.

The Survey Repository Database

The Survey Repository database is pretty simple as far as databases go. Its sole purpose is to store and version survey profiles, survey runs, users, and associated user security settings, such as roles and permissions.

One important thing to keep in mind is that we are not actually storing any information about the survey profiles or the runs themselves. The database doesn't store the list of questions or the list of respondents. Instead, the database simply stores the XML serialization of the typed data sets, along with some indexing and version information to make retrieval and browsing easier.

Stored Procedures in Survey Repository

Table 3.7 lists the stored procedures that have been developed to support the Survey Repository Web services.

TABLE 3.7 Stored Procedures in the Survey Repository SQL 2000 Database

Stored Procedure	Description
`SVY_Add_RevisionRun`	Adds a new revision of a run to the database. The run XML file is passed along with the survey profile and revision ID.
`SVY_CheckInProfile`	Sets the status of a profile to checked-in.
`SVY_CreateProfile`	Creates a new survey profile.
`SVY_Delete_User`	Deletes a user (and his or her related information) from the system.

TABLE 3.7 Stored Procedures in the Survey Repository SQL 2000 Database (continued)

Stored Procedure	Description
`SVY_Get_AllRevisions`	Obtains all the revision indexing information for all profiles in the system.
`SVY_Get_Effective_Permissions`	Gets the effective permissions granted to a user by virtue of the user's role membership.
`SVY_Get_Profile`	Gets a specific profile from the system. Note that the XML data belongs to a revision, not to the profile itself.
`SVY_Get_ProfileRuns`	Gets a list of all runs that belong to a given survey profile.
`SVY_Get_UserProfiles`	Gets a list of all profiles that are visible to the given user. This includes profiles the user created and nonprivate profiles created by others.
`SVY_GetProfiles`	Gets all profiles in the system.
`SVY_GetMaxRevisionId`	Obtains the highest revision ID from the profile history for a given profile.
`SVY_GetProfileHistory`	Gets all the different versions of a given profile in the system.
`SVY_GetProfileRevision`	Gets the indexing data for a specific revision of a profile.
`SVY_GetRun`	Obtains all the information, including the serialized XML, for a given run.
`SVY_GetSurveyProfile`	Gets all the indexing data for a specific survey profile.
`SVY_Update_User`	Commits changes to a specific user.
`SVY_Validate_User`	Validates a given user's password and username. If the user is valid, the user ID is returned.

Tables in Survey Repository

Table 3.8 briefly summarizes the tables contained within the Survey Repository database and the purpose of each. You'll see for yourself how these tables are used throughout the book, as you spend more time working with the application code.

TABLE 3.8

Tables in the Survey Repository Database

Table	Description
SVY_Categories	Contains all the permission categories.
SVY_Permissions	Has a list of all the permissions and their descriptions.
SVY_ProfileHistory	Stores the revision history of each survey profile in the system. Each row of this table contains an XML string that can be turned into a disk file containing a survey profile.
SVY_RolePermissions	Stores a mapping of all the permissions that have been granted to the various roles.
SVY_Roles	Contains an index of roles and their descriptions.
SVY_Runs	Contains all the various runs being managed by the repository. Each row of this table contains an XML string that can be used to produce a disk file containing a survey run.
SVY_SurveyProfiles	Is a top-level index of all the profiles being managed by the repository.
SVY_UserRoles	Maps the roles granted to users.
SVY_Users	Is an index of all the users in the system, including their usernames and passwords.

Listing 3.9 shows some of the most interesting stored procedures found in the database, in no particular order. You will be seeing more of these and learning more about their purposes and functions later. To keep the SQL as portable as possible, there are very few fancy tricks in the stored procedures and there is very little, if any, SQL Server–specific code.

LISTING 3.9

Selected Stored Procedures in the Survey Repository Database

```
CREATE PROCEDURE SVY_Validate_User
@UserName varchar(8),
@Password varchar(8),
@UserId int output,
@FullName varchar(40) output
AS
```

LISTING 3.9

Selected Stored Procedures in the Survey Repository Database (continued)

```
SELECT @UserId = UserId, @FullName = FullName  FROM
SVY_Users WHERE UserName = @UserName AND Password = @Password

IF @UserId IS NULL
BEGIN
  SET @UserId = -1
  SET @FullName = 'Invalid User'
END
GO

CREATE PROCEDURE SVY_GetProfileHistory
@ProfileId int
AS
  SELECT h.ProfileID, h.RevisionId, h.RevisedBy,
         h.RevisedOn, h.XMLSource, h.RevisionComment,
         u.UserName, u.FullName
  FROM SVY_ProfileHistory h INNER JOIN
       SVY_Users u ON h.RevisedBy = u.UserId
  ORDER BY h.RevisionId ASC
GO

CREATE PROCEDURE SVY_Get_AllRevisions
AS

  SELECT p.ProfileId, p.CreatedBy, p.CreatedOn,
         p.State, p.CheckedOutBy, p.CheckedOutOn,
         p.ShortDescription, u.FullName as CreatedByName,
         u2.FullName as CheckedOutByName,
         ph.RevisionId, ph.RevisedBy, ph.RevisedOn, ph.RevisionComment
  FROM SVY_SurveyProfiles p INNER JOIN SVY_Users u ON p.CreatedBy = u.UserId
  INNER JOIN SVY_ProfileHistory ph ON p.ProfileId = ph.ProfileId
  LEFT JOIN SVY_Users u2 ON p.CheckedOutBy = u2.UserId
  ORDER BY p.ShortDescription ASC
GO

CREATE PROCEDURE SVY_CreateProfile
@ShortDescription varchar(50),
```

LISTING 3.9
Selected Stored Procedures in the Survey Repository Database
(continued)

```
@LongDescription varchar(4000),
@CreatedBy int,
@Private bit,
@XMLSource text,
@ProfileId int output
AS

BEGIN TRANSACTION

  INSERT INTO SVY_SurveyProfiles(ShortDescription,
     LongDescription, CreatedBy,
     Private, CreatedOn, State)
  VALUES(@ShortDescription,
         @LongDescription, @CreatedBy,
         @Private, getdate(), 0)

  SET @ProfileId = @@IDENTITY

  INSERT INTO SVY_ProfileHistory(ProfileId, RevisionId,
     RevisedBy, RevisedOn, RevisionComment, XMLSource)
     VALUES(@ProfileId, 1, @CreatedBy, getdate(),
     'Created', @XMLSource)

  COMMIT TRANSACTION
GO

CREATE PROCEDURE SVY_Create_User
@UserName varchar(8),
@Password varchar(8),
@FullName varchar(40),
@UserId int output
AS
  INSERT INTO SVY_Users(UserName, Password, FullName)
  VALUES(@UserName, @Password, @FullName)

  SET @UserId = @@IDENTITY
GO
```

As you can see, there really isn't anything particularly complex going on in the stored procedures. The code uses a lot of joins and filters. The only transaction that Survey Repository makes use of is a transaction used when creating a new survey profile. When the stored procedure to create a new profile is called, it creates a new profile as well as the first revision of that profile. Other than that, the stored procedures all perform pretty basic `INSERT`, `UPDATE`, `DELETE`, and `SELECT` operations.

Survey Development Studio

So far in this chapter we've been talking only about the Survey Repository Web service and all the back-end code that supports it. Now, we're going to talk about the Survey Development Studio Windows Forms application and all its supporting code. While we may have covered a lot of code in the previous sections, we have by no means covered all the code. If you understand the basic concepts behind the code we're discussing in this chapter, you should definitely take the time to read through the code within Visual Studio .NET. There is no substitute for the understanding you can achieve just by getting your hands dirty and digging through the code for a while.

The Survey Profile Editor

Earlier in this chapter you saw a little bit of how the profile editor works when we took a tour of the application and how the application works. The following sections take you through some of the highlights of building and editing a survey profile and the code that makes it all happen.

Editing Questions

Editing questions with the Survey Development Studio application is fairly straightforward. When you have selected a question on the survey profile, you can click the `Edit` button. You are then prompted for the short and long versions of the question, as well as the question type. If the question type is one that requires a list of items to be presented to the user, you can select that list or create a new list from within the question editor.

Prompting to Save Changes

Because the Survey Development Studio application is an MDI application, it is possible to have open a document (in this case, a survey profile) that has not had the recent changes saved. One thing I decided to build into the Survey Development Suite to illustrate one of the often-overlooked properties of an MDI application is the ability to detect when the user attempts to close a document and automatically save that document if the user chooses.

This functionality hinges on the `Closing` event. Listing 3.10 shows the `Closing` event handler and some of the other methods related to saving changes. All the code in this listing is part of the `frmSurvey` form class.

LISTING 3.10 `SurveyV1\SurveyStudio\frmSurvey.cs`
The `frmSurvey_Closing` Event Handler and Other Related Event Handlers

```
private void frmSurvey_Closing(object sender, System.ComponentModel.CancelEventArgs e)
{
  DialogResult dr =
    MessageBox.Show(this,
     "You are about to close a Survey Profile, would you like to save?",
     this.Text, MessageBoxButtons.YesNoCancel, MessageBoxIcon.Question);

  switch (dr)
  {
    case DialogResult.Cancel: e.Cancel = true; break;
    case DialogResult.Yes: menuItem8_Click(sender, e); CloseChildWindows(); break;
    case DialogResult.No: CloseChildWindows(); break;
  }
}

private void menuItem8_Click(object sender, System.EventArgs e)
{
  if (currentFileName == string.Empty)
    SaveSurveyAs();
  else
    SaveSurvey();
  MessageBox.Show(this,
   "Survey Profile (" + currentFileName + ") has been saved to disk.",
   "Save Profile",
   MessageBoxButtons.OK, MessageBoxIcon.Information );
}

private void SaveSurvey()
{
  surveyProfile.WriteXml( currentFileName );
}
```

LISTING 3.10 `SurveyV1\SurveyStudio\frmSurvey.cs`
The `frmSurvey_Closing` Event Handler and Other Related Event Handlers (continued)

```
private void SaveSurveyAs()
{
  if (saveFileDialog1.ShowDialog() == DialogResult.OK)
  {
    currentFileName = saveFileDialog1.FileName;
    SaveSurvey();
  }
}
```


The `frmSurvey_Closing` event handler is called every time the form is about to be closed, regardless of what action triggered the closing. This means that it will be triggered if the `Close()` method is called programmatically or if the user clicks the Close button.

When the `Close()` method is called, we ask the user if he or she wants to save the profile, if he or she wants to cancel (and therefore not close the profile form), or if he or she wants to continue closing without saving.

You can see that saving the survey profile is as simple as calling the `WriteXml` method of the typed data set that contains all the survey profile information.

Another thing that you might notice is that we invoke a method called `CloseChildWindows`. This method is responsible for closing all the windows that are only relevant within the context of the survey profile window. The following section deals with managing MDI child windows to keep the user interface clean.

CODE TOUR: Managing MDI Child Windows

Windows Forms has built-in support for MDI parents and child windows. If you close an MDI parent, all the child windows close. However, you cannot make an MDI child window the logical parent of another window.

In our case, the survey profile window is the logical parent of all sub-editors you can launch based on that profile, such as questions. This is a problem because we need to have more logic involved in which windows can be open at any given time. One solution to this is to make the question editors modal. However, this would preclude us from being able to have more than one profile open at a time; that's a sacrifice I didn't want to make.

The workaround here is really just that—nothing more than a workaround. Each time a question editor is loaded, the instance is added to a collection of question editors that each profile window maintains. When that profile window is closed, the collection is then iterated through, allowing all the open question editors to be closed.

A handy side effect of this approach is that when the user tries to edit an existing question, we can go through the collection of question editor windows and look for one that is already open for that question. If one is open, we can simply bring it to the foreground instead of creating a new window. We definitely don't want to have two windows open and editing the same data. Listing 3.11 shows some of the various event handlers within the code that are responsible for maintaining the MDI child windows.

LISTING 3.11 SurveyV1\SurveyStudio\frmSurvey.cs
Various Event Handlers That Deal with Managing MDI Child Windows

```
private void button1_Click(object sender, System.EventArgs e)
{
  SurveyProfile.Question question = surveyProfile.Questions.NewQuestion();
  surveyProfile.Questions.AddQuestion( question );

  frmQuestion newQuestion = new frmQuestion( this, question.ID );
  newQuestion.MdiParent = this.MdiParent;
  newQuestion.Show();
  questionEditors.Add( newQuestion );
}

public void RemoveQuestionEditor( frmQuestion qeditor )
{
  questionEditors.Remove( qeditor );
}
private void button6_Click(object sender, System.EventArgs e)
{
  int questionId = surveyProfile.Questions[ dgQuestions.CurrentRowIndex ].ID;
  string surveyId = surveyProfile.Profiles[0].GlobalID;
  bool alreadyOpen = false;
```

LISTING 3.11 SurveyV1\SurveyStudio\frmSurvey.cs
Various Event Handlers That Deal with Managing MDI Child Windows
(continued)

```
  foreach (object qe in questionEditors)
  {
    frmQuestion fq = (frmQuestion)qe;
    if ((fq.questionId == questionId) &&
        (fq.SurveyID == surveyId) )
    {
      alreadyOpen = true;
      fq.Focus();
      break;
    }
  }
  if (!alreadyOpen)
  {
    frmQuestion currentQuestion = new frmQuestion( this, questionId );
    currentQuestion.MdiParent = this.MdiParent;
    currentQuestion.Show();
    currentQuestion.Focus();
    questionEditors.Add( currentQuestion );
  }
}

private void CloseChildWindows()
{
  if (contactManager != null)
  {
    contactManager.Close();
    contactManager.Dispose();
  }
  foreach (object qe in questionEditors)
  {
    ((frmQuestion)qe).Close();
    ((frmQuestion)qe).Dispose();
  }
}
```

The button1_Click event handler creates a new question and loads a new question editor to allow the user to enter the details for that question. The button6_Click handler is invoked when the user chooses to edit the currently selected question.

The ID of the question is obtained from the `data set`. Then the list of question editor forms is iterated through. If an open question editor is found that has the appropriate question ID, that form is then brought to the foreground with the `Focus()` method. Otherwise, a new form is created to manage the selected question, the form instance is added to the collection of editors, and then the form instance is opened.

All this wouldn't work if the question editor didn't have some way of removing its own instance from the editor collection when it closes because the parent form doesn't inherently know when child forms close. This is because we're going one level deeper than the supported MDI framework, and we have to do all the parent/child management on our own.

The question editor form has a `Closing` event handler of its own:

```
private void frmQuestion_Closing(object sender,
                               System.ComponentModel.CancelEventArgs e)
{
  this.parentForm.RemoveQuestionEditor( this );
}
```

The `parentForm` variable is a variable of type `frmSurvey` and is set at the time that the question editor is instantiated. This serves to link the question editors to the parent survey editor, allowing the user to have multiple survey profiles open without getting the question editors mixed up. The `frmQuestion_Closing` method removes the current question editor from the parent survey profile form's editor list when the form closes. This completes the custom implementation of parent/child forms at a level beneath what Windows Forms already provides in the form of an MDI application.

CODE TOUR: The Run Editor

The run editor form consists of a tab control. The first tab contains a list of all the response sheets submitted for the current run. The second tab, which is read-only, contains a list of all the respondents who have submitted sheets. Note that not every sheet needs to have a specific respondent, so you may often see more response sheets than respondents. From the main form, you can create a new sheet, edit an existing sheet, remove a sheet, or import sheets that were retrieved, using the Pocket PC application.

A lot of the issues that we had to deal with for the survey profile form are the same issues we have to deal with on the run editor form. Listing 3.12 shows one of the most complex routines that support the run editor, adding the run itself to the repository.

LISTING 3.12 SurveyV1\SurveyStudio\frmRunEditor.cs
Adding a Run to Survey Repository

```
private void menuItem7_Click(object sender, System.EventArgs e)
{
  // add run to repository
  frmRepositoryProfileList profList = new frmRepositoryProfileList();
  profList.LoadProfiles();
  if (profList.ShowDialog() == DialogResult.OK)
  {
    int selProfileId = profList.SelectedProfileId;
    int selRevisionId = profList.SelectedRevisionId;

    string xmlSource =
      RepositoryClient.GetProfileRevision( selProfileId,
        selRevisionId );
    DataSet tmpDs = new DataSet();
    tmpDs.ReadXml( new System.IO.StringReader( xmlSource) );
    DataSet tmpDs2 = new DataSet();
    tmpDs2.ReadXml(
       new System.IO.StringReader(
         tmpDs.Tables[0].Rows[0]["XMLSource"].ToString() ) );
    string existingSurveyId =
       tmpDs2.Tables["Profile"].Rows[0]["GlobalID"].ToString();
    tmpDs.Dispose();
    tmpDs2.Dispose();

    if (existingSurveyId != this.surveyRun.RunDataItems[0].SurveyID)
    {
      MessageBox.Show(this,
        "You cannot add this run to this Survey Profile, the Surveys are not the same.");
    }
    else
    {
      frmRepositoryAddRun repAdd = new frmRepositoryAddRun();
      repAdd.ProfileLabel = this.surveyTitle;
      repAdd.ShortDescription = string.Empty;
```

LISTING 3.12 SurveyV1\SurveyStudio\frmRunEditor.cs
Adding a Run to Survey Repository
(continued)

```
      repAdd.LongDescription = string.Empty;
      if (repAdd.ShowDialog() == DialogResult.OK)
      {
     managed_runId = RepositoryClient.AddRun( selProfileId, selRevisionId,
       repAdd.ShortDescription, repAdd.LongDescription,
       surveyRun.GetXml() );
     managed = true;
     MessageBox.Show(this,
               "Current run added to repository",
               "Repository",
               MessageBoxButtons.OK,
               MessageBoxIcon.Information);
       }
   }
}
}
```


When the user chooses to add the run to the repository, he or she is prompted with a dialog that contains a list of all the profiles and revisions to which that user has access. When a profile and a revision are chosen, that survey profile has to be loaded so that the global ID (a GUID) can be examined. The global ID of the survey is compared with the ID of the survey against which the run was taken. If they don't match, the run cannot be added to that profile in Survey Repository. This is another measure to make sure that data remains consistent.

If the survey destination chosen from Survey Repository does in fact match the survey profile against which the run was taken, the `RepositoryClient` class (which you'll see a little later in this chapter) is invoked to communicate with the Web service to add the run to the database. After the run has been added to the database, various internal state variables (for example, `managed`, `managed_runId`) are modified so that the form behaves like a form that is editing a repository-managed run.

Repository and Disk Storage

Whether the survey runs or profiles are being stored in the repository or on disk, they are stored in XML format. The XML format is actually dictated by the typed data sets that were built to allow for easy programmatic access to survey information.

Figure 3.4 shows the typed data set for a survey profile, in the XSD designer view. (Showing the XSD in XML view is not only lengthy and painful but makes it much harder to view relationships.)

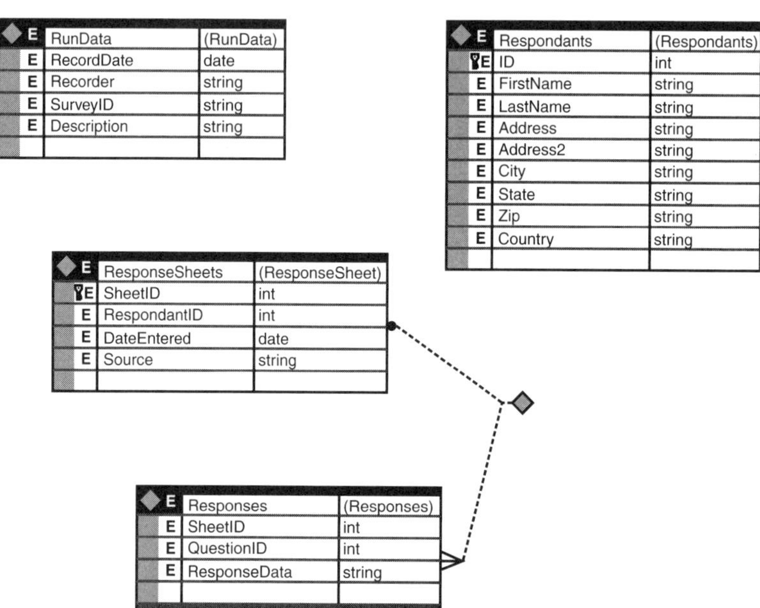

FIGURE 3.4
The `SurveyProfile` typed data set (relational view).

Figure 3.5 shows the data structure for the survey run.

These two data structures are used in multiple places throughout the Survey Development Suite. The Windows Forms application makes the most direct use of them, although their XML formats are stored in string form in the database through the Web service.

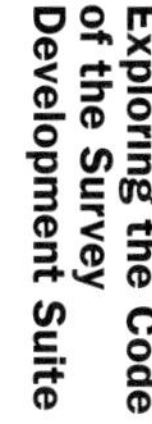

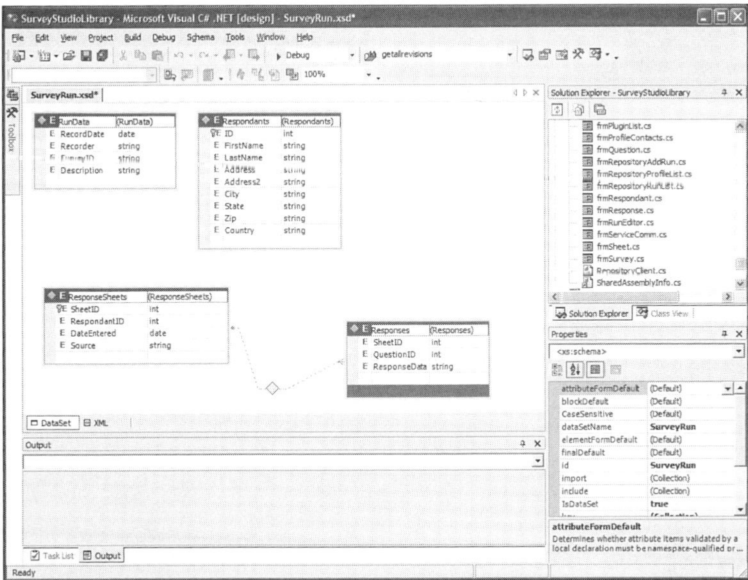

FIGURE 3.5

The `SurveyRun` typed data set (relational view).

CODE TOUR: The `RepositoryClient` Class

`RepositoryClient` is a class with static methods and variables that I created to function as a global wrapper for the method calls to the Web service. The reason I did this was to abstract the action of calling the Web service so that if I wanted to build in layers of detail later, I wouldn't have to modify all my GUI code—just the `RepositoryClient` class.

In addition to wrapping all the methods exposed by the Web service, the `RepositoryClient` class keeps track of the current user's credentials and his or her authorization token so that each time a Windows Forms application needs to make a call, it doesn't need to keep track of that information. Listing 3.13 shows the `RepositoryClient` class.

LISTING 3.13 `SurveyV1\SurveyStudio\RepositoryClient.cs`
The `RepositoryClient` Class

```
using System;
using System.Timers;
using System.Data;
using System.Text;
using System.IO;
```

LISTING 3.13 SurveyV1\SurveyStudio\RepositoryClient.cs
The RepositoryClient Class
(continued)

```
namespace SAMS.Survey.Studio
{
 public class RepositoryClient
 {
   private static repositoryLogin.Login loginService;
   private static repositoryMain.RepositoryService repositoryService;

   private static string userToken;
   private static System.Timers.Timer reloginTimer;

   private static RepositoryClient singletonInstance;
   private static string clientUserName;
   private static string clientPassword;

   private static bool loggedIn;

   public delegate void LoginDelegate(string userName, string password);

   public static event LoginDelegate OnLogin;


   static RepositoryClient()
   {
     loggedIn = false;
     loginService = new repositoryLogin.Login();
     repositoryService = new repositoryMain.RepositoryService();
     singletonInstance = new RepositoryClient();
   }

   public static void Login(string userName, string password)
   {
     clientUserName = userName;
     clientPassword = password;

     PerformLogin();
     reloginTimer = new Timer(3600000); // every hour
     reloginTimer.AutoReset = true;
```

LISTING 3.13 `SurveyV1\SurveyStudio\RepositoryClient.cs`
The `RepositoryClient` Class
(continued)

```
    reloginTimer.Elapsed += new ElapsedEventHandler( OnTimerElapsed );
    reloginTimer.Start();
  }

  public static void LogOff()
  {
    reloginTimer.Stop();
    loggedIn = false;
  }

  private static void OnTimerElapsed(object sender, ElapsedEventArgs e )
  {
    PerformLogin();
  }

  public static string GetProfile( int profileId )
  {
    string xmlProfile = repositoryService.GetProfile( userToken, profileId );
    return xmlProfile;
  }


  public static string GetProfileRevision( int profileId, int revisionId )
  {
    return repositoryService.GetProfileRevision( userToken, profileId, revisionId );
  }

  public static int CheckInProfile( int profileId, string revisionComment,
    string xmlSource )
  {
    return repositoryService.CheckInProfile( userToken,
                                             profileId, revisionComment,
                                             xmlSource );
  }

  public static int CreateProfile( string shortDescription,
                                   string longDescription, bool isPrivate,
                                   string xmlSource)
  {
```

LISTING 3.13 SurveyV1\SurveyStudio\RepositoryClient.cs
The RepositoryClient Class
(continued)

```
    return repositoryService.CreateProfile( userToken, shortDescription,
                                            longDescription, isPrivate, xmlSource );
  }

  public static DataSet GetUserProfiles()
  {
    string xmlProfiles = repositoryService.GetUserProfiles( userToken );
    DataSet ds = new DataSet();
    StringReader sr = new StringReader( xmlProfiles );
    ds.ReadXml( sr );
    return ds;
  }

  public static DataSet GetProfileRuns( int profileId )
  {
    string xmlRuns = repositoryService.GetProfileRuns( userToken, profileId );
    DataSet ds = new DataSet();
    StringReader sr = new StringReader( xmlRuns );
    ds.ReadXml( sr );
    return ds;
  }

  public static DataSet GetRun( int runId )
  {
    string xmlRun = repositoryService.GetRun( userToken, runId );
    DataSet ds = new DataSet();
    StringReader sr = new StringReader( xmlRun );
    ds.ReadXml( sr );
    return ds;
  }

  public static DataSet GetAllRevisions()
  {
    string xmlRevisions = repositoryService.GetAllRevisions( userToken );
    DataSet ds = new DataSet();
    StringReader sr = new StringReader( xmlRevisions );
    ds.ReadXml( sr );
    return ds;
  }
```

LISTING 3.13 `SurveyV1\SurveyStudio\RepositoryClient.cs`
The `RepositoryClient` Class
(continued)

```
public static int GetProfileStatus( int profileId )
{
  return repositoryService.GetProfileStatus( userToken, profileId );
}

public static int AddRun( int profileId, int revisionId,
                          string shortDescription, string longDescription,
                          string xmlSource )
{
  return repositoryService.AddRun( userToken, profileId, revisionId,
                                   shortDescription, longDescription, xmlSource );
}

private static void PerformLogin()
{
  userToken = loginService.LoginUser(clientUserName, clientPassword);
  if (userToken != string.Empty)
    loggedIn = true;
  else
  loggedIn = false;
  if (OnLogin != null)
  {
   OnLogin( clientUserName, clientPassword );
  }
}

public static string UserToken
{
  get
  {
  return userToken;
  }
}

public static string CurrentUser
{
  get
  {
```

LISTING 3.13 SurveyV1\SurveyStudio\RepositoryClient.cs
The RepositoryClient Class
(continued)

```
    if (loggedIn)
      return clientUserName;
    else
      return string.Empty;
      }
  }

  public static bool LoggedIn
  {
    get
    {
   return loggedIn;
    }
  }
 }
}
```


The first thing to point out about this class is that right at the top of the class definition, we can see the declaration for an event handler:

```
public delegate void LoginDelegate(string userName, string password);
public static event LoginDelegate OnLogin;
```

This event handler allows the Windows Forms application to respond to a successful login without blocking the execution of the foreground thread. Having this class expose the event handler like this makes it very easy for the application to respond to events triggered by the Web service. One thing you might notice is that this particular structure may also lend itself quite well to allowing this class to be converted in such a way that all access to the Web service can be made asynchronously so as not to block the application during network activity.

Another interesting piece of this class is the use of a re-login timer. One thing you may have noticed while browsing the code for the Survey Repository Web service is that when authorization tokens are added to the application cache, they are added with a sliding expiration time period of one hour. This is to ensure the security of the system. If, for some reason, someone has been sniffing packets and manages to peel an authorization token out of one of those packets, that token will be valid for only a short period of time. When the token has expired, any hijacked-token messages fail when the service attempts to establish a user identity.

PocketSurvey

So far we've seen some of the code that drives the Web service: the back-end code, the database tier, and the code that makes the Windows Forms application possible. Now let's take a look at some of the code that was written for the PocketSurvey application.

As we discussed in Chapter 2, "Using the Survey Development Suite," PocketSurvey is an application that loads a survey profile and then lets people enter their responses. It is designed to take responses to the same survey profile over and over again, assisting survey administrators in conducting a survey run in remote locations such as shopping malls, outside movie theaters, and so on.

The two things that make this application possible are dynamically generated forms and the ability to store and retrieve data on the Pocket PC device.

CODE TOUR: Dynamic Forms with the `DynaFormHelper` Class

Dynamically generated forms are possible because of the fact that we can do programmatically everything that the designer can do. This includes creation of controls, placement and sizing of controls, and everything else you want to do with controls. In fact, if you expand the region-collapsed area of C# code that the Visual Studio .NET designer creates for you, you see all the code statements that create everything that the designer has done in the design view.

All the dynamic form creation for the PocketSurvey application is made possible through the use of a helper class. This helper class, as shown in Listing 3.14, is responsible for taking information about a question and creating the appropriate input controls on the form to deal with that question. To do this, it uses four main methods:

- `Initialize_SingleNumericQuestion`
- `Initialize_NumberListQuestion`
- `Initialize_CheckboxQuestion`
- `Initialize_RadioQuestion`

These methods create and position all the input controls necessary to prompt a respondent for the answer to a question. Listing 3.14 shows the `DynaFormHelper` class.

LISTING 3.14 `SurveyV1\PocketSurvey\DynaFormHelper.cs`
The `DynaFormHelper` Class

```
using System;
using System.Drawing;
using System.Windows.Forms;
using System.ComponentModel;
using System.Collections;

using SAMS.Survey.Studio.Library;

namespace SAMS.Survey.PocketSurvey
{
public class DynaFormHelper
{
  private static void InitializeQuestion( frmBlank blank, string question )
  {
    Label lblQuestion = new Label();
    lblQuestion.Text = question;
    lblQuestion.Location = new Point(8, 8);
    lblQuestion.Width = blank.Width - 10;
    lblQuestion.Height = 30;
    blank.Controls.Add( lblQuestion );
  }

  public static void Initialize_SingleNumericQuestion( frmBlank blank, string question )
  {
    InitializeQuestion( blank, question );

    TextBox tb = new TextBox();
    tb.Width = 32;
    tb.Location = new Point(8, 40);
    blank.Controls.Add( tb );
  }

  public static void Initialize_NumberListQuestion(
        frmBlank blank,
        string question, string[] options )
```

LISTING 3.14 `SurveyV1\PocketSurvey\DynaFormHelper.cs`
The `DynaFormHelper` Class
(continued)

```
{
  InitializeQuestion( blank, question );

  int yOffset = 40;

  foreach (string option in options)
  {
  TextBox tb = new TextBox();
  tb.Width = 16;
  tb.Location = new Point(8, yOffset);
  blank.Controls.Add( tb );
  Label lblOption = new Label();
  lblOption.Text = option;
  lblOption.Location = new Point(30, yOffset +2);
  yOffset += 22;
  blank.Controls.Add( lblOption );
  }

}

public static void Initialize_CheckboxQuestion(
  frmBlank blank, string question,
  string[] options )
{
  InitializeQuestion( blank, question );
  int yOffset = 40;

  foreach (string option in options)
  {
    CheckBox cb = new CheckBox();
    cb.Text = option;
    cb.Location = new Point(8, yOffset);
    cb.Checked = false;
    blank.Controls.Add( cb );
    yOffset += 20;
  }
}
```

LISTING 3.14 `SurveyV1\PocketSurvey\DynaFormHelper.cs`
The `DynaFormHelper` Class
(continued)

```
public static void Initialize_RadioQuestion(
  frmBlank blank, string question, string[] options )
{
  InitializeQuestion( blank, question );

  int yOffset = 34;
  Panel pnl = new Panel();
  pnl.Location = new Point(0, yOffset);
  pnl.Height = blank.Height - yOffset - 23;
  pnl.Width = blank.Width;
  blank.Controls.Add(pnl);

  foreach (string option in options)
  {
    RadioButton rb = new RadioButton();
    rb.Text = option;
    rb.Checked = false;
    rb.Location = new Point(8, yOffset);
    pnl.Controls.Add( rb );
    yOffset += 20;
  }
}

public static void Initialize_DynaForm( frmBlank blank,
  QuestionType questionType, string question, string[] options  )
{
  blank.QuestionType = questionType;

  switch (questionType)
  {
    case QuestionType.ChoiceListMultipleAnswers:
  // this should be a checkbox next to each response option
  Initialize_CheckboxQuestion( blank, question, options );
  break;
    case QuestionType.ChoiceListNumericalRank:
  // this should be a text box next to each response option
  Initialize_NumberListQuestion( blank, question, options );
  break;
```

LISTING 3.14 SurveyV1\PocketSurvey\DynaFormHelper.cs
The DynaFormHelper Class
(continued)

```
      case QuestionType.Essay:
    // there should be no initialization for essay questions
    break;
      case QuestionType.MultipleChoiceSingleAnswer:
    Initialize_RadioQuestion( blank, question, options );
    break;
      case QuestionType.SingleResponseNumericalRank:
    Initialize_SingleNumericQuestion(blank, question );
    break;
    }
  }
 }
}
```


Now that we've looked at the helper class, let's take a look at the code that makes use of the helper class. When the PocketSurvey application starts up, there is a Take Survey button on the main form. When you click this button, the event handler in Listing 3.15 is triggered.

LISTING 3.15 SurveyV1\PocketSurvey\frmMain.cs
The Take Survey Button Click Event Handler

```
private void btnStart_Click(object sender, System.EventArgs e)
{
  SAMS.Survey.Studio.Library.QuestionType questionType;
  string questionText;

  DataRow newSheet = dsRun.Tables["ResponseSheets"].NewRow();
  newSheet["DateEntered"] = DateTime.Now;
  newSheet["Source"] = "PocketSurvey";
  dsRun.Tables["ResponseSheets"].Rows.Add( newSheet );

  // for each question in the profile, prompt the user for a response
  // then store the responses in a new run
  foreach ( DataRow question in dsProfile.Tables["Questions"].Rows )
  {
```

LISTING 3.15 `SurveyV1\PocketSurvey\frmMain.cs`
The Take Survey Button `Click` Event Handler
(continued)

```
    // obtain the question type
    questionType = (SAMS.Survey.Studio.Library.QuestionType)((int)question["Type"]);
    questionText = (string)question["LongText"];
    int choiceListId = (int)question["ChoiceListId"];
    string[] options = null;
    if (choiceListId > 0)
    {
      DataRow[] items =
       dsProfile.Tables["ChoiceListItems"].Select("ChoiceListId=" +
       choiceListId.ToString());
      options = new string[ items.Length ];
      int i=0;
      foreach (DataRow item in items)
      {
        options[i] = item["Description"].ToString();
        i++;
      }
    }
    // grab the options (if any)
    frmBlank blankForm = new frmBlank();
    blankForm.Text = question["ShortDescription"].ToString();
    DynaFormHelper.Initialize_DynaForm( blankForm, questionType, questionText, options );
    if (blankForm.ShowDialog() == DialogResult.OK)
    {
      // do something with the result
      string response = blankForm.Response;
      DataRow newResponse = dsRun.Tables["Responses"].NewRow();
      newResponse["QuestionId"] = (int)question["ID"];
      newResponse["SheetId"] = (int)newSheet["SheetId"];
      newResponse["ResponseData"] = response;
      dsRun.Tables["Responses"].Rows.Add( newResponse );
    }
  }
  dsRun.AcceptChanges();
  dsRun.WriteXml( @"\Program Files\PocketSurvey\CurrentRun.svr" );
 }
}
```

In a couple pieces of Listing 3.15, it might not be immediately obvious what is going on. Before this button is even clicked, the survey profile has been loaded from disk (you'll see this code in the next section), and if there is data existing for the current run, that information has also been loaded from disk.

The basic logic is this: For each question loaded in the profile, a dynamic form is created and displayed, the response to that form is then stored, and the form is destroyed when the user clicks Next.

CODE TOUR: Data Storage

Data storage gave me a bit of a challenge that I wasn't expecting. Having spent so much of my time with .NET using typed data sets, I naturally assumed that I would be able to use typed data sets within the Compact Framework.

The truth is that typed data sets are not supported in the Compact Framework. Even if you attempt to take the class generated by a standard typed data set and compile it within the Compact Framework, it won't work. Getting something resembling a typed data set to work involves a considerable amount of time and effort. Another issue I had was that you can't automatically reuse assemblies between the .NET Framework and the Compact Framework. The reason for this is that the references are strongly typed. What this boils down to is that if your .NET Framework assembly references `System.Data`, it references a nonportable, platform-specific `System.Data` namespace. When you build a Compact Framework project, it might also reference `System.Data`, but that assembly is not the same assembly as the `System.Data` namespace referenced by a standard Windows Forms application. If you attempt to use an assembly with a platform-specific assembly reference on a mobile device, at best it will simply not load, and at worst it could cause your application to fail.

All I wanted was to be able to verify that the XML that I was loading was of a format that guaranteed my software the capability to load a profile and take response sheets. For that, I could do with some simple schema validation.

Because I didn't want to have any more file dependencies than necessary, I took the XSD that I used to build the typed data set for Survey Development Studio and embedded it directly in the assembly for the PocketSurvey application. In Listing 3.16 you'll see some of the initialization code from PocketSurvey, including the code that creates a schema-backed data set from the assembly-embedded XSD.

LISTING 3.16 SurveyV1\PocketSurvey\frmMain.cs
The Initialization Code for PocketSurvey

```
public frmMain()
{
  InitializeComponent();
  Stream s =
    Assembly.GetExecutingAssembly().GetManifestResourceStream(
      "SAMS.Survey.PocketSurvey.SurveyProfile.xsd");
   XmlTextReader xr = new XmlTextReader( s );
   dsProfile = new DataSet();
   dsProfile.ReadXmlSchema( xr );
   xr.Close();
   s.Close();

   dsRun = new DataSet();
   s =     Assembly.GetExecutingAssembly().GetManifestResourceStream(
      "SAMS.Survey.PocketSurvey.SurveyRun.xsd");
   xr = new XmlTextReader( s );
   dsRun.ReadXmlSchema( xr );
   xr.Close();
   s.Close();

   dsProfile.ReadXml( @"\Program Files\PocketSurvey\CurrentSurvey.svp" );
   lblCurrent.Text =
     "Current Profile: " + dsProfile.Tables["Profile"].Rows[0]["Title"].ToString() +
     "\n\r" + dsProfile.Tables["Profile"].Rows[0]["Notes"].ToString();

    if (File.Exists( @"\Program Files\PocketSurvey\CurrentRun.svr" ) )
    {
      dsRun.ReadXml( @"\Program Files\PocketSurvey\CurrentRun.svr" );
    }
}
```

In Listing 3.16 you can see that we're using GetManifestResourceStream to take hold of the embedded XSD file that we compiled into the assembly. Then a data set is created, and that schema is read into the profile data set. This ensures that no attempt to load invalid XML will ever succeed. If the load succeeds, the data conforms to the format and requirements of a proper survey profile.

If a current run (that is, collection of response sheets) is found in the application directory, the contents are loaded into memory. This is done because each time someone supplies a response to the system, the data set (`dsRun`) is written to disk.

Moving On

This chapter takes a look at the code that is on the CD provided with the book. It looks at the code used to create a set of common infrastructure services. This chapter also looks at business objects as well as the code behind two .asmx Web services that make up the Survey Repository application.

Moving further away from the back end, this chapter looks at the code that drives the Windows Forms application Survey Development Studio. It shows how to manage MDI child windows with deeper relationships than Windows Forms allows for out of the box. You have learned about communicating with Web services and storing and reading data from XML files, and you have seen some interesting event handling.

Finally, this chapter looks at the PocketSurvey application and shows how, with very little code, you can create dynamic forms that automatically drop the appropriate controls onto their surfaces, depending on what kind of question the application is asking the user.

I hope that not too much of this chapter seems overly complex. The goal of this chapter is to familiarize you with the stock, out-of-the-box code that was produced for this book and is available on the book's CD. The real meat of the book is about tweaking, enhancing, improving, and even adding to the code described in this chapter. In Chapter 4, "Experimenting with the Code for the Survey Development Suite," you'll be experimenting with the code. Chapter 4 examines in detail certain parts of the code, and you'll see what happens when you change values and poke and prod the existing codebase.

Experimenting with the Code for the Survey Development Suite

4

CHAPTER

So far in this book all we've done is examine the code and take a look at how the Survey Development Suite works. Finally, in this chapter you'll be getting into the code and actually tinkering with the application.

Everyone learns new things in different ways. However, a lot of people learn and retain more about a subject if they get a chance to tinker than if they just attend a lecture on that topic. For that reason, this chapter is all about tinkering. In this chapter you'll experiment with the following:

- Changing cache expiration times
- Inserting a typo in the object-relational meta-data
- Changing security permissions
- Changing the modality of forms
- The dangers of relying on assumptions
- Missing data files
- Limited form factors

In this chapter you'll poke around in the Survey Development Suite, make changes, recompile, and see how the changes affect the code. They might have no visible effect, or they might break the entire application. I hope that you'll learn a little something about the technology underneath the application by playing with it and that you'll be able to apply that knowledge in applications you build in the future.

Survey Repository

The following sections deal with the Survey Repository database. We're going to take a look at how modifying certain bits of code within Survey Repository affects the application, and then we'll talk about why those changes take place. Hopefully you'll be able to pick up some useful coding tips from these exercises.

EXPERIMENT: Changing the Cache Expiration Time

In the Survey Repository application as it stands now, when a user logs in to the system, a new GUID, called a *token*, is generated for the user. This token is then cached for one hour. Essentially, this allows any client that knows the exact token to use the Web service for that hour-long period. The token expires after an hour to avoid having the valid token values "sniffed" off of the wire, or hijacked, and used by someone who isn't paying for the service—or worse, used maliciously to damage the service.

To see what it looks like when the client's token expires, you can modify the token expiration time so that it is extremely short. When you're done with this code change, the tokens will all expire after just one short minute. After that minute, you can take a look at what happens to the client.

First you need to change the code in Survey Repository to decrease the token cache expiration time. Bring up the `Login.asmx.cs` code-behind file in Visual Studio .NET (with the main solution open, of course). Scroll down until you find the section of code in the `LoginUser` method that looks like this:

```
string returnGuid = Guid.NewGuid().ToString();
string cacheKey = "Security-" + returnGuid;
if (cache[cacheKey] != null)
    cache.Remove( cacheKey );
cache.Insert( cacheKey,
    pl, null, Cache.NoAbsoluteExpiration, TimeSpan.FromHours(1),
    CacheItemPriority.High,
    null );
return returnGuid;
```

What you're looking to change is the `TimeSpan.FromHours(1)` section of the code. Go ahead and change that to `TimeSpan.FromMinutes(1)`. This should quickly and easily change the expiration time from 1 hour to 1 minute. Build the project (`RepositoryV1`) and open the Survey Development Studio client application for debugging.

As you can see in Figure 4.1, you've just logged in to Survey Repository and haven't attempted to perform any Survey Repository functions such as opening a profile or a run.

Don't worry about timing yourself exactly. Just sit and wait for a few minutes to make sure that the cache has expired. A cache item does not expire exactly 60 seconds from when it was created; it expires when the cache system examines the item, sees that it is old enough to expire, and removes it. To be safe, wait two minutes and then attempt to open a survey profile from Survey Repository.

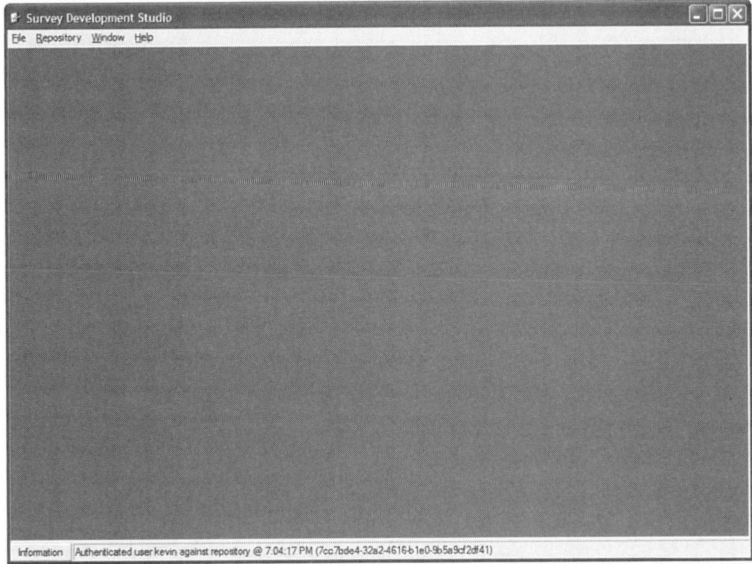

FIGURE 4.1
The Survey Development Studio application, immediately after a successful login.

A few seconds pass, and if you were using the Visual Studio .NET 2003 debugger to run the Survey Development Studio application, you receive an error message that breaks into the current debugging session and that looks something like the dialog shown in Figure 4.2.

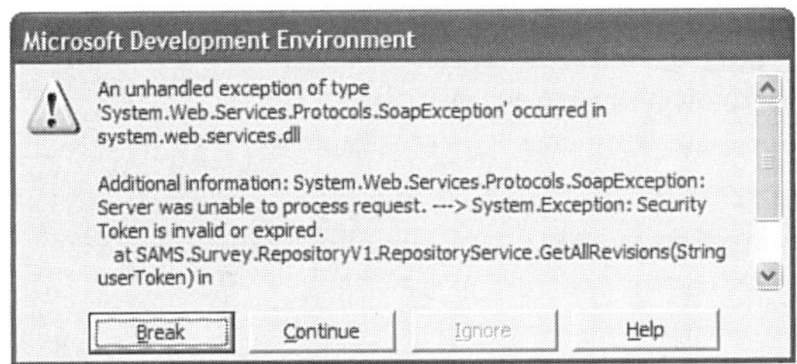

FIGURE 4.2
An error message received when a security token expires.

A couple of really interesting things are going on here. The first thing that you should immediately notice is that the Survey Development Studio application does not have any centralized error handling. You'll deal with that in Chapter 8, "Improving the Code of the Survey Development Suite." For now, you can just leave the error handling system alone.

The second thing that you should notice is that somehow an exception has managed to travel, completely intact, across the wire from the Web service application to the client application. This exception will make it across whether you're dealing with an Internet connection or an intranet connection. The beauty of this is that the exception itself is being stuffed into the SOAP envelope that is returned from the Web server that contains the results of the method call. The proxy class then detects that error from within the SOAP envelope and then rethrows a client-side error that contains all the same information as the server-side error.

What a lot of people don't notice is that this allows you to put calls to a Web service within a `try/catch` block and it actually works as if you were invoking local code or invoking code via remoting.

This application handles the case of a security token expiring in a slightly different manner. As soon as Survey Development Studio logs in to Survey Repository, it starts a timer. This timer waits for one hour and then performs another login to the Web service, obtaining a new security token or GUID. The problem arises in the case just illustrated: if the token expires before the application has had a chance to log in again.

EXPERIMENT: A Rolling Typo Gathers No Meta-Data

To quickly recap: The object-relational system in Survey Repository loads XML information from an embedded XML document in an assembly via reflection. After the information is loaded, it is used to create an instance of a command object. That command object is then executed. After it is executed, the results of the command execution are placed back onto the persistence object instance. This truly allows two-way relating between object instances and tabular information in the SQL Server database.

Again, the theme of this chapter is that one of the best ways to learn how something works is to break it—and break it hard. What happens if you dig into one of the XML mappings and create a typo? Typos happen all the time, every single day. Let's see what happens to the application if you inject a typo.

Open the `SurveyRepository` project (it's a class library) and double-click the `ORM.xml` file. You should immediately be confronted with quite a few stored procedure-object mapping records.

Take a look at the following code from the `ORM.xml` file. About halfway down, the `SVY_Get_AllRevisions` command mapping is highlighted:

```
<relationalmapping>
<type fullname="SAMS.Survey.Repository.SurveyProfile">
  <commandmap storedproc="SVY_GetSurveyProfile"
      multiple="false" type="Select">
    <propertymap member="ProfileId" dbtype="int"
      dbsize="4" parameter="@ProfileId"
      direction="Input"></propertymap>
    <propertymap member="ShortDescription" dbtype="varchar"
      dbsize="40" parameter="@ShortDescription"
      direction="Output"></propertymap>
    <propertymap member="LongDescription" dbtype="varchar"
      dbsize="4000" parameter="@LongDescription"
      direction="Output"></propertymap>
    <propertymap member="CreatedBy" dbtype="int"
      dbsize="4" parameter="@CreatedBy"
      direction="Output"></propertymap>
    <propertymap member="CreatedOn" dbtype="datetime"
      dbsize="8" parameter="@CreatedOn"
      direction="Output"></propertymap>
    <propertymap member="Private" dbtype="boolean"
      dbsize="1" parameter="@Private" direction="Output"></propertymap>
    <propertymap member="CheckedOutBy" dbtype="int"
      dbsize="4" parameter="@CheckedOutBy"
      direction="Output"></propertymap>
    <propertymap member="CheckedOutOn" dbtype="datetime"
      dbsize="8" parameter="@CheckedOutOn"
      direction="Output"></propertymap>
    <propertymap member="State" dbtype="int"
      dbsize="4" parameter="@State" direction="Output"></propertymap>
    <propertymap member="CreatedByUserName" dbtype="varchar"
      dbsize="10" parameter="@CreatedByUserName"
      direction="Output"></propertymap>
    <propertymap member="CheckedOutByUserName" dbtype="varchar"
      dbsize="10" parameter="@CheckedOutByUserName"
      direction="Output"></propertymap>
  </commandmap>
  <commandmap storedproc="SVY_CheckOutProfile"
     multiple="false" type="Checkout">
    <propertymap member="ProfileId" dbtype="int"
      dbsize="4" parameter="@ProfileId"
```

```
        direction="Input"></propertymap>
      <propertymap member="CheckedOutBy" dbtype="int"
        dbsize="4" parameter="@UserId" direction="Input"></propertymap>
    </commandmap>
    <commandmap storedproc="SVY_CreateProfile"
      multiple="false" type="Insert">
      <propertymap member="ShortDescription" dbtype="varchar"
        dbsize="150" parameter="@ShortDescription"
        direction="Input"></propertymap>
      <propertymap member="LongDescription" dbtype="varchar"
        dbsize="4000" parameter="@LongDescription"
        direction="Input"></propertymap>
      <propertymap member="CreatedBy" dbtype="int"
        dbsize="4" parameter="@Createdby"
        direction="Input"></propertymap>
      <propertymap member="Private" dbtype="boolean"
        dbsize="1" parameter="@Private" direction="Input"></propertymap>
      <propertymap member="NewXmlSource" dbtype="text"
        dbsize="-1" parameter="@XMLSource"
        direction="Input"></propertymap>
      <propertymap member="ProfileId" dbtype="int"
        dbsize="4" parameter="@ProfileId"
        direction="Output"></propertymap>
    </commandmap>
  </type>
  <type fullname="SAMS.Survey.Repository.ProfileList">
    <commandmap storedproc="SVY_Get_Profiles"
     multiple="true" type="SelectMultiple">
    </commandmap>
    <commandmap storedproc="SVY_Get_UserProfiles"
     multiple="true" type="GetUserProfiles">
      <propertymap member="UserId" dbtype="int"
        dbsize="4" parameter="@UserId" direction="Input"></propertymap>
    </commandmap>
  </type>
  <type fullname="SAMS.Survey.Repository.UserList">
    <commandmap storedproc="SVY_Get_Users" multiple="true"
     type="SelectMultiple">
    </commandmap>
  </type>
  <type fullname="SAMS.Survey.Repository.ProfileHistory">
    <commandmap storedproc="SVY_GetProfileHistory" multiple="true"
     type="SelectMultiple">
```

```
    <propertymap member="ProfileId" dbtype="int"
      dbsize="4" parameter="@ProfileId"
      direction="Input"></propertymap>
  </commandmap>
  <commandmap storedproc="SVY_GetMaxRevisionId"
   multiple="false" type="GetNewestRevisionId">
    <propertymap member="ProfileId" dbtype="int"
      dbsize="4" parameter="@ProfileId"
      direction="Input"></propertymap>
    <propertymap member="NewestRevisionId" dbtype="int"
      dbsize="4" parameter="@RevisionId"
      direction="Output"></propertymap>
  </commandmap>
  <commandmap storedproc="SVY_Get_AllRevisions" multiple="true"
  ➥type="GetAllRevisions">
  </commandmap>
</type>
<type fullname="SAMS.Survey.Repository.ProfileRevision">
  <commandmap storedproc="SVY_GetProfileRevision"
   multiple="true" type="Select">
    <propertymap member="ProfileId" dbtype="int"
      dbsize="4" parameter="@ProfileId"
      direction="Input"></propertymap>
    <propertymap member="RevisionId" dbtype="int"
      dbsize="4" parameter="@RevisionId"
      direction="Input"></propertymap>
  </commandmap>
  <commandmap storedproc="SVY_CheckInProfile"
   multiple="false" type="CheckIn">
    <propertymap member="ProfileId" dbtype="int"
      dbsize="4" parameter="@ProfileId"
      direction="Input"></propertymap>
    <propertymap member="RevisedBy" dbtype="int"
      dbsize="4" parameter="@RevisedBy"
      direction="Input"></propertymap>
    <propertymap member="RevisionComment" dbtype="varchar"
      dbsize="150" parameter="@RevisionComment"
      direction="Input"></propertymap>
    <propertymap member="XmlSource" dbtype="text"
      dbsize="-1" parameter="@XMLSource"
      direction="Input"></propertymap>
  </commandmap>
</type>
```

```
<type fullname="SAMS.Survey.Repository.RunHistory">
  <commandmap storedproc="SVY_Get_ProfileRuns"
   multiple="true" type="GetProfileRuns">
    <propertymap member="ProfileId" dbtype="int"
      dbsize="4" parameter="@ProfileId"
      direction="Input"></propertymap>
  </commandmap>
  <commandmap storedproc="SVY_GetRun" multiple="true" type="GetRun">
    <propertymap member="RunId" dbtype="int"
      dbsize="4" parameter="@RunId" direction="Input"></propertymap>
  </commandmap>
</type>
<type fullname="SAMS.Survey.Repository.RevisionRun">
  <commandmap storedproc="SVY_Add_RevisionRun"
    multiple="false" type="AddRun">
    <propertymap member="ProfileId" dbtype="int"
      dbsize="4" parameter="@ProfileId"
      direction="Input"></propertymap>
    <propertymap member="RevisionId" dbtype="int"
      dbsize="4" parameter="@RevisionId" direction="Input">
    </propertymap>
    <propertymap member="XMLSource" dbtype="text"
      dbsize="-1" parameter="@XMLSource" direction="Input">
    </propertymap>
    <propertymap member="SubmittedBy" dbtype="int"
       dbsize="4" parameter="@SubmittedBy"
       direction="Input"></propertymap>
    <propertymap member="SubmittedOn" dbtype="datetime"
       dbsize="8" parameter="@SubmittedOn"
       direction="Input"></propertymap>
    <propertymap member="ShortDescription" dbtype="varchar"
       dbsize="50" parameter="@ShortDescription"
       direction="Input"></propertymap>
    <propertymap member="LongDescription" dbtype="varchar"
       dbsize="4000" parameter="@LongDescription"
       direction="Input"></propertymap>
    <propertymap member="RunId" dbtype="int" dbsize="4"
       parameter="@RunId" direction="Output"></propertymap>
  </commandmap>
</type>
</relationalmapping>
```

You're going to make a little bit of a change to this meta-data and see what happens to the application. Change `SVY_Get_AllRevisions` to `SVY_Get_SomeRevisions`. After you do this, rebuild the `RepositoryV1` project. Visual Studio .NET will detect the change in the `SurveyRepository` project and will rebuild that as well, copying the assemblies to the appropriate place.

Now you can test the freshly broken meta-data. Open the `SurveyStudio` project in a new debug instance. Log in to Survey Repository and choose File, Open, From Repository. You should hear the horrible sound of your hard drive spinning while the .NET Framework generates a nice juicy exception for you. Figure 4.3 shows a screenshot of the exception generated.

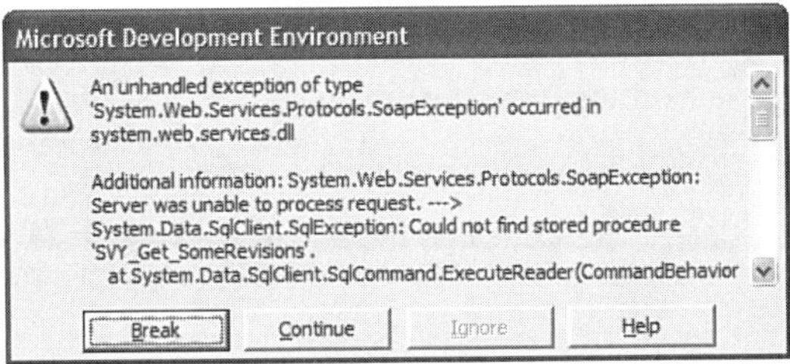

FIGURE 4.3

An error message caused by incorrect meta-data in an `ORM.xml` file.

The important part of this screenshot is the phrase "Could not find stored procedure `'SVY_Get_SomeRevisions'`." What this tells you is that when you changed the text in the `commandmap` node for the `storedproc` attribute, you directly changed the stored procedure to which the object maps. Without a stored procedure with that new name, the `SqlClient` library is going to throw an exception, and you won't be able to accomplish the ORM.

Again, you saw that the exception itself made it across the wire completely intact, even though you didn't manually throw the exception. In the previous example, dealing with cache expiration times, the code throws the exception when validating user credentials. In this case, Microsoft's own code throws the exception when `SqlClient` tries to find a stored procedure named `SVY_Get_SomeRevisions`.

The information you can take away from this is that your own code should probably be a little bit more flexible when it comes to the meta-data. You've already seen that your application should be handling errors more aggressively. The other lesson to be learned here is that this XML file is highly prone to error. Any time a human is responsible for entering data like this, there is room for typos and other human error. Therefore, at some future date, you might want to produce some kind of tool that creates the `ORM.xml` file for you, to reduce the chance of human error corrupting that file.

EXPERIMENT: Changing Security Permissions

The situation described in this section is one that you might encounter more often than you'd think. In a real-world environment, not everything is deployed to a development machine that has a completely open configuration and allows everyone access. What if the `.asmx` files were not accessible by the `ASPNET` account? What if the `.config` file were modified to use Windows authentication and prevented anonymous access to the service files? Well, in this section you'll find out exactly what does happen and what kind of things you'll see on a client if something like that happens.

To test this, right-click the `Login.asmx` file (probably in your `Inetpub\RepositoryV1` directory). You might want to make a backup of this file so you can restore the security permissions later. Click the Security tab and remove all the entries in the permission list except for Administrators. If you have inherited security involved, you have to disable that from the Advanced section before you can remove entries for Everyone and so on. When you've completely cleaned out all the security entries for `Login.asmx`, click Apply and then start a new debug instance of Survey Development Studio. When you attempt to log in to Survey Repository, you receive the error that is displayed in Figure 4.4.

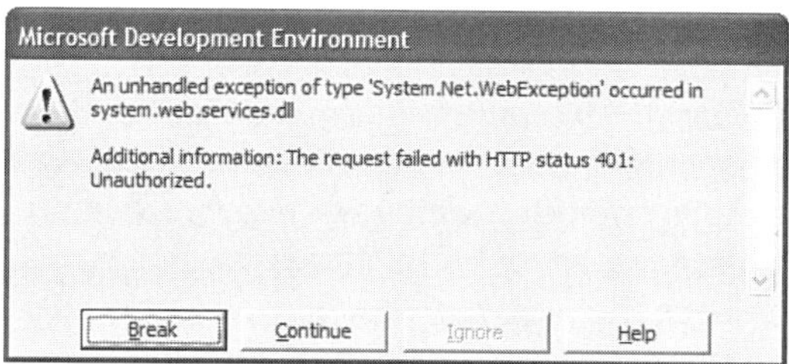

FIGURE 4.4
An HTTP 401 (Unauthorized) error that is returned from a Web service call.

As you can see, the error that you get is an exception that is thrown. This exception contains enough information for you to determine that the Web server generated a "401: Unauthorized" error. What happens if you give all the privileges back to the `Login.asmx` file and do something similar through `Web.config`?

To test this theory, go ahead and restore `Login.asmx` to its original security state. Open the `Web.config` file (shown in Listing 4.1) and locate the `<authorization>` element. Where it contains the element `<allow users="*"/>`, change that to `<deny users="*"/>`.

LISTING 4.1 `RepositoryV1/Web.config`
The `Web.config` File for the `RepositoryV1` Application

```
<?xml version="1.0" encoding="utf-8" ?>
<configuration>

  <system.diagnostics>
    <switches>
      <add name="SystemTrace" value="4"></add>
    </switches>
  </system.diagnostics>
  <system.web>

    <!--  DYNAMIC DEBUG COMPILATION
          Set compilation debug="true" to enable
          ASPX debugging.  Otherwise, setting this value to
          false will improve runtime performance of this application.
          Set compilation debug="true" to insert debugging symbols (.pdb information)
          into the compiled page. Because this creates a larger file that executes
          more slowly, you should set this value to true only when debugging and to
          false at all other times. For more information, refer to the
          documentation about
          debugging ASP.NET files.
    -->
    <compilation
         defaultLanguage="c#"
         debug="true"
    />

    <!--  CUSTOM ERROR MESSAGES
          Set customErrors mode="On" or "RemoteOnly" to enable
          custom error messages, "Off" to disable.
          Add <error> tags for each of the errors you want to handle.

          "On" Always display custom (friendly) messages.
          "Off" Always display detailed ASP.NET error information.
          "RemoteOnly" Display custom (friendly) messages only to users not running
```

LISTING 4.1 RepositoryV1/Web.config
The Web.config File for the RepositoryV1 Application
(continued)

```
        on the local Web server. This setting is recommended for security purposes, so
        that you do not display application detail information to remote clients.
-->
<customErrors
mode="RemoteOnly"
/>

<!-- AUTHENTICATION
      This section sets the authentication policies of the application.
      Possible modes are "Windows",
      "Forms", "Passport" and "None"

      "None" No authentication is performed.
      "Windows" IIS performs authentication (Basic, Digest, or
      Integrated Windows) according to
       its settings for the application. Anonymous access must be disabled in IIS.
      "Forms" You provide a custom form (Web page) for users to
       enter their credentials, and then you authenticate them in your
       application. A user credential token is stored in a cookie. "Passport"
       Authentication is performed via a centralized authentication service provided
       by Microsoft that offers a single logon and core profile
       services for member sites.
-->
<authentication mode="Forms" >
   <forms name="reposAdminApp" loginUrl="sitelogin.aspx" protection="All"></forms>
</authentication>
<!-- AUTHORIZATION
      This section sets the authorization policies of the application.
      You can allow or deny access to application resources by user or
      role. Wildcards: "*" mean everyone, "?" means anonymous
      (unauthenticated) users.
-->

<authorization>
    <deny users="*" />
        <!-- <allow    users="[comma separated list of users]"
                       roles="[comma separated list of roles]"/>
             <deny     users="[comma separated list of users]"
```

LISTING 4.1 `RepositoryV1/Web.config`
The `Web.config` File for the `RepositoryV1` Application
(continued)

```
                                        roles="[comma separated list of roles]"/>
                -->
    </authorization>



    <!--  APPLICATION-LEVEL TRACE LOGGING
          Application-level tracing enables trace log output for every
          page within an application. Set trace enabled="true" to enable
          application trace logging.  If pageOutput="true", the trace
          information will be displayed at the bottom of each page.
          Otherwise, you can view the application trace log by browsing
          the "trace.axd" page from your web application
          root.
    -->
    <trace
        enabled="true"
        requestLimit="20"
        pageOutput="true"
        traceMode="SortByTime"
           localOnly="true"
    />

    <!--  SESSION STATE SETTINGS
          By default ASP.NET uses cookies to identify which requests
          belong to a particular session. If cookies are not available,
          a session can be tracked by adding a session identifier to the URL.
          To disable cookies, set sessionState cookieless="true".
    -->
    <sessionState
            mode="InProc"
            stateConnectionString="tcpip=127.0.0.1:42424"
            sqlConnectionString="data source=127.0.0.1;Trusted_Connection=yes"
            cookieless="false"
            timeout="20"
    />
```

LISTING 4.1 RepositoryV1/Web.config
The Web.config File for the RepositoryV1 Application
(continued)

```
    <!--  GLOBALIZATION
          This section sets the globalization settings of the application.
    -->
    <globalization
            requestEncoding="utf-8"
            responseEncoding="utf-8"
   />

 </system.web>

<location path="login.asmx">
        <system.web>
            <authorization>
                <allow users="*"/>
            </authorization>
         </system.web>
</location>


    <location path="repositoryservice.asmx">
      <system.web>
         <authorization>
            <allow users="*"/>
         </authorization>
      </system.web>
    </location>


    <location path="GenerateChart.aspx">
       <system.web>
          <authorization>
            <allow users="*"/>
          </authorization>
       </system.web>
    </location>
```

LISTING 4.1 RepositoryV1/Web.config
The Web.config File for the RepositoryV1 Application (continued)

```
<appSettings>
    <add key="DefaultDSN"
        value="server=localhost; user id=survey; password=survey;
➥initial catalog=SurveyRepository;"></add>
</appSettings>

</configuration>
```

This will completely block every single user from the Web service. Will the result be the same as in the preceding example? If you block access to the service via NTFS permissions, you get a 401 error. If you block access via `Web.config`, will you get the same 401 error, or will you get some kind of different message or exception? There's only one (good) way to find out: Try it yourself.

Start a new debug instance of Survey Development Studio with the modified `Web.config` file set to deny all users. When you attempt to log in to Survey Repository, you should see the same error dialog that you saw in the previous example (refer to Figure 4.4): a message indicating a "401: Unauthorized" error.

The good point to take away from this little experiment is that there is more than one way to restrict access to a Web application. You can use standard NTFS permissions, you can use IIS to set up restrictions based on networking information such as IP address ranges, or you can use `Web.config` to prevent access to one or more locations within the application.

The authorization scheme that we're using for Survey Repository doesn't require any of these measures. A custom set of credentials is passed to the login service, and the login service returns a reusable, expiring token. That token is then handed to the main service as proof of valid identity. If you wanted to employ a system like this, you could make changes as you did here to prevent people from outside your domain from using the login service or you could set up an IP address range belonging to authorized machines that can log in. The possibilities are endless, and deciding on which method to use is often more of a business decision than a technical one.

Survey Development Studio

Now that you've found a few creative ways to break the Repository Web service and the back-end code, let's take a look at the Survey Development Studio application. In the following sections you'll poke around, change some things, and see how those changes affect how the application performs.

EXPERIMENT: Modal and Nonmodal Forms

Believe it or not, the decision as to whether a form is modal or not is a fairly important design concern. If you decide incorrectly, it could cause you a lot of headache in terms of development effort.

When you're working with modal and nonmodal forms, there are generally two different kinds of forms: input, or "prompt," forms and controller forms.

An input (or prompt) form is designed to request a certain set of information from the user. When users are done submitting that information, they generally click a confirmation button (Submit, Save, Send, and so on). If they don't like what they've entered, they can back out their input with a Cancel button. These modal forms are generally referred to as *dialogs*.

A controller form is basically a host for multiple dialogs and other input controls. Instead of this form's sole purpose being to prompt the user for input, this form's purpose is to guide the user through various other tasks, some of which might require additional forms to be opened.

That is the logical or design difference between the form types. Code-wise, what does all this boil down to? With a modal dialog, no other input can take place. Forms do not receive user interface events while a modal dialog is in the foreground. This means you don't have to worry about some action from another form interfering with the action of the foreground form. With a nonmodal form, the foreground form starts up with focus, but it can also lose that focus. It allows any other form in the application to take focus, to move in front of it, and so on. In addition, while the nonmodal form is visible, other forms are able to receive and respond to events. With nonmodal forms it is extremely important to prevent two forms from working with the same data at the same time. This is essentially the core of the experiment in this section.

For this first experiment with forms, let's take a look at the code for editing contacts. On the main survey form, if you want to edit the contacts for a given survey profile (*contacts* are the survey administration personnel, not respondents), the following bit of code (found in the `frmSurvey.cs` file) is triggered when you click the appropriate button:

```
if (contactManager == null )
{
    contactManager = new frmProfileContacts( this.surveyProfile);
    contactManager.MdiParent = this.MdiParent;
    contactManager.Show();
}
else
{
    contactManager.Show();
}
```

The survey form has a private member variable called `contactManager`. This member variable is used to store an instance of the contact manager form. The preceding code prevents you from ever having more than one contact manager open at the same time. Make a backup of the `frmSurvey.cs` file and remove the conditional elements from the preceding code so that your code now looks like this:

```
contactManager = new frmProfileContacts( this.surveyProfile);
contactManager.MdiParent = this.MdiParent;
contactManager.Show();
```

With this code in place, rebuild the Survey Development Studio application and run it in a new debug instance. What do you think is going to happen when you click the Edit/View Contacts button? Each time you click it, you get a new form that is responsible for editing the *same* data.

Go ahead and click the Edit/View Contacts button twice. Navigate to the same contact record (if you don't have one, create one with the first contact editor before you open the second form). Now, when you make changes to this record, the *last* form to make changes will be the one whose changes are persisted. In addition, the second form will not "see" the changes made by the first form because it doesn't periodically refresh its data.

As you can see, by just removing a couple lines of code designed to prevent multiple concurrent uses of a nonmodal form, you give the users the ability to completely mess up the data and the application.

So, why don't you just make the form modal and forget about it? The problem is that if you made it modal, no other forms in the entire application would be able to function. You don't care if the user has two surveys open and each of those survey profiles has an open contact editor. The problem arises when the same profile has two contact editors open. This makes the situation slightly more complex than simply modal versus nonmodal. Essentially what you've done with the above logic that you removed for the experiment is create a singleton form. This means that for each survey profile, there is one and only one contact editor form.

A lot of examples on how to work with Windows Forms give you information on how to create modal dialogs and how to create nonmodal MDI child windows. What they don't normally tell you is that those two situations don't cover everything, and you often need to have much more complex logic for dealing with windows.

Even more complex than the contact editor form is the question editor. The survey profile can have an unlimited number of questions. You can be editing one or more of those questions at any given time. The rule or restriction is that you cannot have two question editors for the same question open at the same time. Again, you can't simply get by with just a choice of modal or nonmodal. In essence, you're looking at an array or a list of singleton forms or question editors.

As another experiment, take a look at the event handler for the Edit Question button, shown in Listing 4.2.

LISTING 4.2 SurveyV1\SurveyStudio\frmSurvey.cs
The Edit Question Event Handler

```
private void button6_Click(object sender, System.EventArgs e)
{
  int questionId = surveyProfile.Questions[ dgQuestions.CurrentRowIndex ].ID;

  bool alreadyOpen = false;

  foreach (object qe in questionEditors)
  {
    frmQuestion fq = (frmQuestion)qe;
    if  (fq.questionId == questionId )
    {
      alreadyOpen = true;
```

LISTING 4.2 `SurveyV1\SurveyStudio\frmSurvey.cs`
The Edit Question Event Handler
(continued)

```
      fq.Focus();
      break;
    }
  }
  if (!alreadyOpen)
  {
    frmQuestion currentQuestion = new frmQuestion( this, questionId );
    currentQuestion.MdiParent = this.MdiParent;
    currentQuestion.Show();
    currentQuestion.Focus();
    questionEditors.Add( currentQuestion );
  }
}
```

The code in Listing 4.2 iterates through a private member variable called `questionEditors`. This variable is a collection of instances of type `frmQuestion`. Each time a user clicks the Edit Question button to edit a question, a new question editor form is created to edit that one particular question. If the user clicks the Edit Question button with that same question highlighted, the existing form gains focus instead of a new form being created. This prevents concurrent editing of the same data, as you saw before, but it is a bit more complex because you're dealing with a collection of singleton forms.

To completely mess this code up, you can do to it the same thing you did with the previous code. Instead of iterating through the private members, you can just create a brand new question editor. Change the preceding method to the following:

```
private void button6_Click(object sender, System.EventArgs e)
{
    int questionId =
      surveyProfile.Questions[ dgQuestions.CurrentRowIndex ].ID;
    frmQuestion currentQuestion =
      new frmQuestion( this, questionId );
    currentQuestion.MdiParent = this.MdiParent;
    currentQuestion.Show();
    currentQuestion.Focus();
}
```

This should give you plenty of ability to completely wreck the data. Click the Edit Question button for the same question two or three different times. Now, start changing the data in each window. You'll notice that because you used data binding to a class instance that has scope outside the boundaries of the question editor forms, the secondary editors do in fact see the changes *as soon as focus leaves the edit field*. This means that when you change the name of a question and then press Tab, all other windows that are open and editing that question are informed of the change. While the consequences of losing the concurrency code here are not quite as harmful to the data as in other circumstances, it is still something the user would find frustrating and confusing.

The lesson to be learned here is that deciding between modal and nonmodal doesn't always cover all the bases. If you're going to make a nonmodal form, you need to decide whether you can have multiple instances of the same form open and editing the same bits of data and, if so, how you will handle concurrent updates. You can either prevent multiple instances from working on the same bits of data, as is done in the sample application, or you can get a little advanced and make each instance aware of the other instances and handle the updates intelligently. I think that unless you have a very specific business case that requires that you have multiple instances editing the same data, you should avoid that scenario at all costs.

EXPERIMENT: We All Know What We Get When We Assume

Regardless of how much we try to deny it, making assumptions about code's environment is something that every programmer does. Sometimes these assumptions are safe, such as assuming that the operating system will be Windows 2000/XP/2003. This is something that might be listed in your application requirements, and your code can safely assume that such an environment exists.

Unsafe assumptions can cause a lot of problems. For example, back in the good old days of manually programming PalmOS synchronization code, one could not even assume the nature of integers. On the PalmOS device, integers are stored with the bytes in the reverse order as on the desktop. Equally as dangerous is assuming that input from a user will follow a given format. Without validation code, a user who doesn't conform to your assumption could easily break your code.

To take a look at the consequences of assuming something that can easily change, let's take a look at the code that retrieves all the survey profiles and their revisions from the database when the user chooses to open a profile from Survey Repository.

When the user follows the menus to open a profile from Survey Repository, an instance of `frmRepositoryProfileList` is created, and the `LoadProfiles` method is invoked. This method retrieves all the profiles and revisions from the database and displays them in a `TreeView` control. Take a look at the code in Listing 4.3 and see if you can spot the dangerous assumption before reading further.

LISTING 4.3 `SurveyV1\SurveyStudio\frmRepositoryProfileList.cs`
The `LoadProfiles` Method

```
public void LoadProfiles()
{
  dsProfiles = RepositoryClient.GetAllRevisions();
  DataTable tblProfiles = dsProfiles.Tables[0];

  int lastProfileId = -999;
  int currentProfileId;
  TreeNode newNode;

  foreach (DataRow row in tblProfiles.Rows)
  {
    newNode = null;
    currentProfileId = Int32.Parse( row["ProfileId"].ToString() );
    if (currentProfileId != lastProfileId)
    {
      newNode = new TreeNode( row["ShortDescription"].ToString());
      newNode.Tag = Int32.Parse( row["ProfileId"].ToString() );
      if (row["State"].ToString() == "1")
    newNode.ForeColor = Color.Red;
      trvProfiles.Nodes.Add( newNode );
      AddRevision( newNode, row );
    }
    else
    {
      // this row is a revision of the previous row
      AddRevision( trvProfiles.Nodes[trvProfiles.Nodes.Count-1], row );
    }
    lastProfileId = currentProfileId;
  }
}
```

LISTING 4.3 SurveyV1\SurveyStudio\frmRepositoryProfileList.cs
The LoadProfiles Method
(continued)

```
private void AddRevision( TreeNode parent, DataRow row )
{
  TreeNode newNode = new TreeNode( row["RevisionComment"].ToString() );
  if (row["State"].ToString() == "1")
  {
    newNode.ForeColor = Color.Red;
  }
  newNode.Tag = Int32.Parse( row["RevisionId"].ToString() );
  parent.Nodes.Add( newNode );
}
```


The code in Listing 4.3 invokes the GetAllRevisions method of the Survey Repository Web service, storing the results in a data set. As you can see from the main loop, the top-level elements of the tree are profiles, and the child elements are profile revisions. Basically, if the current profile ID is not the same as the previous profile ID, the code knows to create a new top-level node. If the current and previous profile IDs are the same, the code makes the *assumption* that the current item is a revision, and so it is placed as a second-level element. The problem here is that this code relies completely on the fact that the rows appear in a specific order. Let's take a look at the code for the stored procedure that fills the code in Listing 4.3 with results:

```
CREATE PROCEDURE SVY_Get_AllRevisions
AS

SELECT p.ProfileId, p.CreatedBy, p.CreatedOn, p.State, p.CheckedOutBy,
       p.CheckedOutOn, p.ShortDescription, u.FullName as CreatedByName,
       u2.FullName as CheckedOutByName,
       ph.RevisionId, ph.RevisedBy,
       ph.RevisedOn, ph.RevisionComment
       FROM SVY_SurveyProfiles p INNER JOIN
         SVY_Users u ON p.CreatedBy = u.UserId
       INNER JOIN
         SVY_ProfileHistory ph ON p.ProfileId = ph.ProfileId
       LEFT JOIN SVY_Users u2 ON p.CheckedOutBy = u2.UserId
       ORDER BY p.ShortDescription ASC
```

This stored procedure performs a join of the survey profile and profile revision tables to prevent a flattened view of all profiles and all revisions in the system. The profiles are then sorted by the field `ShortDescription`. The code listed here relies on the concept that the profile IDs of all revisions are in the right position. What happens if there are two different profiles, and they have the same short description? You might get the information in the right order or you might not. The fact that the code works properly with the data you have isn't an excuse to leave it this way. If you changed the sort order so that you sorted based on `RevisionComment`, you would surely break the code.

Change the stored procedure `SVY_Get_AllRevisions` to order by `ph.RevisionComment` instead of by `p.ShortDescription`. Then run the Survey Development Studio application and try to open a profile from Survey Repository. Figure 4.5 shows what my application displays when I do this.

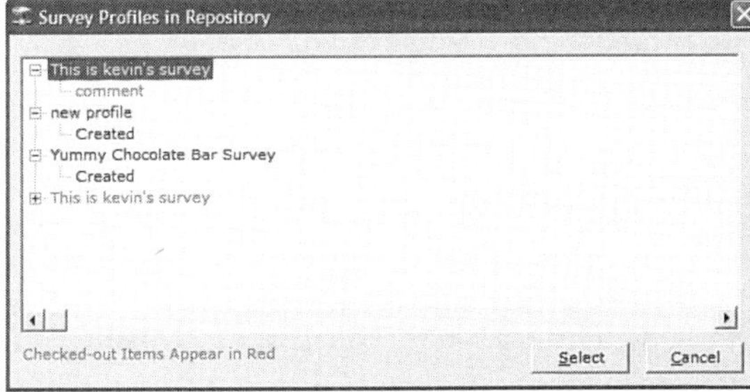

FIGURE 4.5
The Survey Profiles in Repository dialog, grouping out of order.

As you can see, the same survey profile actually appears twice in the tree. Revisions belonging to the same survey profile no longer belong to the same node in the tree view. Although you would hope the sort order would never change in the application, it is possible that a database person could change it, and you might not be informed of the change. Rather than assume or hope that the database code will never change, you can make code more reliable by doing things differently.

Change the contents of the `LoadProfiles` method to the following code:

```
public void LoadProfiles()
{
  dsProfiles = RepositoryClient.GetAllRevisions();
  DataTable tblProfiles = dsProfiles.Tables[0];
```

```
    TreeNode newNode;
    object node;

    foreach (DataRow row in tblProfiles.Rows)
    {
      node = GetProfileNodeFromTag( row["ProfileId"].ToString() );
      if (node == null)
      {
        // that profile isn't in the tree yet
        newNode = new TreeNode( row["ShortDescription"].ToString() );
        newNode.Tag = Int32.Parse( row["ProfileId"].ToString());
        if ( Int32.Parse(row["State"].ToString()) == 1 )
          newNode.ForeColor = Color.Red;
        trvProfiles.Nodes.Add( newNode );
        AddRevision( newNode, row );
      }
      else
        AddRevision( (TreeNode)node, row );
    }
  }
```


The new version of this code makes use of a new method, `GetProfileNodeFromTag`. This method looks for a top-level node with the tag that matches the current row's profile ID. If it is found, it returns the appropriate node. Otherwise, it returns null. By using "agile" code like this, you can remove the damage that assumptions cause. The new version of the code couldn't care less what the sort order of the result set is, nor does it care about any aspect of the data other than the columns contained in that data. Here's the `GetProfileNodeFromTag` method:

```
private TreeNode GetProfileNodeFromTag( string tag )
{
  // iterate through the top-level nodes.
  foreach (TreeNode node in trvProfiles.Nodes )
  {
    if (node.Parent == null)
    {
      if (node.Tag.ToString() == tag)
        return node;
    }
  }
  return null;
}
```

The moral of the story is that if you ever find yourself putting comments in your code that start with `// Assumes that ...`, you might want to take another look at the code and see if you can write it so that it works without the assumption. This might seem like more work up front, but a year after your code has been written, and someone makes a change to the information on which your code bases an assumption, you'll be glad you went back and modified the code to work without any unsafe assumptions.

PocketSurvey

The PocketSurvey application is a relatively sensitive application. It doesn't take much to make it perform in an unexpected way. By poking, prodding, and looking for some weaknesses in the application, we may find some ways to improve the application in terms of reliability and usability.

EXPERIMENT: When Data Files Go Missing

The section "Survey Development Studio," earlier in this chapter, describes what might happen if code makes unsafe assumptions. One of those unsafe assumptions is to assume the presence of a required file. The code for PocketSurvey does just that: It assumes that a file called `CurrentSurvey.svp` is located in the `\Program Files\PocketSurvey` directory. If the file isn't there, the application will break.

To test this, open the `PocketSurvey` project from within the main solution. Highlight the `CurrentSurvey.svp` test profile and change the build action from `Content` to `None`. This prevents the file from being deployed with the application to the Pocket PC device or emulator.

Start a new instance of PocketSurvey in debug mode. Very shortly after starting up, as expected, you get a "File Not Found" exception. An exception like this on a real device would likely confuse and irritate the user, and you really should do more to handle this situation gracefully.

Listing 4.4 shows the code that executes when the main form of PocketSurvey loads.

LISTING 4.4 `SurveyV1\PocketSurvey\frmMain.cs`
Main Form Initialization Code

```
Stream s = Assembly.GetExecutingAssembly().GetManifestResourceStream(
  "SAMS.Survey.PocketSurvey.SurveyProfile.xsd");
XmlTextReader xr = new XmlTextReader( s );
dsProfile = new DataSet();
dsProfile.ReadXmlSchema( xr );
xr.Close();
s.Close();

dsRun = new DataSet();
s = Assembly.GetExecutingAssembly().GetManifestResourceStream(
   "SAMS.Survey.PocketSurvey.SurveyRun.xsd");
xr = new XmlTextReader( s );
dsRun.ReadXmlSchema( xr );
xr.Close();
s.Close();

dsProfile.ReadXml( @"\Program Files\PocketSurvey\CurrentSurvey.svp" );
lblCurrent.Text = "Current Profile: " +
  dsProfile.Tables["Profile"].Rows[0]["Title"].ToString() + "\n\r" +

dsProfile.Tables["Profile"].Rows[0]["Notes"].ToString();
if (File.Exists( @"\Program Files\PocketSurvey\CurrentRun.svr" ) )
{
  dsRun.ReadXml( @"\Program Files\PocketSurvey\CurrentRun.svr" );
}
```


In Listing 4.4, you can see that you're actually very close to having the code you need. You're already making a check to see if the run file exists, so it should be easy enough to wrap the entire set of code with a `File.Exists` call to handle the error gracefully:

```
if (File.Exists(@"\Program Files\PocketSurvey\CurrentSurvey.svp") {
  // ... code from previous listing
}
else
{
  lblCurrent.Text = "No Survey Profile was Found.";
  btnStart.Enabled = false;
}
```

After putting in a simple change like the wrapper you just inserted into the code, you get the user-friendly screen shown in Figure 4.6 instead of an application-breaking exception.

FIGURE 4.6
The main form of PocketSurvey when no survey profile has been found.

The goal here isn't to show you *how* to make an application more reliable. The goal is to show you how *easy* it is to make an application more reliable. There is a big difference between an application that does what it is supposed to and an application that does what it is supposed to without breaking and under unusual conditions. If you spend just a little bit of effort looking back at an application and think to yourself, "How can I break this?" and then you patch those holes, the application will be a much more solid, reliable piece of software.

EXPERIMENT: Dealing with Limited Form Factors

Whenever you are dealing with a device that has limited form factor, the number of problems the application might experience grows exponentially. You have to worry about whether there is enough room on the device to display the data you need to display.

In a standard Windows Forms application, if you set a label control to auto-size, and the form can be sized, chances are that the user can make room for the text contained in that label. On a Pocket PC or another mobile device, the options are far more limited. For one thing, the user can't grab a corner of the window with the mouse and simply drag it to make more room.

In Figure 4.7 you can see some of the limitations of the small form factor, as some of the survey profile description has been cut off and some has word-wrapped.

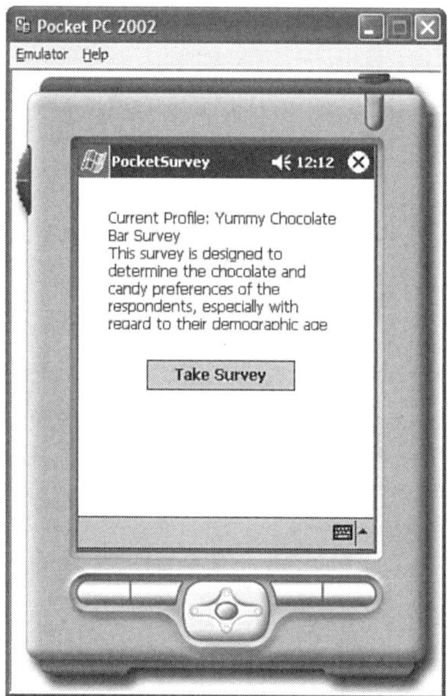

FIGURE 4.7 The main form of the PocketSurvey application, cutting off long string data in the survey profile.

An easy way to get around this limitation, at least on the main title form of the application, is to place the text inside scrollable regions. Take a look at Figure 4.8, which shows the application after I've separated the main text label into a label and a scrollable, read-only text box.

I won't go over the code required to make this change as it is fairly trivial. The point of this experiment is to illustrate that when you're dealing with limited form factors, the change in environment is so fundamental that it is dangerous to assume that if a layout works in Windows Forms it will work on a Pocket PC, a SmartPhone, and so on.

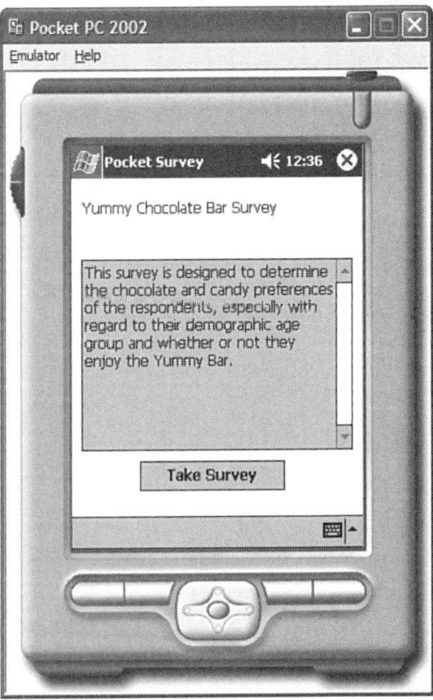

FIGURE 4.8
The main form of the PocketSurvey application, with a new multiline text box.

Moving On

This chapter is about experimenting with code. If there is one piece of information that you can take away from this chapter, it is to remember that just because your code compiles doesn't mean that it is done. If you are creating professional, production-quality code, you should seriously consider using peers review the code. Having peers experiment and examine your code in the same fashion we did during this chapter may produce a wealth of improvements.

You saw in this chapter that sometimes an assumption that the programmer makes in code can introduce a weak spot in the code that might break tomorrow, or in a year. You saw how security settings can radically affect the usability and even the functionality of an application. In addition, you took a look at some design issues related to MDI applications and applications for limited form factors.

You should never be afraid to tinker with your code or someone else's code. Not only is experimenting with code an extremely good way to learn, it is extremely beneficial for the product. All too often, weak, unreliable, or poorly designed code makes it into a production environment simply because programmers were intimidated by it and didn't want to experiment with it. Get into code, get your hands dirty, and break an application every way you can possibly imagine. When you're all done, you will know all of the application's vulnerabilities and you'll know how to fix them. You will be a better programmer, and your application will be a more solid, professional application as a result of taking the time to tinker with your so-called complete code.

Customizing Survey Repository

CHAPTER 5

This chapter and those that follow are all about customization. You're going to customize and enhance the existing codebase. Hopefully you'll see how some of the good decisions made in the creation of the existing codebase make it easier to enhance, customize, and add on to the code that's already built. This chapter covers the following:

- Extending the role-based security system
- Creating an administrative Web site

In this chapter you'll work on a few different things. First, you'll modify the Web service that already exists so that it contains full support for the role-based security (RBS) system that is already partially implemented. When you're done, the Web service will prevent users from performing actions for which they're not authorized. In addition, you're going to create an administrative Web site that allows people to create, modify, and delete users, roles, and more. From this you'll see the true benefits of object-relational mapping and the design of the business objects you've seen in earlier chapters.

Understanding RBS Systems

Using RBS for secure systems is so ubiquitous these days that a lot of programmers take it for granted that when they are building a security system, it will be role based.

What exactly is RBS? Before we get into that, let's talk a little bit about the problem that RBS solves. Assume that you are an administrator of a very large financial application. Employees from banks all across the country log in to this application to do their work throughout the day.

Different kinds of employees have access to different menus and different options. For example, a branch manager would have far more control and power within the application than a newly hired teller. Customer service representatives would also need to have their own limited set of access that may or may not overlap with permissions granted to other employee types.

For the sake of argument, let's assume that this particular financial application does not use RBS. Instead, each user is explicitly assigned each permission on an as-needed basis. If there are 50 permissions available to assign to each user and there are 5,000 users, that is a considerably large number of available combinations.

If you need to modify a single user, then the task might not seem all that daunting. However, what would you do if you wanted to increase the privilege level of all branch managers to include the ability to view the transaction logs of their employees? First, you would have to find out who all the branch managers are (there could be hundreds, even thousands). Second, you would have to manually edit each and every branch manager and hope that after editing hundreds of them, you didn't make any mistakes.

To counter this problem, using RBS has become the standard way of creating user security systems. A *role* is an abstraction that represents the collective permissions and restrictions that belong to the abstract concept of a particular user role.

In the financial application example, Branch Manager would become a role, as would Teller and Customer Service Representative. Instead of assigning specific permissions to specific users, you assign permissions to the roles. Let's say the financial application has a permission called View Employee Transactions.

When you have these well-defined roles that provide a logical interaction model for your users, you can start assigning roles to users. This might seem just like assigning permissions, but when you consider that each role holds its own set of permissions, you can see that you create an exponential savings in time and effort.

Setup is only the first savings. Maintenance is the other huge savings. In the financial application example, say the administrator wanted to add permissions to all the branch managers. Using the strict user-permission model, this task could take days and would be extremely error prone. In an RBS system, all the administrator would have to do is add a new permission to the Branch Manager role, and all users who had that role would automatically gain that permission.

The true elegance of this system starts to shine when you consider that each user can be assigned more than one role. You might have users with both the Teller role and the Customer Service Representative, who needs to perform both tasks. Such users would have two roles and still not have all the permissions associated with the Branch Manager role.

The way this is handled is that the user's permissions are resolved through some process. This process starts off with the assumption that the user has absolutely no permissions. For each role assigned to the user, permissions are granted to the user accordingly. In this way, the role-permission assignments are additive.

More complex systems have the ability to both grant and deny permissions to a role. A system like this allows the concept that a user belonging to a particular role can prevent that user from ever being granted a specific permission, even if the user's other roles grant that same permission.

As you can see, the possibilities for complex RBS design are virtually limitless. The point I want to make here is that if the application you are developing has both users and permissions, you would do yourself a disservice not to try to implement role abstractions instead of assigning permissions to individual users.

Enforcing RBS

Something that you might have noticed from previous chapters or from exploring the code of the Survey Repository application on your own is that we already have a partially implemented RBS system. We have the data structures, some of the stored procedures, and even some code for caching user permissions. Unfortunately, we don't actually do anything to enforce permissions above and beyond the simple authentication test. Essential to all security systems is the idea of implementing *both* authentication *and* authorization. Not only does the system need to know who is using it, but it needs to know what that person can and cannot do, assuming that they are who they say they are.

Before we get implement code to really tighten up the security on the Survey Development Suite, let's do a quick overview of what we have now.

The first thing we'll look at is the data structures. We used a number of tables to implement the RBS system. Table 5.1 describes the `SVY_Users` table.

TABLE 5.1

The `SVY_Users` Table

Column	Description
`UserId`	The database identity of the user
`UserName`	The user's login name (8-character limit)
`FullName`	The user's real full name
`Password`	The user's password (8-character limit)

The SVY_Users table is a basic table that stores user identities. It contains enough information to support password-based authentication and to store the names of the users within the system. In general, more complex systems that need more information than this generally leave the stock user table alone and add extra details with additional tables that key off of a user ID. Tables 5.2 through 5.4 describe more of the RBS data structure.

TABLE 5.2 The SVY_Roles Table

Column	Description
RoleId	The database identity of the role
Description	A description of the role

TABLE 5.3 The SVY_Categories Table

Column	Description
CategoryId	The Database identity of the permission category
Description	A description of the permission category

TABLE 5.4 The SVY_Permissions Table

Column	Description
PermissionId	The Database identity of the permission (not an auto-incrementing value)
Description	A description of the permission
CategoryId	The category ID to which the permission belongs

The SVY_Permissions table is slightly different from the others. The PermissionId column does not auto-increment like the other primary key columns in other tables. The main reason for this is that users and administrators should not be adding permissions to the system. This table exists solely for the purpose of providing user-friendly names and categorization for permissions. When the code (which you'll write later in this chapter) checks whether a user has a given permission, it checks by ID and not by the permission name. The idea behind this particular design is that after the application is built, the kinds of tasks a user might need permission for will not change; however, the set of permissions that belong to given users should be able to change frequently. If a new version of the application that has more tasks is released, we can simply add more permissions to the SVY_Permissions table. Tables 5.5 and 5.6 describe the permission- and role-related tables.

TABLE 5.5

The SVY_UserRoles Table

Column	Description
RoleId	The role ID of the user-role mapping
UserId	The user ID of the user-role mapping

TABLE 5.6

The SVY_RolePermissions Table

Column	Description
RoleId	The role ID of the role-permission mapping
PermissionId	The permission ID of the role-permission mapping
AccessMode	The access mode, which is a bitmasked integer value

Bitmasking and Access Modes

Over the years, I have built dozens of systems that have required authentication and authorization. Many of those have been role based, in which permissions are granted to roles and then roles are assigned to users. The set of permissions granted to the user is considered to be all the permissions granted to all the roles to which the user has been assigned.

We have a couple options for setting up permissions. One option would be to create permissions such as Create Profile, Edit Profile, and Delete Profile, and then if the user has the permission, he or she has the permission. That is a somewhat cumbersome system. Another alternative (my favorite) is to create permissions such as Profile, and then when you assign that permission to a role, you assign it with an access mode. An *access mode* is a description of *how* a role can access a particular item. A role might have the permission Profile and only the Read mode, while another might have Read, Update, Delete, and Create modes. This system allows administrators a lot of flexibility.

How do you use an access mode? You could create a long list of Boolean or bit columns. There might be a column for Read, a column for Update, one for Create, and so on. This is functional but not optimal. Sometimes there are finer degrees of access than the four CRUD (Create, Retrieve/Read, Update, Delete) operations. What if someone wants to transfer a record from one location to another? You could use the Read access mode, but that might not cover it. You could use the Update mode, but that might be too much because changing the location of a record (for example, moving it from one folder to another, changing category) might not be considered an actual update. To give users the ability to transfer a record without being able to modify it in other ways, you might create an access mode called Transfer. If you were using the Boolean or bit-column method, this might create some headaches.

However, if you use the bitmask method, it shouldn't bother you at all. Essentially, this method goes back to the "good old days" of programming. The binary representation of any integer is a string of 0s and 1s, and you can convert that list of 0s and 1s into a list of true and false assertions. By setting and checking individual bits, you can use a single 32-bit integer to store 32 individual true or false assertions. In the past, this kind of technique was used to overcome memory and speed limitations in the underlying hardware. Now it's used to make the permission system scalable. You can continue to add access modes as you need them, without worrying about whether the additions will break any existing code.

CODE TOUR: The Existing RBS Code

Before we start clamping down on security by writing new code, we should take stock of what code we already have, to see what we can use.

The first, and probably most useful, piece of the RBS system that is already intact is the code that caches user permissions each time a user logs in via the `Login.asmx` Web service.

Listing 5.1 contains the entire listing of the code that runs when a user logs in via the Web service. Pay close attention to the code that uses the application's cache object.

LISTING 5.1 SurveyV1\RepositoryV1\Login.asmx
The LoginUser Method

```
[WebMethod]
public string LoginUser(string userName, string password)
{
  SystemTrace.MethodStart( MethodBase.GetCurrentMethod() );
  // authenticate user
  // cache user security data (permissions, etc)
  // return GUID as authentication token.

  User testUser = new User();
  testUser.UserName = userName;
  testUser.Password = password;

  int userValid = testUser.Validate();
  if (userValid < 0)
  {
    SystemTrace.TraceVerbose("User failed login attempt: {0}/{1}",
      userName, password);
    return string.Empty;
  }
  else
  {
    // fetch the security permissions that belong to the user according to
    // their assigned roles.
    PermissionList pl = new PermissionList();
    pl.FetchPermissions( userValid );
    SystemTrace.TraceVerbose("Permissions fetched {0}",
      pl.ResultSet.Tables[0].Rows.Count);
    System.Web.Caching.Cache cache = System.Web.HttpContext.Current.Cache;

    string returnGuid = Guid.NewGuid().ToString();
    string cacheKey = "Security-" + returnGuid;
    if (cache[cacheKey] != null)
    cache.Remove( cacheKey );
    cache.Insert( cacheKey,
    pl, null, Cache.NoAbsoluteExpiration, TimeSpan.FromHours(60),
    CacheItemPriority.High,
    null );
    return returnGuid;
  }
}
```

The parts of this code that are important for adding new features is the `PermissionList` class and the `cache.Insert` method call. By calling `pl.FetchPermissions`, you can retrieve all the permissions that the user has available by virtue of his or her role membership. This list of permissions is then stored in the application cache. At the moment, you don't do anything with that list of permissions. In the next section you're going to write some code that will help you enforce these permissions and prevent users from calling unauthorized functions.

There is one more thing you should look at before customizing the code: the stored procedure that retrieves the user permissions. This procedure contains some logic that automatically resolves the issue of a user having multiple roles that have varying access modes for the same permission. For example, one role might grant the user Create mode on the Profile permission. A second right might grant the user Read and Update modes on the Profile permission. By using the `SUM` operator, you effectively grant the user the sum of all permissions granted by their roles:

```
CREATE PROCEDURE SVY_Get_Effective_Permissions
@UserId int
AS
select rp.PermissionId, p.Description, SUM(rp.AccessMode) as Access
    FROM SVY_Permissions p
INNER JOIN SVY_RolePermissions rp
      ON p.PermissionId = rp.PermissionId
    INNER JOIN SVY_UserRoles ur ON rp.RoleId = ur.RoleId
    INNER JOIN SVY_Users u ON
    ur.UserId = u.UserId
WHERE u.UserId = @UserId
GROUP BY rp.PermissionId, p.Description
GO
```

There are some flaws with this idea (for example, if enough roles grant the same permission, it could create false-positives in other access modes), but for now, this code will suffice for our needs.

STEP-BY-STEP GUIDE: Enforcing RBS on the Web Service with New Code

Now that you've seen the code that already exists to support RBS, you can create some new code to build on top of that and create a solid set of code that enforces permission checks. You should be able to reuse a considerable amount of the underlying code to make this an easy enhancement to the existing application. Here's what you need to do:

1. Add some more helper methods to the `SecurityHelper` class. As mentioned earlier in this chapter, you're going to be doing some work with bitmasks, and I want to make sure that as much of that is abstracted and hidden from the programmer as possible. With that in mind, take a look at some of the new methods you can add to `SecurityHelper` (see Listing 5.2).

LISTING 5.2 `SurveyV1\SecurityServices\SecurityHelper.cs`
Methods Added to `SecurityHelper` for RBS Enforcement

```
public static int BuildStandardAccessMode( bool create,
  bool read, bool update, bool delete )
{
  int accessMode = 0;
  if (create)
    accessMode += (int)AccessMasks.Create;
  if (read)
    accessMode += (int)AccessMasks.Read;
  if (update)
    accessMode += (int)AccessMasks.Update;
  if (delete)
    accessMode += (int)AccessMasks.Delete;
  return accessMode;
}

public static bool CheckCacheForAccess( string userToken,
  int permissionId, int accessMode )
{
  System.Web.Caching.Cache cache = System.Web.HttpContext.Current.Cache;
  string cacheKey = "Security-" + userToken;
  if (cache[cacheKey] == null)
  {
    SystemTrace.TraceVerbose(
      "User data no longer in cache {0}, cache item count {1}",
        cacheKey, cache.Count);
    return false;
  }
```

LISTING 5.2 `SurveyV1\SecurityServices\SecurityHelper.cs` **Methods Added to `SecurityHelper` for RBS Enforcement (continued)**

```
  PermissionList pl = (PermissionList)cache[cacheKey];
  return pl.HasPermission( permissionId, accessMode );
}

public static string AccessModeToString( int accessMode )
{
  string accessString = "";

  if (SecurityHelper.CheckAccess( accessMode, (int)AccessMasks.Create ))
    accessString += "C";
  else
    accessString += "-";
  if (SecurityHelper.CheckAccess( accessMode, (int)AccessMasks.Read))
    accessString += "R";
  else
    accessString += "-";
  if (SecurityHelper.CheckAccess( accessMode, (int)AccessMasks.Update))
    accessString += "U";
  else
    accessString += "-";
  if (SecurityHelper.CheckAccess( accessMode, (int)AccessMasks.Delete))
    accessString += "D";
  else
    accessString += "-";

  return accessString;
}
```


2. The first method, `BuildStandardAccessMode`, is a helper function that does some of the tedious math that is a hallmark side effect of using bitmasked value fields. It allows the programmer to pass in four Boolean values, and the result is an integer that represents the combined access mode that can be used to check permissions.

3. The next method, `CheckCacheForAccess`, retrieves an instance of the `PermissionList` class from the application cache. This instance contains a list of all permissions granted to the user via his

or her role membership (as explained earlier). This class has a method called `HasPermission` that checks whether a given permission is in the list, with a specific access mode.

4. Finally, the helper method, `AccessModeToString`, takes a numeric access mode and returns a string that represents which bits are on and which are not. This outputs a string that looks very much like the access permissions that Unix file systems display. If the Create bit is turned on in the number, a `C` is output in the appropriate location; otherwise, it is a `-`. Therefore, a role that has been assigned the Create, Update, and Delete modes of a given permission outputs the string `C-UD`. The access mode string follows the CRUD pattern, so the positions are the same. If at some later date you add more access modes, you can just change the output string so that it contains new positions.

5. Now you've added several methods to the `SecurityHelper` class, and you've taken a look at how the permissions are being stored in the cache for us to reuse. There's just one more thing you need to do before you actually wrap the Web service calls in secured code. To make it easy for clients to clarify exactly what went wrong when an exception is thrown, and to make it easy to track when security exceptions occur, you need to create a new class that derives from `ApplicationException`. Listing 5.3 shows the SecurityException class derived from ApplicationException.

LISTING 5.3 `SurveyV1\SecurityServices\SecurityException.cs`
The `SecurityException` Class

```
using System;
using System.Runtime.Serialization;
using System.Collections;
using System.ComponentModel;
using System.Data;
using System.Diagnostics;
using System.Web;


namespace SAMS.Survey.SecurityServices
{
  public class SecurityException : System.ApplicationException
  {
```

LISTING 5.3 `SurveyV1\SecurityServices\SecurityException.cs`
The `SecurityException` Class
(continued)

```
    public SecurityException() :
      base("Insufficient Permissions to Perform Current Action")
    {

    }

   public SecurityException( string message) : base(message)
   {
   }

   public SecurityException( SerializationInfo info,
                            StreamingContext context) : base(info, context)
   {
   }

  }
}
```

Listing 5.3 might not look like much, but the potential for expansion is certainly here. Because this class inherits from `ApplicationException`, it automatically gains all the behavior of standard CLR exceptions. In addition, you can override all the constructor methods, as is done here. They're currently blank, but you can easily add code that makes use of the `ExceptionManager` class that is part of the Microsoft application block for exception management handler to publish the exception to a database, send emails, or even send SMS messages.

With this new exception class in hand, you can actually start wrapping some of the methods of the Survey Repository Web service with permission checks. Listing 5.4 shows some of the methods of the Survey Repository service that now check for various permissions before allowing the operation to take place.

LISTING 5.4 SurveyV1\RepositoryV1\RepositoryService.asmx.cs
Some of the Newly Secured Methods in RepositoryService.asmx.cs

```
[WebMethod()]
public int AddRun( string userToken, int profileId, int revisionId,
string shortDescription, string longDescription, string xmlSource )
{
  int userId = SecurityHelper.GetUserIdFromToken( userToken );
  if (userId == -1)
    throw new SecurityException("Security Token is invalid or expired.");
  else
  {
    if (!SecurityHelper.CheckCacheForAccess( userToken,
    (int)StandardPermissions.Runs,
    SecurityHelper.BuildStandardAccessMode( true, true, false, false ) ) )
    throw new SecurityException();
    SecurityHelper.SetIdentityContext( userId );

    RevisionRun rr = new RevisionRun();
    rr.SubmittedBy = userId;
    rr.SubmittedOn = DateTime.Now;
    rr.ProfileId = profileId;
    rr.RevisionId = revisionId;
    rr.ShortDescription = shortDescription;
    rr.LongDescription = longDescription;
    rr.XMLSource = xmlSource;
    rr.Add();

    return rr.RunId;
  }
}


[WebMethod()]
public string GetProfile(string userToken, int profileId )
{
  int userId = SecurityHelper.GetUserIdFromToken( userToken );
  if (userId == -1)
    throw new SecurityException("Security Token is invalid or expired.");
  else
  {
```

LISTING 5.4 SurveyV1\RepositoryV1\RepositoryService.asmx.cs
Some of the Newly Secured Methods in RepositoryService.asmx.cs
(continued)

```
    if (!(SecurityHelper.CheckCacheForAccess( userToken,
          (int)StandardPermissions.Profiles,
          SecurityHelper.BuildStandardAccessMode( false, true, false, false ) ) ))
      throw new SecurityException();

    SecurityHelper.SetIdentityContext( userId );
    SurveyProfile sp = new SurveyProfile();
    sp.ProfileId = profileId;
    sp.Load();
    return sp.ToXmlString();
  }
}

[WebMethod()]
public string GetProfileHistory(string userToken, int profileId )
{
  int userId = SecurityHelper.GetUserIdFromToken( userToken );
  if (userId == -1)
    throw new SecurityException("Security Token is invalid or expired.");
  else
  {
    if (!SecurityHelper.CheckCacheForAccess( userToken,
    (int)StandardPermissions.Profiles,
    SecurityHelper.BuildStandardAccessMode( false, true, false, false ) ) )
      throw new SecurityException();

    SecurityHelper.SetIdentityContext( userId );
    ProfileHistory ph = new ProfileHistory( profileId );
    ph.GetProfileHistory();
    return ph.ResultSet.GetXml();
  }
}
```


As you can see, it's a pretty simple procedure to wrap the public Web methods in permission-checking security. All you do is invoke `CheckCacheForAccess` for the appropriate permission. If the access check fails, you throw a security exception with no argument to the constructor. As shown previously in Listing 5.3, the default constructor creates the exception, with a message that indicates a permission failure.

After entering the code in Listing 5.4 and doing the same type of thing to all the other methods for the Survey Repository service, you can be certain that if a user attempts to invoke a method from a client and that user doesn't have permission to do so, an exception will be thrown and the operation will not be completed.

In this example I illustrated that when you need to add new features or functionality to an application, the first thing you should do is look at the application to find out how much code you can reuse. If you have a good infrastructure in place and the application has been designed for scalability, it should be a fairly straightforward process to add features.

STEP-BY-STEP GUIDE: Testing the RBS Additions

One unfortunate side effect of being programmers is that we like to program a lot more than we like to test. If this weren't the case, we would all be working in QA departments instead of programming. However, no matter how much we want to avoid it, we need to test our own code.

You added some code to the existing security system to enforce permission-level security checks on users making requests of the Web service by checking their RBS permission lists. To make sure it is working properly, you need to test it:

1. First, see if the method calls work properly when the user has the permissions necessary. To make sure the user has the permissions needed, you can run the appropriate stored procedure in SQL Query Analyzer, as shown in Figure 5.1.

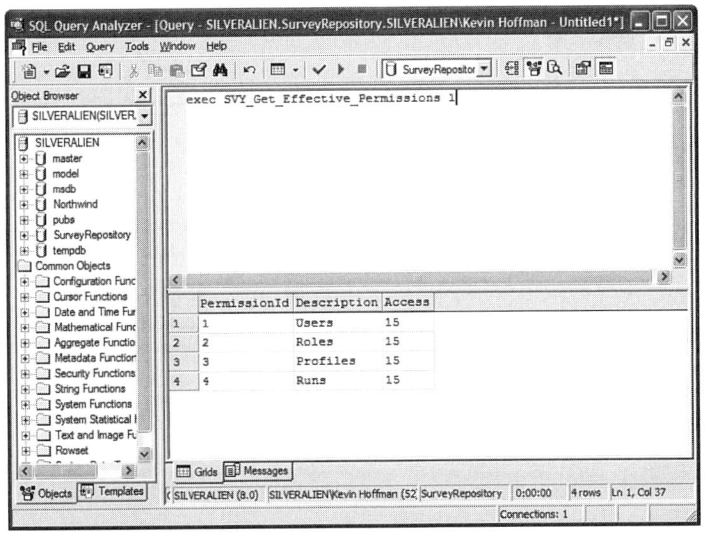

FIGURE 5.1 SQL Query Analyzer, used to determine the effective permissions of a specific user.

According to Figure 5.1, this user account has all the permissions required to perform whatever task the user needs to perform. By this point, you know enough about Survey Development Studio to log in to Survey Repository and perform a few operations.

2. Run a few sample tests against method calls that you know are wrapped in security checks. If any of them fail, you'll have to go back and double-check the code and stored procedure for accuracy.

3. Test the case where the user account has insufficient permission to perform a given task. To test this, you just remove the administrative role from the user, and the user will lose all associated permissions. You can do this by removing the appropriate row from the `SVY_UserRoles` table. After you remove that row and query the effective permission list, you can look at the SQL Query Analyzer screen (see Figure 5.2).

FIGURE 5.2

SQL Query Analyzer, illustrating a lack of permissions associated with a given user.

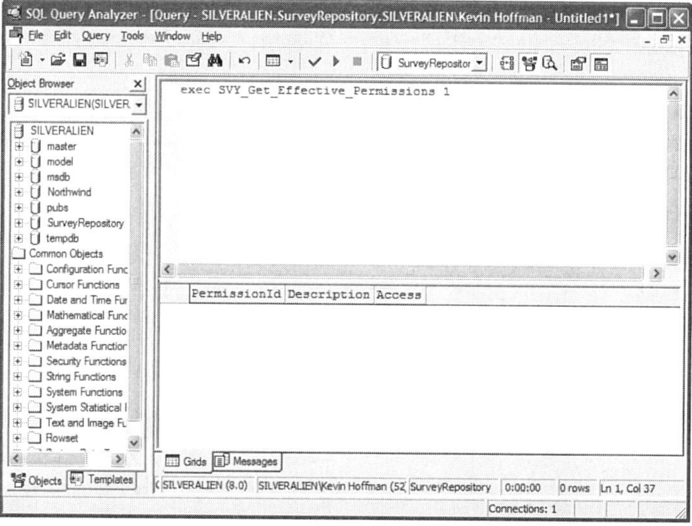

4. Now that you know that the user doesn't have any permissions, use the Windows Forms application to log in to Survey Repository and try to open a survey profile from Survey Repository. Figure 5.3 illustrates the security exception that is thrown on the Web service and propagated via SOAP headers to the client automatically.

After you've tested the additions to the RBS code to your satisfaction, you are ready to continue to the next section.

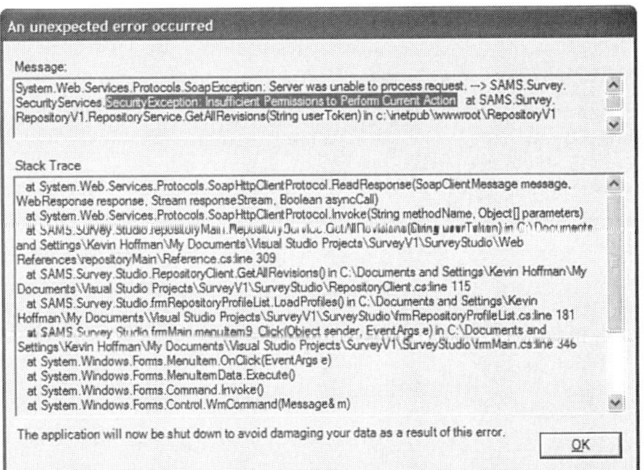

FIGURE 5.3
An exception thrown when a user attempts to perform a Web service action for which he or she has not been authorized.

Creating an Administrative Web Site

The design process is just as important (if not more important) as the actual build process. This section walks you through adding an administrative Web site to Survey Repository. There are two ways you can do this. You can simply open Visual Studio .NET and start coding, or you can do some preliminary design to make the coding job easier.

If you immediately chose the "open Visual Studio .NET and start coding" option, you might be a good coder, but most IT shops don't operate on that principal. Carpenters have a saying, "Measure twice, cut once." That saying is applicable to programming as well, except it sounds like this: "Design twice, code once." One of the worst positions to be in as a programmer, an architect, or a project manager is to be stuck rewriting portions of an application due to a design failure.

The first thing you should do is come up with a list of features that the Web site will support, as well as a list of implementation requirements, such as authentication, authorization, use of session state, and so on. After that, you can move on to creating a conceptual site map.

The list of requirements for this Web site might be determined as follows:

- Allow the creation of new users.
- Allow the modification of existing user details.
- Allow the deletion of users.
- Allow the creation of new roles.
- Allow the modification of existing roles.

- Allow the deletion of existing roles.
- Allow the assignment of roles to users.
- Allow the assignment of permissions to roles.
- Restrict access to the site according to user permissions.
- Restrict access to the site via ASP.NET Forms authentication.

With the list of requirements firmly in hand, you can go ahead and start producing further design documents. The number of artifacts produced for an application during the design phase typically varies both by the application and by the size of the shop producing it. In this case, the only extra document you need is a conceptual site map, which Visio conveniently supports by default. The site map for the new administration site is shown in Figure 5.4.

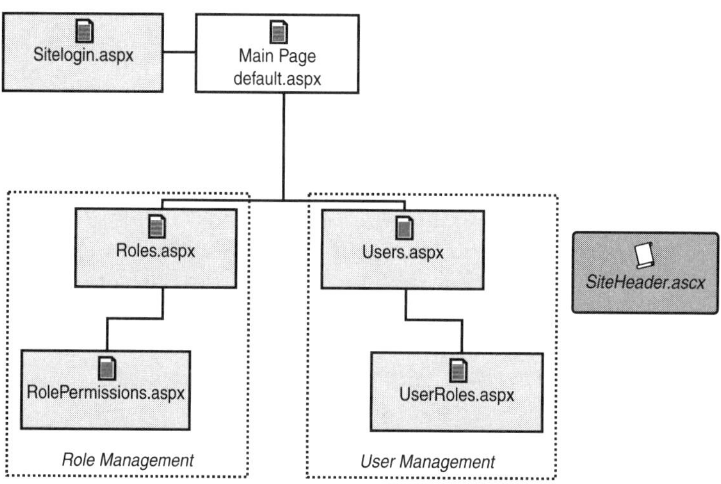

FIGURE 5.4
The conceptual site map for the Survey Repository administration Web site.

Now that you know what you're trying to accomplish with the Web site and you have the site map and list of requirements in hand, you can start creating some code for the site.

STEP-BY-STEP GUIDE: Reusing Existing Code to Build an Administrative Web Site

We'll continue with the theme of building additional features on top of the existing code. In this section you'll build an administrative Web site that reuses a lot of the structure and business objects that you've already put in place to support the Web services. The goal here is to add this administrative site by writing as little new code as possible.

The first thing you need to do for an administrative site is to make sure that only the right people can use it. You don't want to go through all the trouble of restricting access to the Web service and leave the administration site wide open.

One thing to keep in mind is that even though you currently have only Web services in the Web project, you can actually add Web forms to this project. Before you do that, however, you need to add some information to the `Web.config` file to set it up for cookie-based authentication. Follow these steps:

1. Configure the Web application to support forms-based authentication:

   ```
   <authentication mode="Forms" >
     <forms name="reposAdminApp"
       loginUrl="sitelogin.aspx"
       protection="All"></forms>
   </authentication>
   ```

   This entry, when put in the `<system.web>` section of the `Web.config` file, activates forms-based authentication. In addition, it specifies the location of the login page in case a user attempts to load a secured page.

2. In order to secure a page, you need to define which pages will allow anonymous access and which will not. In the case of an administration application, you don't want anonymous users to be allowed to view any pages (except the login page). Therefore, you can add the following lines to the `<system.web>` section of `Web.config`:

   ```
   <authorization>
     <deny users="?" />
   </authorization>
   ```

The `<authorization>` section tells ASP.NET which users to deny. The `?` character indicates anonymous (unauthenticated) users. By denying access to all anonymous users, you force every user to go to the login page until he or she has completed the authentication process.

If you left the `Web.config` file as it now stands and you wrote the login page and the rest of the administration Web site right now, you would quickly find out that you've done something wrong. In fact, if you add the preceding code to the `Web.config` file and then used it as is, you would break the Survey Development Studio application, and it would be unable to use the Web services.

The reason for this is that the calls to the Web service application have no credentials associated with them. You're supplying your own means of authentication. As a result, when you deny anonymous access to the application, you are also denying access to the Web service, even the `Login.asmx` file.

3. To fix the denial-of-access problem, you can add two `<location>` directives at the bottom of the `Web.config` file (outside the `<system.web>` tag):

```
<location path="login.asmx">
  <system.web>
    <authorization>
      <allow users="*"/>
    </authorization>
  </system.web>
</location>


<location path="repositoryservice.asmx">
  <system.web>
    <authorization>
      <allow users="*"/>
    </authorization>
  </system.web>
</location>
```

This allows anonymous access to the two Web services files while still preventing anonymous access to any Web forms that you might create in the future.

When the user tries to go to the `RepositoryV1` administration Web site that you're building, the first time he or she attempts to access it, that person is taken to a login page. Figure 5.5 shows the login page in action.

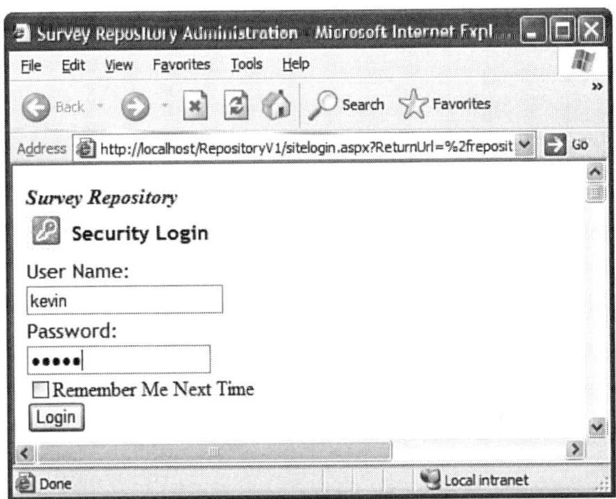

FIGURE 5.5
The Security Login page.

4. Use the code in Listing 5.5 to actually perform the login.

LISTING 5.5 `SurveyV1\RepositoryV1\SiteLogin.aspx.cs` **`btnLogin_Click` Login Button Event Handler**

```
private void btnLogin_Click(object sender, System.EventArgs e)
{
  SystemTrace.MethodStart( MethodBase.GetCurrentMethod() );
  // authenticate user
  // cache user security data (permissions, etc)
  // return GUID as authentication token.

  User testUser = new User();
  testUser.UserName = txtUserName.Text;
  testUser.Password = txtPassword.Text;

  int userValid = testUser.Validate();
  if (userValid < 0)
  {
```

LISTING 5.5 SurveyV1\RepositoryV1\SiteLogin.aspx.cs
btnLogin_Click Login Button Event Handler
(continued)

```
    SystemTrace.TraceVerbose(
      "User failed login attempt: {0}/{1}",
      txtUserName.Text, txtPassword.Text );
    Response.Write("<font color=\"red\">Login Failed.</font><br><br>");
  }
  else
  {
    Response.Cookies.Add( new HttpCookie( "USERNAME", testUser.FullName ) );
    FormsAuthentication.RedirectFromLoginPage(
      testUser.UserId.ToString(), chkRememberMe.Checked );
  }
}
```

This code is run when the user clicks the Login button on the `sitelogin.aspx` page. The important thing to notice is that it all boils down to these four lines of code:

```
User testUser = new User();
testUser.UserName = txtUserName.Text;
testUser.Password = txtPassword.Text;
int userValid = testUser.Validate();
```

Remembering the code that drives the `Login.asmx` Web service, you might recognize the `Validate()` method. It is a method on the standard `User` business object, a class that is part of the `SecurityServices` project. Instead of indexing a permission list in the cache with a GUID, you're using the `FormsAuthentication` class to create and write an authentication cookie. After this cookie is written, the user has the ability to use the administration site.

5. As an exercise on your time, check the permission levels of the users. It should be a simple matter to take some of the things you learned in the previous example about the application cache and permission checking and apply that to the administration Web site.

   After the user has been logged in, it all really boils down to data grids. There is a page for editing roles and a page for editing users, and there are pages for editing the mappings between roles and users as well as roles and permissions.

One of the most difficult things to remember about ASP.NET data grids is that they make some data binding tasks extremely simple and others far more difficult. The key thing to never forget is that ASP.NET data binding is one way; it is completely read-only. The only way that modifications ever make their way back to the database is if you, as the programmer, write event handlers and invoke the database code yourself. This differs radically from the two-way, read/write binding that you find in Windows Forms data binding.

6. To see some of the intricacies of templated, data-bound data grids as well as how you're going to reuse the business classes you've already built for the application, look at a few of the data grids that are part of the administrative Web site.

   The first of the grids to look at is the user editor. Listing 5.6 is the `.aspx` definition of the data grid that displays users and allows editing of a user's full name, username, and password. It also contains a button labeled Security that redirects to the user-role mapping editor page. I have used boldface to highlight some of the most notable sections of the data grid's declaration to make it easier to follow.

LISTING 5.6 `\RepositoryV1\Users.aspx.cs`
The User Editor Data Grid

```
<asp:datagrid id="dgUsers" Runat="server" BorderColor="#999999"
    BorderStyle="None" BorderWidth="1px" BackColor="White"
    CellPadding="3" GridLines="Vertical"
    AutoGenerateColumns="False" DataKeyField="UserId">
  <SelectedItemStyle Font-Bold="True"
    ForeColor="White" BackColor="#008A8C">
  </SelectedItemStyle>
  <AlternatingItemStyle BackColor="#DCDCDC">
  </AlternatingItemStyle>
  <ItemStyle ForeColor="Black" BackColor="#EEEEEE">
  </ItemStyle>
  <HeaderStyle Font-Bold="True" ForeColor="White"
    BackColor="#000084">
  </HeaderStyle>
  <FooterStyle ForeColor="Black"
   BackColor="#CCCCCC">
  </FooterStyle>
  <Columns>
```

LISTING 5.6 \RepositoryV1\Users.aspx.cs
The User Editor Data Grid
(continued)

```
<asp:ButtonColumn ButtonType="LinkButton"
   CommandName="Delete" Text="Delete">
</asp:ButtonColumn>
<asp:ButtonColumn ButtonType="LinkButton" CommandName="Security"
   Text="Security">
</asp:ButtonColumn>
<asp:EditCommandColumn ButtonType="LinkButton"
  CancelText="Cancel" EditText="Edit"
  UpdateText="Update">
</asp:EditCommandColumn>
<asp:TemplateColumn HeaderText="User ID"
   HeaderStyle-Font-Bold="true" HeaderStyle-ForeColor="white">
   <ItemTemplate>
  <%# DataBinder.Eval( Container.DataItem, "UserId" ) %>
   </ItemTemplate>
   <EditItemTemplate>
 <%# DataBinder.Eval( Container.DataItem, "UserId" ) %>
   </EditItemTemplate>
</asp:TemplateColumn>
<asp:TemplateColumn HeaderText="Full Name"
   HeaderStyle-Font-Bold="True" HeaderStyle-ForeColor="white">
   <ItemTemplate>
      <%# DataBinder.Eval( Container.DataItem, "FullName" ) %>
   </ItemTemplate>
   <EditItemTemplate>
  <asp:TextBox id="txtFullName" Runat=server
         TextMode=SingleLine
         Text='<%# DataBinder.Eval( Container.DataItem, "FullName") %>' />
   </EditItemTemplate>
</asp:TemplateColumn>
<asp:TemplateColumn HeaderText="User Name"
   HeaderStyle-Font-Bold="True" HeaderStyle-ForeColor="white">
   <ItemTemplate>
  <%# DataBinder.Eval( Container.DataItem, "UserName" ) %>
   </ItemTemplate>
   <EditItemTemplate>
  <asp:TextBox ID="txtUserName" Runat=server
         TextMode=SingleLine
         Text='<%# DataBinder.Eval( Container.DataItem, "UserName") %>' >
```

LISTING 5.6 `\RepositoryV1\Users.aspx.cs`
The User Editor Data Grid
(continued)

```
        </asp:TextBox>
      </EditItomTemplate>
    </asp:TemplateColumn>
    <asp:TemplateColumn HeaderText="Password"
        HeaderStylc Font-Bold-"True"  HeaderStyle-ForeColor="white">
    <ItemTemplate>
   *****
    </ItemTemplate>
    <EditItemTemplate>
   <asp:TextBox ID="txtPassword" Runat=server
          TextMode=Password
          Text='<%# DataBinder.Eval( Container.DataItem, "Password" ) %>' >
        </asp:TextBox>
    </EditItemTemplate>
  </asp:TemplateColumn>
</Columns>
</asp:datagrid>
```

Figure 5.6 shows the data grid from this code, rendered in a browser.

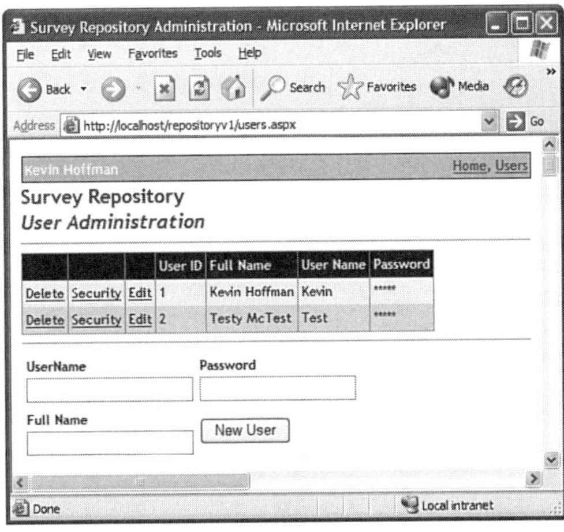

FIGURE 5.6
The User editor data grid.

You are likely to have seen the code that creates a data grid before. I see a lot of people use the `DataKeyField` field, which sets the field that the data grid uses to determine the key for the set of rows displayed. In this case, you're using the `UserId` field. That means that whenever an event related to a data grid item takes place, you will be able to determine the key to which that data grid item applies. This makes it remarkably easy to figure out what data needs to be edited, removed, and so on.

7. The code in step 6 displays the appropriate data for the user when the item is in its default mode. In addition, it creates `TextBox` controls when the item is in edit mode. By doing this, you can obtain a reference to those controls when the user is done editing the row. You can see how this works in this next piece of code, taken from the `users.aspx.cs` code-behind file:

```
private void dgUsers_UpdateCommand(object source,
  System.Web.UI.WebControls.DataGridCommandEventArgs e)
{
  SystemTrace.MethodStart( MethodBase.GetCurrentMethod() );
  DataGridItem dgi = e.Item;
  int userId = (int)dgUsers.DataKeys[ dgi.ItemIndex ];
  TextBox txtUserName = (TextBox)dgi.FindControl("txtUserName");
  TextBox txtFullName = (TextBox)dgi.FindControl("txtFullName");
  TextBox txtPassword = (TextBox)dgi.FindControl("txtPassword");
  SystemTrace.Trace( TraceLevel.Verbose,
    "About to update User {0}| Fullname: {1}, UserName: {2}",
    userId.ToString(), txtFullName.Text, txtUserName.Text );

  User user = new User();
  user.UserId = userId;
  user.Password = txtPassword.Text;
  user.FullName = txtFullName.Text;
  user.UserName = txtUserName.Text;
  user.Update();

  dgUsers.EditItemIndex = -1;
  LoadData();
}
```

After you get a reference to the current item, you can get a reference to the key for that item by using the `DataKeys` collection. The `DataKeys` collection is populated by the data grid, based on the field you defined for the `DataKeyField` property. When we have the information you need to perform an update, all you do is create an instance of the `User` object, call the `Update` method, and you're done. Again, it is to our advantage that you have these business objects that are not only completely indifferent to the database but have no direct ties to the user interface. This model of having user interface *and* data-independent business objects is extremely useful when you need to expand existing applications, as shown here.

8. You use the following methods to respond to `DataGrid` events in the `users.aspx` page:

```
private void dgUsers_EditCommand(object source,
  System.Web.UI.WebControls.DataGridCommandEventArgs e)
{
  // as usual, need to re-bind grid after changing edititemindex
  dgUsers.EditItemIndex = e.Item.ItemIndex;
  LoadData();
}

private void dgUsers_CancelCommand(object source,
  System.Web.UI.WebControls.DataGridCommandEventArgs e)
{
  dgUsers.EditItemIndex = -1;
  LoadData();
}

private void dgUsers_DeleteCommand(object source,
  System.Web.UI.WebControls.DataGridCommandEventArgs e)
{
  // respond to user pressing the delete button
  DataGridItem dgi = e.Item;
  int userId = (int)dgUsers.DataKeys[ dgi.ItemIndex ];
  User user = new User();
  user.UserId = userId;
  user.Delete();

  LoadData();
}

private void dgUsers_ItemCommand(object source,
  System.Web.UI.WebControls.DataGridCommandEventArgs e)
{
  DataGridItem dgi = e.Item;
```

```
    if (e.CommandName == "Security")
    {
      Response.Redirect("userroles.aspx?userId=" +
        dgUsers.DataKeys[ dgi.ItemIndex ].ToString());
    }
  }

  private void btnNewUser_Click(object sender, System.EventArgs e)
  {
    User user = new User();
    user.UserName = txtNewUserName.Text;
    user.FullName = txtNewFullName.Text;
    user.Password = txtNewPassword.Text;
    user.Create();
    LoadData();
  }
```

9. The `LoadData` method is pretty much the same in all the pages in the administration Web site. Its sole purpose is to load all the information that is being edited or viewed on that page and bind it to the appropriate controls. By placing all that logic into the same method, you can make the page fairly easy to understand as well as maintain. The next few lines of code show the `LoadData` method:

```
private void LoadData()
{
  ul = new UserList();
  ul.GetAllUsers();
  dgUsers.DataSource = ul.ResultSet;
  dgUsers.DataBind();
}
```

The information and techniques used in this particular data grid are used throughout the rest of the administration application and should not only provide you with a good example of building data grids in ASP.NET, but should also demonstrate how to make the data grid binding code work so that you write as little new code as possible and can reuse as much of the existing business tier classes as possible.

In addition to data grids, the administration application also uses list boxes. I'm sure you've seen this kind of GUI pattern before. Two list boxes are rendered: The one on the left contains a list of items that are currently assigned, and the one on the right contains a list of items that are available for assignment (meaning that they're not currently assigned). As you add items from one list box, they move into the other box. Figure 5.7 shows what the implementation of this pattern looks like for editing the list of roles assigned to a given user.

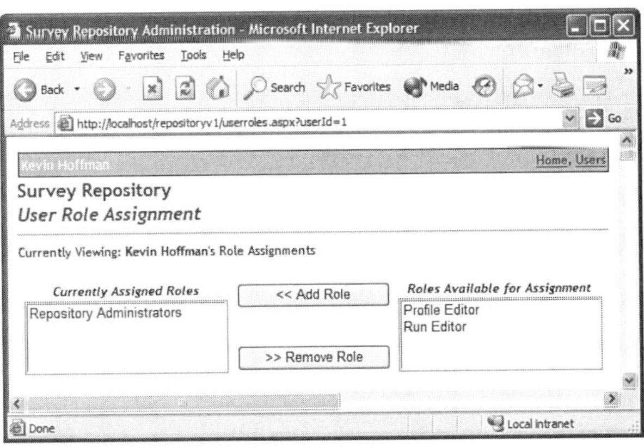

FIGURE 5.7
Assigning roles to a user.

The .aspx code is considerably smaller to maintain two list boxes than it is to maintain a single dynamic, templated data grid:

```
<table width="100%" border="0" cellspacing="0" cellpadding="2">
  <tr>
    <td width="40%" valign="top" align="center">
      <b><i>Currently Assigned Roles</i></b>
      <br>
      <asp:ListBox ID="lbAssigned"
         Runat="server" Width="200px">
      </asp:ListBox>
    </td>
    <td width="20" valign="middle" align="center">
      <asp:Button ID="btnAddRole"
         Text="<< Add Role" Runat="server" Width="150px">
      </asp:Button><br>
      <br>
      <br>
      <asp:Button id="btnRemoveRole"
         Text=">> Remove Role" Runat="server" Width="150px">
      </asp:Button><br>
    </td>
    <td width="40%" valign="top" align="center">
```

```
        <b><i>Roles Available for Assignment</i></b><br>
        <asp:ListBox ID="lbAvailable"
           runat="server" Width="200px">
        </asp:ListBox>
     </td>
  </tr>
</table>
```

The tricky part about this kind of user interface style is determining when to hide the various pieces of the interface. For example, when one of the boxes becomes empty (nothing is available or nothing is assigned), you need to hide the list box and hide the button that can transfer an item from one list box to the other. The reason for this is that the currently selected item carries through on view state, even if the box becomes empty. If you don't hide the button, all kinds of problems could occur. Take a look at the event-handling code that supports these two list boxes, including the code to load the data:

```
private void Page_Load(object sender, System.EventArgs e)
{
  SecurityHelper.SetIdentityContext(
    Int32.Parse( User.Identity.Name ));
  GetCurrentUser();

  lblUserName.Text = currentUser.FullName;

  if (!Page.IsPostBack)
    LoadRoles();
}

private void GetCurrentUser()
{
  userId = Int32.Parse(Request["UserId"]);
  currentUser = new User();
  currentUser.UserId = userId;
  currentUser.Load();
}

private void LoadRoles()
{
```

```
  btnAddRole.Visible = true;
  btnRemoveRole.Visible = true;
  lbAssigned.Visible = true;
  lbAvailable.Visible = true;

  lbAssigned.DataTextField = "Description";
  lbAssigned.DataValueField = "RoleId";

  lbAvailable.DataTextField = "Description";
  lbAvailable.DataValueField = "RoleId";

  rolesAssigned = new RoleList();
  rolesAssigned.UserId = currentUser.UserId;
  rolesAssigned.GetUserRoles();

  if (rolesAssigned.ResultSet.Tables[0].Rows.Count == 0)
  {
    lbAssigned.Visible = false;
    btnRemoveRole.Visible = false;
  }
  else
  {
    lbAssigned.DataSource = rolesAssigned.ResultSet.Tables[0];
    lbAssigned.DataBind();
  }

  rolesAvailable = new RoleList();
  rolesAvailable.UserId = currentUser.UserId;
  rolesAvailable.GetAvailableRoles();

  if (rolesAvailable.ResultSet.Tables[0].Rows.Count == 0)
  {
    lbAvailable.Visible = false;
    btnAddRole.Visible = false;
  }
  else
  {
    lbAvailable.DataSource = rolesAvailable.ResultSet.Tables[0];
    lbAvailable.DataBind();
  }
}
```

```
private void btnAddRole_Click(object sender, System.EventArgs e)
{
  if (lbAvailable.SelectedIndex > -1)
  {
    GetCurrentUser();
    int roleId = Int32.Parse(
      lbAvailable.Items[ lbAvailable.SelectedIndex ].Value);
    currentUser.AddRole( roleId );
    LoadRoles();
  }
}

private void btnRemoveRole_Click(object sender, System.EventArgs e)
{
  if (lbAssigned.SelectedIndex > -1)
  {
    GetCurrentUser();
    int roleId = Int32.Parse(
      lbAssigned.Items[ lbAssigned.SelectedIndex ].Value );
    currentUser.RemoveRole( roleId );
    LoadRoles();
  }
}
```

It's pretty obvious that 90% of the work being done here has to do with manipulating the user interface. The actual work of getting the data through the business tier is already done for you; that part of the application was written before you started working on the administration Web site. There are really only two important pieces of code on this page. First, the method call to `GetUserRoles` on the `RoleList` class retrieves the list of roles currently assigned to the given user. Second, the method `GetAvailableRoles` on the `RoleList` class retrieves the list of roles that are *not* currently assigned to the given user. `GetAvailableRoles` populates the list box on the right side of the GUI, and `GetUserRoles` populates the list box on the left. All the other code is simply user interface manipulation.

Moving On

This chapter is all about customizing the Survey Repository Web service application. The goal isn't just to customize the application, but to customize it by enhancing the code that already exists. By implementing the code with a clearly defined, data agnostic, GUI-agnostic business tier, you are able to reuse all the business logic code to create new features and to enhance existing ones.

In this chapter you took a look at securing the calls to the Web service by enforcing the RBS permission checks. You do this by reusing existing code and adding just a few lines here and there. In addition, you saw how to reuse the existing business code and logic and security infrastructure to create an administrative Web site for administering users, roles, and permissions assignments.

Something to take away from this chapter is that if you're adding a new feature or customizing or enhancing an existing application, and you find that it is taking too much time or too much effort or you've having to rewrite too much code, the infrastructure or existing code might be at fault. If you are creating all new code and you can either design it to get the code out the door sooner or you can design it for scalability and to support extension later, it is definitely worth your time and effort to examine the latter option. In the case of the Survey Repository application, you can build the infrastructure to support extensibility and reuse, and all throughout this chapter, you've been taking advantage of that fact, creating quick and easy enhancements and customizations.

Customizing Survey Development Studio

6

CHAPTER

I have always held the strong belief that the best way to learn about something new is to tinker with it. Experimentation and exploration give us new ways to look at something we might already have some experience with. The more unique and different ways we have to look at something, the more we will understand it and the longer we will retain that information. In this chapter, you're going to tinker with the following:

- Creating an error provider
- Creating a help provider
- Applicationwide exception handlers
- Application globalization

Many of us are guilty of laughing at the programmers who think that if you press Compile and the IDE comes up with no errors and no warnings, the application is done. The ironic thing is that most of us started out that way. At some point in our growth from amateur programmer to professional, we realized that there is far more to a "prime time" application than simply getting it to compile.

Throughout this chapter, you're going to customize various elements of Survey Development Studio, a Windows Forms application with which you should already be at least somewhat familiar. By customizing and enhancing existing pieces of the application, not only will you get the opportunity to tinker (and increase your understanding in the process), but you'll get the opportunity to make changes to an application to take it further from being a sample application and closer to being a production-ready application.

Error Providers

As much as a lot of us would like to be able to focus solely on the data, we often have to deal with the user interface. This is especially true when dealing with a Windows Forms application. Users not only expect the application to look good, run fast, and respond fast, they expect to be able to use it and make mistakes that don't cause catastrophic problems.

One way to make sure that the user's input doesn't wreak havoc with the application's back-end code or business logic is to never let the bad data reach the back end. In order to do that, you have to implement some kind of validation on the Windows Forms application. Whereas ASP.NET contains `Validator` controls to give the user feedback as to the validity of their input, Windows Forms has something called an *error provider*.

An `ErrorProvider` control is a control that has no user interface. Instead of having its own interface, it adds properties to other controls on the form. These properties can be set at runtime to turn on error indicators that can blink and display ToolTip information.

STEP-BY-STEP GUIDE: Implementing an `ErrorProvider` Control

There are a couple ways that you can use an `ErrorProvider` control. The first way is to drag one from the Toolbox in the designer view and place it anywhere on a form. When the control is on the form, it will appear in the nonvisible component tray at the bottom of the designer view. There you can set any of the properties you want.

I prefer to use `ErrorProvider` controls at runtime because I will not actually be setting any error messages until after a user triggers the `Validated` event of a control on the form.

Basically, all you need to do is attach an `ErrorProvider` control to a control that you want to provide visual validation feedback. When it is attached, if you set the error string for that control, some sort of visual indicator will appear, with the appearance properties that you specified when you created the `ErrorProvider` control. For example, if a user leaves an edit field (either by pressing Tab or clicking somewhere else), you could have a red X appear next to that field if the input doesn't match an appropriate mask, such as a telephone number or valid email address.

To start tinkering with the application, you're going to put a couple `ErrorProvider` controls onto the login prompt form. It's a small enough form that it should be a pretty painless exercise, but it will give you enough information to go ahead and do some of the customization on the rest of the application on your own. Follow these steps:

1. Open the `SurveyV1` solution in Visual Studio .NET 2003 and open the code for the `dlgSecurityPrompt` form from the `SurveyStudio` project. Add the following code after the `InitializeComponent()` method call:

```
errUserName = new ErrorProvider();
errUserName.SetIconAlignment( txtUserName,
    ErrorIconAlignment.MiddleRight );
errUserName.SetIconPadding( txtUserName, 5 );
errUserName.BlinkStyle = ErrorBlinkStyle.NeverBlink;
```

This sets up an error provider that will provide feedback regarding the validation status of the `txtUserName` `TextBox` control. If an error occurs, the icon (which you have left as the default) will appear five pixels to the right, aligned horizontally with the middle of the `TextBox` control. The icon will not blink at all when it appears.

2. Go back to the Visual Studio designer surface and click the `txtUserName` control.
3. Switch to the events view (with the lightning bolt in the Properties tool window) and double-click the blank area next to the `Validated` event.
4. Enter the following lines of code in the newly generated event handler:

```
if (IsUserNameValid())
    errUserName.SetError(txtUserName, "");
else
   errUserName.SetError(txtUserName,
        "User Name must be between 1 and 8 characters." );
```

You have just one more thing to do, and you should have your first working `ErrorProvider` control.

5. Create the `IsUserNameValid` method to provide some logic for validating the username input box:

```
private bool IsUserNameValid()
{
  return ((txtUserName.Text.Length >0) &&
    (txtUserName.Text.Length < 9));
}
```

From this code, you can tell that if the username entered in the text box is not between 1 and 8 characters, the code sets an error message on the `ErrorProvider` control. Realistically, all values, such as minimum and maximum lengths for validation fields, should be stored in a database or as constants rather than placed as literals directly in the code.

6. To see what this looks like in action, debug a new instance of Survey Development Studio and try to log in to Survey Repository. But instead of actually logging in, just press Tab in and out of the username field. You should see a red circle with an exclamation point in it. If you hover your mouse over the icon, you see exactly the error message that you set in the `Validated` event handler.

Now that you've seen the error handler in action for one control, you can actually start using the `ErrorProvider` class to its true potential. The great thing about this component is that it lets you manage *all* the errors for all the controls on any given form.

7. Originally, you called the `ErrorProvider` control `errUserName`. Do a quick find-and-replace and rename it to `errLoginDialog`. To attach the error provider to the `txtPassword` control, add the following lines of code at the end of the form's constructor:

```
errLoginDialog.SetIconAlignment( txtPassword,
   ErrorIconAlignment.MiddleRight );
errLoginDialog.SetIconPadding( txtPassword, 5 );
```

8. Go back to the Visual Studio designer surface, highlight the password text box, and create a new `Validated` event handler:

```
private void txtPassword_Validated(object sender,
   System.EventArgs e)
{
  if (IsPasswordValid())
    errLoginDialog.SetError( txtPassword, "");
  else
    errLoginDialog.SetError( txtPassword,
      "Password must be between 1 and 8 characters.");
}
```

9. Create the method that contains the logic for validating the password:

```
private bool IsPasswordValid()
{
  return ((txtPassword.Text.Length >0) &&
          (txtPassword.Text.Length < 9));
}
```

At this point, you have a single error provider on the form. This one error provider can trigger a graphical icon to appear whenever there is some validation problem with something on the form. Another handy thing to remember is that you can set an error message on an `ErrorProvider` control at any time; it doesn't have to be in response to a `Validated` event. With clever use of different icons and multiple providers, you can have a provider that displays warning icons, a provider that displays error icons, and so on.

The possibilities are limitless, and you can accomplish some extremely complex and robust form validation feedback by using an `ErrorProvider` component. Figure 6.1 shows the new login dialog, with the error provider activated.

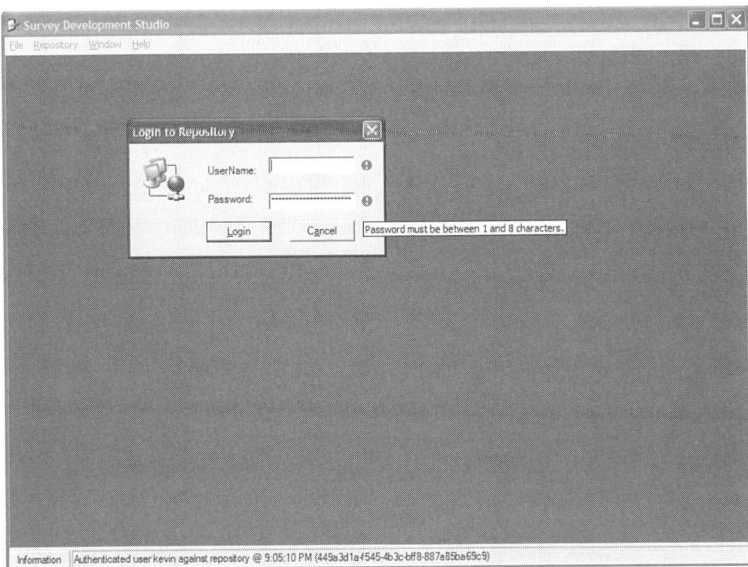

FIGURE 6.1
The Login Repository to dialog, with the error provider active.

If you've been running the code so far, you've probably noticed that the `ErrorProvider` control is an interface-only control. It doesn't do anything to stop the user from clicking the OK button on a form, nor does it prevent data operations. It is up to you, as the programmer, to integrate the `ErrorProvider` control into the form so that it prevents invalid data entry.

10. In the Visual Studio designer surface, double-click the Login button and create the following event handler:

```
private void btnLogin_Click(object sender, System.EventArgs e)
{
  if (errLoginDialog.GetError( txtUserName ) != "")
    this.DialogResult =
      DialogResult.None; // prevent the window from closing
  if (errLoginDialog.GetError( txtPassword ) != "")
    this.DialogResult = DialogResult.None;
}
```

Because the form was invoked with `ShowDialog()`, if you set the `DialogResult` property to `DialogResult.None` when there is a validation problem, the form will not close automatically.

This is just a small example of what you can do with an `ErrorProvider` control. This example is on a small form that does very little that might require dynamic validation. As an exercise, you might want to take a look at one or more of the other forms in the Survey Development Studio application and add `ErrorProvider` controls to them. You don't have to validate against real-world business rules; just come up with something simple that you can test easily so you can get practice integrating `ErrorProvider` components into forms.

Creating an Advanced Error Provider

The previous example shows a quick way to get an error provider up and running on a simple form. You created a simple error provider that displays an error icon on a form when some data is missing. You can accomplish a lot more than that with an error provider, and forms are usually a lot more complex than a simple login dialog box.

This section takes you through creating a slightly more complex error provider. You might be wondering what the big deal is about error providers. They're all about the end user. One of the biggest rules of creating Windows applications is that at no point should bad input from the user negatively affect the application.

Keeping that in mind, you can probably think of quite a few ways in which a user can break an application by inputting bad data. Users can input alphabetic characters in numeric fields, they can input values that are out of range, values that are too big, values that are too small, and so on. A user can do a number of things to cause an application to break or throw an unhandled exception.

In an application that is ready to be consumed by customers, you need to make sure that you not only handle every possible type of incorrect user input, but that you provide visual and possibly audible feedback to indicate to the user that there was an error and the nature of the error. As you've already seen, you can use an error provider to provide this type of feedback. The example in this section shows a way you can set up a form to be completely resilient to poor user input as well as provide feedback when a user enters values that are out of range.

To illustrate some more complex use of the error provider, you can add some validation logic to the `frmQuestion` form. This form is the editor for an individual question. Thinking back to the review of the code in Chapter 3, "Exploring the Code of the Survey Development Suite," you might remember that this form has a set of input boxes on it that prompt the user for a rating scale. The user provides a minimum value and a maximum value.

As an exercise to illustrate the process a lot of user interface designers go through, you should write down some validation requirements for these input boxes, and then you can translate those into code:

- The minimum value must be a valid integer.
- The maximum value must be a valid integer.
- The minimum value must be less than the maximum value.
- The maximum value must be greater than the minimum value.
- The maximum value and minimum value cannot be equal.

You might think that a list like this is overkill, but it really isn't. When complex Windows applications are created, the requirements-gathering process can consume page after page after page simply discussing the validation requirements for each of the input fields on a form.

The first thing you need to do is create an instance of the `ErrorProvider` class. The best place to do this is in the form's constructor. The following code is the modified constructor for the `frmQuestion` form:

```
public frmQuestion( frmSurvey parent, int questId )
{
  parentForm = parent;
  questionId = questId;
  question = parentForm.surveyProfile.Questions.FindByID( questionId );
  //
  // Required for Windows Form Designer support
  //
  InitializeComponent();

  //
  // TODO: Add any constructor code after InitializeComponent call
  //
  erpQuestion = new ErrorProvider();
  erpQuestion.SetIconAlignment(
    txtScaleLow,
    ErrorIconAlignment.BottomRight );
  erpQuestion.SetIconPadding( txtScaleLow, 5 );
```

```
    erpQuestion.SetIconAlignment(
      txtScaleHigh, ErrorIconAlignment.BottomRight );
    erpQuestion.SetIconPadding( txtScaleHigh, 5);

    cboQuestionType.SelectedIndex = (int)(question.Type)-1;
    BindQuestion();
  }
```

In this code, you instantiate the `ErrorProvider` class. Then you call `SetIconAlignment` and `SetIconPadding` to set up where the error icon will appear whenever an error message is set.

As you saw in the previous example, the next thing to do is to set up the event handlers for the Validated event:

```
private void txtScaleLow_Validated(object sender, System.EventArgs e)
{
  ValidateScale();
}

private void txtScaleHigh_Validated(object sender, System.EventArgs e)
{
  ValidateScale();
}
```

You have the code call the `ValidateScale` method in order to perform the multilevel validation that complies with all the requirements previously.

The following code is the `ValidateScale` method that is called each time one of the fields on the form requires validation:

```
private void ValidateScale()
{
  int scaleLow = 0;
  int scaleHigh =0;
  try
  {
    scaleLow = Int32.Parse( txtScaleLow.Text );
    scaleHigh = Int32.Parse( txtScaleHigh.Text );
    if (scaleLow >= scaleHigh)
    {
```

```
        erpQuestion.SetError( txtScaleLow,
          "Minimum scale value cannot be greater than the maximum.");
      }
      else
      {
        erpQuestion.SetError( txtScaleLow, "");
        erpQuestion.SetError( txtScaleHigh, "");
      }
    }
    catch (Exception)
    {
      // ignore it.
    }
}
```

This code has a few things going on. First, all this code is wrapped in a `try/catch` block. This traps the errors that result from an exception that is thrown when `Int32.Parse()` is called on a nonnumeric string, such as `abc`. If that exception does not occur, the code can safely compare the numeric values of the minimum and maximum scale values. If the minimum value is less than or equal to the maximum value, the validation rules have been violated, and the code sets the appropriate error message. Otherwise, the validation conditions have been met, and the code makes sure that no error message is displayed on the form.

If the exception does occur, the code simply ignores the exception. As a result of the exception occurring during this method, the value of the text box prior to the value that caused the exception is reinserted. For example, if you start off with a minimum value of `12`, and then change it to `abc` and press Tab to exit the field, the previous value, `12`, will reappear in the text box. This automatic rollback behavior only occurs because the text box is bound to a numeric data column within a data set. If this binding were not in place, you would need to explicitly do something with the exception when it occurs.

The code you just entered is only part of the package. It's one thing to notify a user that his or her input is incorrect, but you need to be able to prevent users from submitting the bad data to the database, to disk, or to a Web service or any other back end. You can't expect the back end to validate everything for you, so the more bad data you can weed out at the user level, the better things will be for everyone.

Creating an Advanced Error Provider

The way to accomplish this is to insert some additional code into the click event handler for the button that closes the form and submits data. Here's the new, enhanced click event handler for the Done button:

```
private void btnDone_Click(object sender, System.EventArgs e)
{
  string errorMessage;
  errorMessage = erpQuestion.GetError( txtScaleLow );
  if (erpQuestion.GetError( txtScaleHigh ) != "")
    errorMessage += "\n" + erpQuestion.GetError( txtScaleHigh );
  if (errorMessage != "")
    MessageBox.Show(this,
      errorMessage, "Errors On the Form",
      MessageBoxButtons.OK,
      MessageBoxIcon.Error);
  else
    this.Close();
}
```

This code grabs the error messages from the error provider. If there are any error messages, a dialog box appears, displaying the error messages to the user. If this dialog box is displayed, the form does not close, and the user has to fix whatever caused the validation failure before the form will close.

Unfortunately, the `ErrorProvider` class doesn't have a property such as `Errors.Count` with which you can quickly determine whether there are any error messages set on the object. This means that the only way the code can figure out if a form has set any error messages is to go through all the controls and check whether there is a message available for each one.

If you don't know ahead of time what controls might have error messages associated with them, or if you want to create a standardized method that checks for errors, you might be able to use something like the following code:

```
private string GetErrorMessages()
{
  string msg = "";
  string x = "";
  foreach (Control c in this.Controls)
  {
    x = erpQuestion.GetError( c );
    if (x != "")
```

```
    {
      if (msg != "")
        msg += "\n" + x;
      else
        msg = x;
    }
  }
  return msg;
}
```

This code will work on any form, and it uses an error provider called `erpQuestion`. You can further generalize it so that the method takes the error provider as an argument. Such a method could be made part of a standard form that you use in your custom library. Figure 6.2 shows the Errors on the Form dialog box that pops up when a user attempts to submit invalid data on the new validation-enabled form.

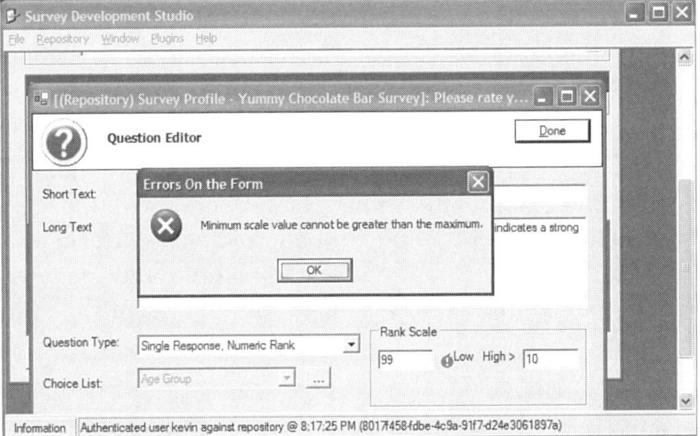

FIGURE 6.2
The new error dialog box, indicating validation failure.

Help Providers

In the previous section you saw just one of the many things that you can do to customize existing applications to make them more reliable and much more user friendly. An `ErrorProvider` control works by adding properties to existing controls. Another control that you can use to add some excellent utility to your application as well as increase its usability is `HelpProvider`.

A `HelpProvider` component maintains a list of controls as well as help information. It can be used to create pop-up help for controls that are triggered by a press of the F1 key or a click of the built-in form Help button. In addition, you can use a `HelpProvider` control to link to external help sources, such as Web sites or Windows help (`.chm`, `.hlp`, and so on) files. There are two main properties that you need to concern yourself with if you're implementing a `HelpProvider` control:

- **`HelpNamespace`**—This property gets or sets the filename of the help file that is associated with the help provider.
- **`HelpNavigator`**—This property gets or sets the kind of navigator that will be used when help is invoked for a particular control. This property allows you to control whether an individual help topic, the entire table of contents, or even the find prompt is displayed.

Integrated help is quite possibly one of the most overlooked aspects of a Windows Forms application. In fact, it's often overlooked in Web applications, as well. A very common misconception is that a printed manual will suffice for an application. In reality, users get easily frustrated if the interface isn't completely intuitive, and if they can't get context-sensitive help, they're just as likely to quit using the application as they are to reach for the printed manual.

In classic Windows 32-bit applications, the task of integrating some kind of electronic help file was often difficult and tedious. With the use of a `HelpProvider` control, this task can be very simple, and the rewards in usability and user acceptance far outweigh the time spent to use it.

STEP-BY-STEP GUIDE: Implementing a `HelpProvider` Control

To see the `HelpProvider` component in action, you're going to add some help to the login form. The login form is small and uncomplicated, so it makes a perfect candidate for a quick customization. Follow these steps:

1. Make sure that you have the `SurveyV1` solution open. Double-click `dlgSecurityPrompt` to bring up the Windows Forms Designer. Open the Toolbox and drag a `HelpProvider` control onto the surface of the form. As soon as you let go of the component, you see it appear in the component tray at the bottom of the Designer. Rename it `hlpLogin`.

As soon as the `HelpProvider` control is placed on the form, something a little unusual happens: All the applicable controls on the form gain several new properties.

2. Click one of the `TextBox` controls and scroll down through the properties list. As shown in Figure 6.3, you should see some new properties, such as `HelpKeyword on hlpLogin` and `HelpString on hlpLogin`. These properties are provided by the `HelpProvider` component that you dragged onto the form earlier. This makes it remarkably easy to set up dynamic, integrated help on any form.

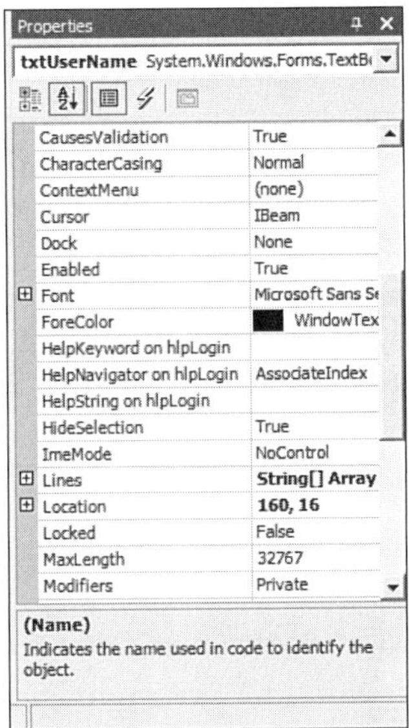

FIGURE 6.3
The Properties view, showing the new `HelpProvider` properties.

3. Type some help text into the right column for the `HelpString on hlpLogin` property for each of the input controls. The help functionality is automatically integrated into your application. You can also use the `ShowHelp` property, a Boolean variable, to toggle whether help information displays for a given control.

4. While you're in the properties list, set the `HelpButton` property on the form to `true`. This enables the question-mark icon that resides in the window's title bar.

5. After you've typed in the help text that you want to display, start Survey Development Studio in a new debug instance. Click Repository and then Log In to bring up the login dialog box.

If you hit F1 while either of the text boxes has focus, the help text that you typed is displayed in a nicely formatted box. This also occurs if you click the question-mark icon in the title bar and then click one of the text boxes. Figure 6.4 shows the security dialog prompt, with integrated help.

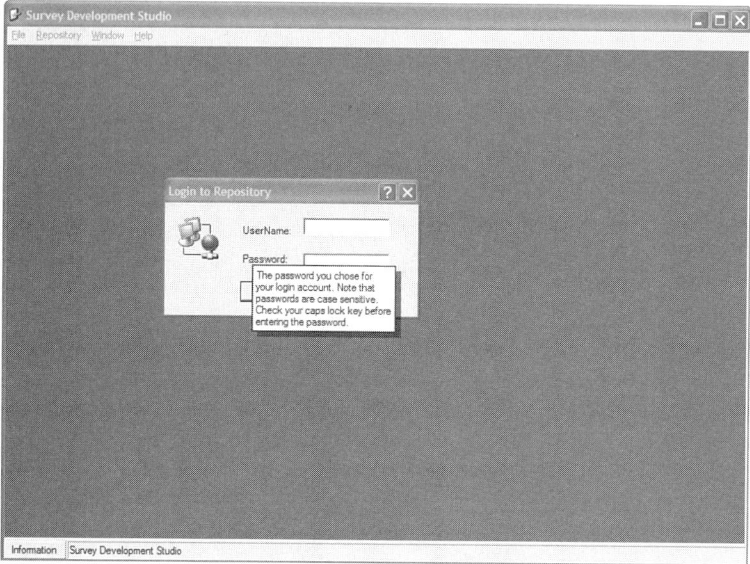

FIGURE 6.4
The security dialog prompt, with integrated help.

Surprisingly, that's all you need to do to implement integrated help in the application. With the advent of the .NET Framework and Windows Forms, there's literally no excuse for not having a full and well-integrated help system in an application.

Applicationwide Exception Handling

You might remember from previous chapters that the Survey Development Studio application has no centralized exception handling. In fact, at this point, it has no exception handling at all. This is obviously a very bad thing.

Before you start peppering the application with exception handling, I think it's good to do a quick review of when you should and should not throw exceptions. Table 6.1 is a rough guide for when to throw exceptions.

TABLE 6.1

When to Throw an Exception

Throw?	Condition
No	User input does not meet business rules or validation requirements.
No	An environmental error is detected, such as a missing file, an operating system version mismatch, and so on.
No	Connectivity to external parts of the application, such as Web services or remoting clients, is lost (in a *detectable* fashion).
Yes	A condition arises in the application that your code could not detect. This is the *only* time you should throw exceptions.

Exception throwing in the .NET Framework consumes a considerable amount of overhead. This overhead is a result of all the extra work that must be done by the CLR to search the stack to find an appropriate exception handler. You may have noticed that while developing, sometimes when you throw an exception, your hard drive grinds for a few seconds before the exception is actually displayed. Microsoft has an excellent guide on exception handling with the .NET Framework. You can find it at `http://msdn.microsoft.com/asp.net/using/understanding/arch/default.asp?pull=/library/en-us/dnbda/html/exceptdotnet.asp`.

Most good programming advice that you will get regarding exceptions typically tells you to use them sparingly, for performance reasons. In addition to causing performance problems, throwing an exception wipes out call contexts. This means that if an application depends on values being carried along a call context (such as a user identity, a current order number, and so on), if an exception is thrown and trapped, that context is no longer valid. That's right. Even if you trap the exception, the call context is invalid. This really means that you should only throw exceptions when something serious enough to invalidate the current chain of method calls (call context) occurs. For Web applications, you can generally get away with trapping an exception and displaying the information to the user without halting the entire application. With a Windows Forms application, untrapped exceptions are generally bad enough to warrant shutting down the application.

That's exactly what you're going to do. In the following section, you're going to add a global exception handler to the Windows Forms application. This exception handler will serve as the last resort; if individual forms and business components fail to trap an error and recover from it, this global exception handler will display a (somewhat) friendly message to the user and halt the application. The information displayed by the global exception handler can be cut and pasted into an email to technical support to help programmers troubleshoot potential problems.

STEP-BY-STEP GUIDE: Creating a Global Exception Handler

The ability to create a global exception handler depends on one property in the `Application` object: the `ThreadException` property, an event to which you can rig an event handler.

The event handler that you need to create will display a dialog box that contains the error information. The user can then copy and paste the error information out of the dialog box and do whatever he or she wants with it, such as sending it to a support address. Follow these steps to create a global exception handler:

1. To create this dialog box, create a new form called `dlgException`.
2. Give the new form an appropriate title and then create two multi-line text boxes—one called `txtMessage` and one called `txtStackTrace`. These text boxes will display the pertinent error information. You can create whatever labels you like.

   Good Windows Forms programming practice dictates that you never publicly expose a control to other forms. Instead, you should create public properties that wrap the information that you want to expose, such as the selected index of a `ComboBox` control or the `Text` property of a `TextBox` control.
3. Create the following properties on the `dlgException` form:

```
public string Message
{
  get
  {
    return txtMessage.Text;
  }
  set
  {
    txtMessage.Text = value;
  }
}
```

```
public string StackTrace
{
  get
  {
    return txtStackTrace.Text;
  }
  set
  {
    txtStackTrace.Text = value;
  }
}
```

These properties give you an easy, readable way of setting the message and stack trace output without having to expose the `TextBox` controls.

4. Now you need a way to trigger the dialog box in case of an unhandled exception. To do that, you need to rig up an event handler to the `ThreadException` event. To do this, add the following line of code to the `frmMain` constructor:

```
Application.ThreadException += new ThreadExceptionEventHandler
➥(Application_ThreadException);
```

5. Now you need to write the event handler by creating the `Application_ThreadException` method:

```
private void Application_ThreadException(
  object sender, ThreadExceptionEventArgs e)
{
  dlgException exception = new dlgException();
  exception.Message = e.Exception.Message;
  exception.StackTrace = e.Exception.StackTrace;
  exception.ShowDialog();
  Application.Exit();
}
```

To test this and see if you are actually trapping exceptions, you can't run the application from within Visual Studio. By default, Visual Studio .NET breaks on an exception, preventing the global exception handler from triggering.

6. Rather than alter a behavior that I normally find extremely useful, just go ahead and run `SAMS.Survey.Studio.exe` from the `bin\debug` directory. To test the error-handling ability of the form,

turn off your SQL Server service and then try to log in to Survey Repository. You should be presented with an error dialog box that looks something like Figure 6.5.

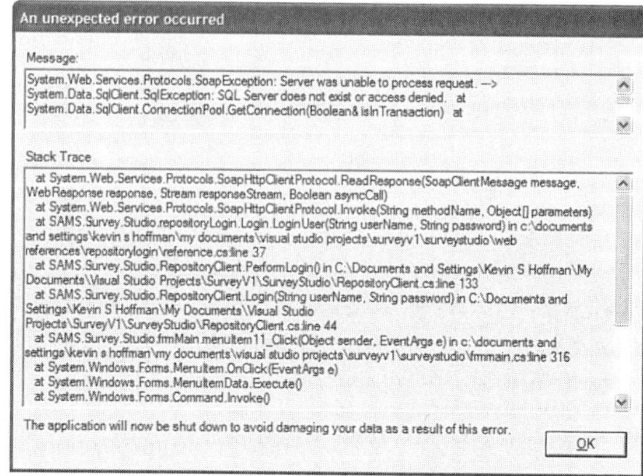

FIGURE 6.5
The global exception handler dialog, displaying a trapped exception.

It might seem like you didn't do much, but you drastically increased the value and reliability of the application. Now, anytime the application encounters an error, the user will get a friendly message indicating that something went wrong, and the user can use that to help the developers troubleshoot the problem. Before you added this global exception handler, the application would simply crash without warning and not tell the user anything about why it crashed.

The beauty of this is that with this little change, you've made room to expand the application even more. As an exercise, you should go through the application and add a few `try/catch` blocks surrounding some points that you know can fail but where you also have no way of predicting that failure (for example, making a Web service call if the network has been unplugged). In addition, you can enhance the error dialog. You can use this error dialog framework to display any error information, not just global errors. One possible enhancement to this would be to create a Web service that accepts errors from the application. This would allow a user to simply push a button to report that an application crashed, and the user would never have to pick up the phone or send an email.

Globalizing an Application

To a lot of programmers, including me until recently, globalization is a nebulous concept. Sure, we might know that the platform on which we're coding supports globalization, but for a lot of us, it isn't something that we deal with on a daily basis. *Globalization* refers to designing and implementing an application that not only supports multiple languages but supports local currency, date formatting, and other regional differences.

Accomplishing globalization before the .NET Framework was incredibly difficult and tedious. With Windows Forms, all the text on a form is stored in resource files that are designed specifically to deal with multiple languages.

Because the .NET Framework is designed to support resources that have multiple variants in different languages and Windows Forms make heavy use of resources, now it is actually quite easy to supply multiple versions of the same form for multiple languages.

In this section, you'll see how to create a Windows form that can be rendered in multiple languages based on the user's current cultural and regional settings. In addition, this section shows you a few different ways to deal with languages that don't have characters in the standard 127-character ASCII set.

When you create a Windows form, by default that form has a property called `Localizable` that is set to `false`. When that value is set to `false`, all the property changes that you make with the Windows Forms Designer will be reflected in the code in the region labeled `Windows Form Designer generated code`. Here's a small piece of code from the main form of the Survey Development Studio application that was built by the Windows Forms Designer:

```
//
// menuItem1
//
this.menuItem1.Index = 0;
this.menuItem1.MenuItems.AddRange(new System.Windows.Forms.MenuItem[] {
   this.menuItem2,
   this.menuItem6,
   this.menuItem13});

this.menuItem1.MergeType = System.Windows.Forms.MenuMerge.MergeItems;
this.menuItem1.Text = "&File";
```

This code creates a top-level menu item called File with the F being an Alt-activated hotkey. There's nothing really new or fancy here, and it looks pretty straightforward. However, take a look at the following code, which creates a menu item for a form that has had its `Localizable` property set to `true`:

```
//
// menuItem7
//
this.menuItem7.Enabled = ((bool)
  (resources.GetObject("menuItem7.Enabled")));
this.menuItem7.Index = 0;
this.menuItem7.MenuItems.AddRange(
    new System.Windows.Forms.MenuItem[] {
      this.menuItem8,
      this.menuItem9});

this.menuItem7.MergeType = System.Windows.Forms.MenuMerge.MergeItems;
this.menuItem7.Shortcut = ((System.Windows.Forms.Shortcut)
    (resources.GetObject("menuItem7.Shortcut")));
this.menuItem7.ShowShortcut = ((bool)
    (resources.GetObject("menuItem7.ShowShortcut")));
this.menuItem7.Text = resources.GetString("menuItem7.Text");
this.menuItem7.Visible = ((bool)
    (resources.GetObject("menuItem7.Visible")));
```

Taking a quick glance at this code, you see that it's pretty obvious that this form is not the same as the simple forms you've been working with up to this point. Instead of assigning hard-coded values to all the properties as you did in the first form, you're actually assigning values by using `resources.GetObject` and `resources.GetString`. The `resources` variable is an instance of the `ResourceManager` class. That class is specifically designed to facilitate the reading of resource data from .NET assemblies. At the very top of the `InitializeComponent()` method, you can see that the resource manager is declared as follows:

```
System.Resources.ResourceManager resources = new
  System.Resources.ResourceManager(typeof(frmSurvey));
```

A little later in this chapter, you'll see some more about how these resources are stored and loaded. When you stop and think about just how much of the work of dealing with resources is handled for you by the .NET Framework itself, it is pretty amazing. It could literally take someone months to build a resource management system like this without the aid of the .NET Framework.

For this experiment in globalization, you're going to make the `frmSurvey` form multilingual. You could do other things to demonstrate localized culture, such as print dates and currency, but changing the language is the most drastic and visible change, so let's stick with that for now.

STEP-BY-STEP GUIDE: Globalizing an Application

The following steps take you through the process of setting up your application to support multiple languages and cultures:

1. Open the survey profile editor dialog by double-clicking the `frmSurvey` form.
2. In the properties box, find the `Localizable` property and change its setting to `true`. At this point, Visual Studio .NET rewrites the entire `InitializeComponent()` method. First, a resource file is created. Then, all the strings, sizes, positions, colors, icons, and so on are copied into that resource as the default culture. After that is done, all the code in the `InitializeComponent()` method is modified so that its data is obtained from the `ResourceManager` instance instead of directly from the code. All this is done after you simply change that one property. Therefore, you might see the hourglass icon for a few seconds, depending on the speed of your machine and hard drive. Take a look at the code in the `InitializeComponent()` method now. It should look quite a bit like the earlier snippet of code that illustrates the nonlocalized `InitializeComponent()` method.
3. Make a copy of the form for a different language. This is also another piece that Visual Studio .NET heavily automates, making it a very painless procedure.
4. Go back to the properties box on the Windows Forms Designer and find the `Language` property. Click the arrow to get the drop-down list of cultures and choose `Hindi`. If you don't see Hindi in that list, your operating system more than likely does not have Indic language support. You can install additional language supports from the Regional Settings control panel applet in Windows 2000 and Windows XP. For more information on installing Indic languages, check your operating system's manual or electronic help. I decided to use Hindi here because I want to demonstrate dealing with a language that doesn't fit within the standard ASCII character set.

When you choose the `Hindi` culture, all the resource strings and data from the default culture are copied entirely to a brand new resource that has been localized to the "hi" culture (that is, the location-neutral Hindi culture).

5. Without changing any text, save the file and rebuild the project. Something new appears in the `bin\debug` directory, as shown in Figure 6.6.

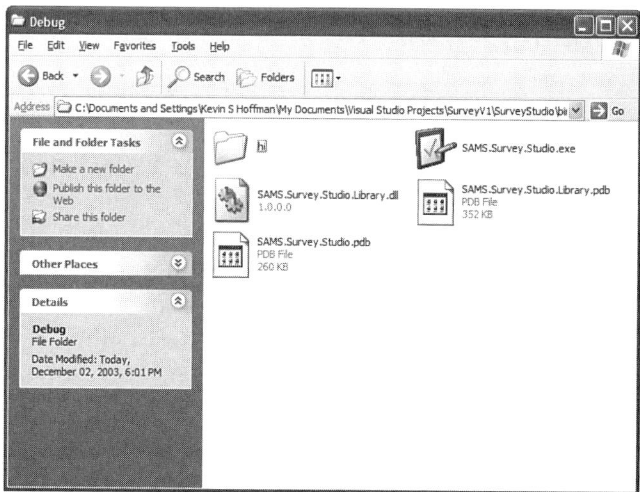

FIGURE 6.6
The `debug` directory after you localize a form to the "hi" culture.

A new directory called `hi` has appeared. Inside that directory is a file called `SAMS.Survey.Studio.resources.dll`. This file contains all the resource data for the "hi" (Hindi) culture for all forms in the entire application. This means that if you converted three other forms in the application to support the Hindi culture, all that resource data would also be in this file. This type of resource-holding assembly is called a *satellite assembly*. Such assemblies are used to keep culturally localized resources and allow them to be loaded dynamically at runtime, depending on the cultural settings of the person running the application.

There are two different ways that you can set up the form to display its contents in Hindi. The first way is to use a standard ANSI font, but the characters below 127 actually display the various glyphs for the foreign script system instead of English characters. One such font is `Khalnayak`. You can find the TTF file for this font on the CD accompanying this book. Simply copy this file into your

\WINNT\FONTS directory and the font is installed on your system. To display the Hindi language text on the form, just change the font of the Label, TextBox, or Button control to Khalnayak and then paste the appropriate character sequence into the property editor. It's a fairly ugly process and not very elegant, but it gets the job done. After pasting in all the Hindi language strings that you can fit on the frmSurvey form, you get a designer that looks something like the form shown in Figure 6.7.

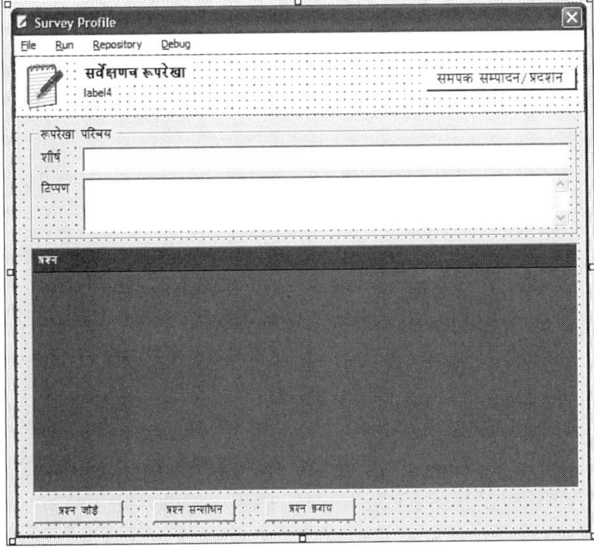

FIGURE 6.7

A localized (Hindi) version of the Survey Profile editor form.

Although this situation actually works, and if you ran the application with your region setting set to Hindi, you would see this form, there are some drawbacks. I think of this particular method as "faking it." Sure, you see the Devanagari script (the scripting system for the Hindi language), but it isn't *really* Hindi. In fact, if you look at the ASCII for the properties of that form, you see that the text looks like ç'u gVk;.

Another thing to note is that by using the glyph font method, you can't actually supply localized menus or form captions. Because Windows itself dictates the font for the menus and window titles, you have no way of putting glyph font characters into a resource and have them show up properly.

This is where Unicode comes in. I deliberately showed you what I consider the "wrong" way to do it so that I could talk about Unicode. Unicode is a mechanism that provides a unique number for every single character, regardless of operating system, font, program, or language. Each Unicode character is a 2-byte character sequence, whereas standard characters only use 1 byte. Take, for example, the Khalnayak font. A semicolon displayed in the Khalnayak font does not look like a semicolon in Wingdings or MS Sans Serif. A Unicode character has *one and only one representation.* The fundamental principal behind Unicode is that it provides one single universal list of numbers that map to characters for all languages. For more information on Unicode and Unicode implementations, check out `www.unicode.org`.

6. To make a Unicode version of the Windows form, go back to `frmSurvey` and change the `Language` property from `Hindi` to `Hindi (India)`. Just like the last time you changed the language, the resource data for the current language is copied to the new language. As a result, after a few seconds of the hard drive spinning, you'll be looking at an exact copy of the previous Hindi form. After rebuilding the project, you've also created another satellite assembly. Figure 6.8 shows the new `bin\debug` directory after you create a new localization for the Hindi (India) culture.

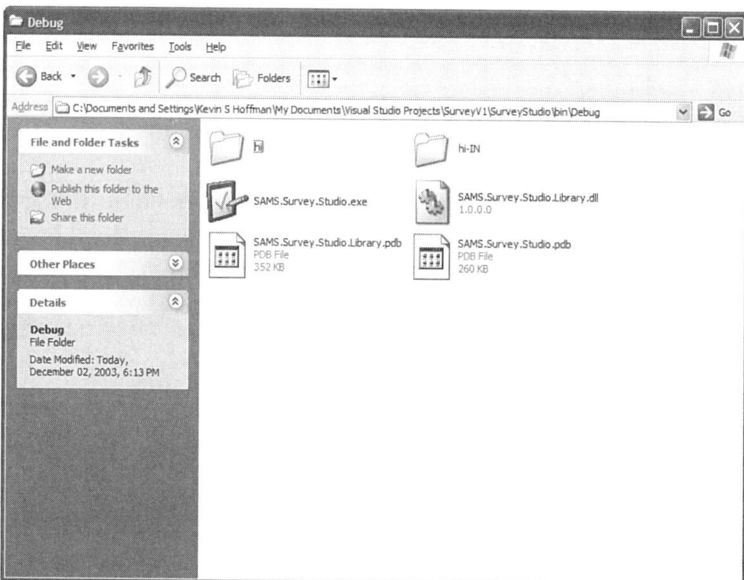

FIGURE 6.8

The `debug` directory after you create a new localized form for the Hindi (India) culture.

By setting a new language, you've created a new directory and yet another satellite assembly. This new satellite assembly contains the Hindi (India) resources for the entire application.

Now that you're dealing with Unicode, you don't need to worry about the font, so we can set it back to MS Sans Serif. The only difficult part about Unicode is actually typing the characters. Because every character has a single unique code, you need some way to enter that code. You can generally find Unicode keyboard mappers and entry tools, or you can use a Hindi specific transliteration tool for the form.

At this point, you have three different forms, but all of them appear to be the same form within Visual Studio .NET. You won't actually see the localized version of the form unless you change your culture settings. Rather than modify your regional settings through the Control Panel, you can write some code to change the regional settings just for this application. This modification is only for testing purposes. In a production application, you would want to either retain the operating system culture settings or use an application `.config` file to store the localization information. Programmatically changing the culture comes in handy if you want the application to give the user the option of which language it should be displayed in, regardless of the user's default operating system language.

7. Add the following lines of code to the constructor for `frmMain` to change the culture and the user interface culture of the application:

```
Thread.CurrentThread.CurrentCulture = new CultureInfo("hi-IN");
Thread.CurrentThread.CurrentUICulture = new CultureInfo("hi-IN");
```

   Modifying the `CurrentCulture` property allows the system to format dates and currency in the appropriate cultural format. By setting `CurrentUICulture`, you control the language from which the resources are loaded.

8. Rebuild the application and run it. To see the new Unicode Hindi version of the form, simply open a survey profile from the CD that accompanies this book or from Survey Repository, and you see the new form, such as the one in Figure 6.9.

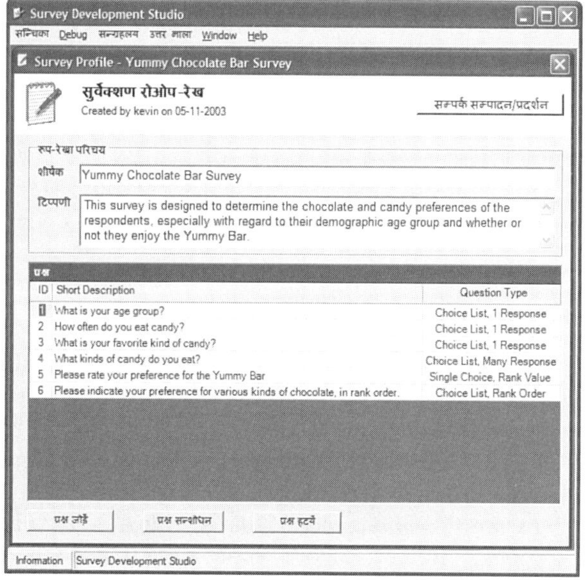

FIGURE 6.9
The localized version of the survey profile editor, enabled using Unicode characters instead of a glyph font.

> You should immediately notice a few things that are different about this form than the previous form. Because you used Unicode characters and not glyph font characters, you were actually able to include Hindi directly in the form's caption and in the form's main menu control.

As you can see, with very little effort (and maybe some people fluent in foreign languages), you can create an application that supports multiple cultures with ease. With the ability to download applications over the Internet, it is no longer safe to assume that the native language of the person using your application is the same as your own. The more languages and cultures that an application supports, the more people will be able to use the application comfortably.

Moving On

Like Chapter 5, "Customizing Survey Repository," this chapter is all about customization. By building new features and improving existing features from an existing codebase, you can convert a mediocre application that serves as a sample into an application that is ready to be used by customers throughout the world.

In this chapter you customized the existing Survey Development Studio application by improving form validation with an error provider. By providing both graphical and textual feedback about user input, you can not only prevent invalid data from being submitted on a form, but you can tell the users what is wrong with the input so they can correct it. This greatly increases the durability and reliability of the application.

By using another provider component, the help provider, you can link to external help files for context-sensitive help or you can provide simple strings that appear in pop-up content windows to provide the user with help on how to use the application. The combination of error providers and help providers on a form creates the rich, error-free, user-friendly experience that users expect from commercial applications.

While you're customizing an application to increase stability and the user experience, you can create a global exception handler that deals with all the unexpected exceptions that might occur that the application has no control over. By doing this, you can ensure that the application will never simply crash to the desktop without providing any feedback. The example you created in this chapter can easily be enhanced to electronically provide exception data to the application publisher via email or Web services.

Finally, one last thing you did to customize the existing Survey Development Studio application and the user experience was to make it able to support multiple cultures. By using localized forms, satellite assemblies, and Unicode characters, the application can support any language in the world, so long as you have a translator handy. The external resource model makes it extremely easy for application developers to hire the services of translators to produce localized versions of the user interface, freeing programmers to work on the business logic and data model.

The goal of this chapter is not only to show you some of the most useful features of the .NET Framework that often get overlooked by application developers, but to show you that just because an application compiles, doesn't mean it's done. If you think back to the state of the Survey Development Studio application before this chapter, it seems pretty limited, doesn't it? That earlier version doesn't handle errors, it doesn't support integrated, context-sensitive help, and it doesn't support foreign languages. A little bit of effort to customize and improve can produce a wealth of extra features that customers will certainly appreciate when they use an application.

Customizing PocketSurvey

CHAPTER 7

In Chapter 6, "Customizing Survey Development Studio," you spent a lot of time customizing and tweaking the Survey Development Studio application. This way, you not only got to learn more about how the application works, but hopefully you learned some good techniques for improving Windows Forms applications. In this chapter you'll learn about the following:

- Adding a timeout period
- Enhancing user interface elements
- Respondent feedback and additional auditing
- Customization and branding

PocketSurvey Customizations

This chapter is all about the PocketSurvey application. As you know, PocketSurvey is a Pocket PC application that allows respondents to supply their answers to a survey profile by using the stylus to click their responses on the Pocket PC. In this chapter, you'll customize the PocketSurvey application in an effort to learn some more about Pocket PC applications and how to make them more ready for commercial distribution, more reliable, and more full featured.

STEP-BY-STEP GUIDE: Adding a Timeout Period

One of the best ways to determine what an application is lacking is to put yourself in the place of the customer. Usability testing often produces some interesting feedback about the application that you might not notice with the standard functional testing. Just because an application meets the requirements you started with doesn't mean that the requirements themselves were complete or accurate.

After I used PocketSurvey for some time, it became apparent that some usage scenarios weren't accounted for in the original design. For example, what if someone was in the middle of taking a survey and then decided to stop? In the original version of PocketSurvey, there is no Quit button, nor is there a Back button. In fact, there's no way to get out of a survey without actually completing it.

One solution to this problem is to create a timeout period. This timeout period can be a timer that is running in the background. Every so often, the application can check to see if the current survey question has changed. If the current question has remained the same for too long a period of time, the survey can abort. This is a nice safeguard to make sure that you never get incomplete results because people simply walked away from the device, gave up, or got confused and didn't know what to do next. If a user simply does nothing for a set amount of time, the current survey can safely abort without altering the results of the current run.

When you're implementing solutions on the Compact Framework, you often have to use some workarounds to deal with the limited amount of support in the Base Class Library for what you're trying to accomplish. Thankfully, the Compact version of `System.Windows.Forms` comes with a fully functioning `Timer` class that you can use just as if you were creating a regular Windows Forms application.

What you can do is set it up so that each time the `Timer` class raises a `Tick` event, you can check to see if the current question has changed. If the current question has not changed since the last time the `Tick` event fired, you can abort the current survey and exit the application.

As you saw in Chapter 3, "Exploring the Code of the Survey Development Suite," when you examined the code for the PocketSurvey application, the main work done by the application is a loop that iterates through the various questions in the survey profile, prompting the user for a response by manually constructing an input form and then recording the response in the local data set. The following steps take you through creating a timeout period:

1. To add the timer, modify the loop so that just before the loop, the timer starts. During each of the iterations through the loop, you'll set a variable that indicates the current question. This way, the event handler for the `Tick` event can tell if the current question has changed since the last tick. This will give you the information you need in order to safely abort the survey at the right time.
2. Modify the `btnStart_Click` method as shown in Listing 7.1. The new, revised version of the event handler that fires when someone clicks the Take Survey button.

LISTING 7.1 `SurveyV1\PocketSurvey\frmMain.cs`
The `btnStart_Click` Method

```
private void btnStart_Click(object sender, System.EventArgs e)
{
  SAMS.Survey.Studio.Library.QuestionType questionType;
  string questionText;

  try
  {
```

LISTING 7.1 `SurveyV1\PocketSurvey\frmMain.cs`
The `btnStart_Click` Method
(continued)

```
surveyAborted = false;
DataRow newSheet = dsRun.Tables["ResponseSheets"].NewRow();
newSheet["DateEntered"] = DateTime.Now;
newSheet["Source"] = "PocketSurvey";
dsRun.Tables["ResponseSheets"].Rows.Add( newSheet );

lastQuestionId = (int)dsProfile.Tables["Questions"].Rows[0]["ID"];
timer = new System.Windows.Forms.Timer();
timer.Tick +=new EventHandler(timer_Tick);
timer.Interval=12000;
timer.Enabled = true;
// for each question in the profile, prompt the user for a response
// then store the responses in a new run
foreach ( DataRow question in dsProfile.Tables["Questions"].Rows )
{
currentQuestionId = (int)question["ID"];
// obtain the question type
questionType =
     (SAMS.Survey.Studio.Library.QuestionType)((int)question["Type"]);
questionText = (string)question["LongText"];
int choiceListId = (int)question["ChoiceListId"];
string[] options = null;
if (choiceListId > 0)
{
  DataRow[] items =
       dsProfile.Tables["ChoiceListItems"].Select("ChoiceListId=" +
          choiceListId.ToString());
  options = new string[ items.Length ];
  int i=0;
  foreach (DataRow item in items)
  {
    options[i] = item["Description"].ToString();
    i++;
  }
}

// grab the options (if any)
blankForm = new frmBlank();
blankForm.Text = question["ShortDescription"].ToString();
DynaFormHelper.Initialize_DynaForm(
```

LISTING 7.1 `SurveyV1\PocketSurvey\frmMain.cs`
The `btnStart_Click` Method
(continued)

```
          blankForm, questionType,
          questionText, options );
      if (blankForm.ShowDialog() == DialogResult.OK)
      {
        // do something with the result
        string response = blankForm.Response;
        DataRow newResponse = dsRun.Tables["Responses"].NewRow();
        newResponse["QuestionId"] = (int)question["ID"];
        newResponse["SheetId"] = (int)newSheet["SheetId"];
        newResponse["ResponseData"] = response;
        dsRun.Tables["Responses"].Rows.Add( newResponse );
      }
      if (surveyAborted)
        break;

    }
    timer.Enabled = false;
    timer = null;

    if (!surveyAborted)
    {
      dsRun.AcceptChanges();
      dsRun.WriteXml( @"\Program Files\PocketSurvey\CurrentRun.svr" );
    }

  }
  catch (Exception ex)
  {
    dsRun.RejectChanges();
    MessageBox.Show( ex.Message, "Error",
       MessageBoxButtons.OK,MessageBoxIcon.Exclamation,
       MessageBoxDefaultButton.Button1 );
  }
}
```

Immediately before the main loop begins, you set the `lastQuestionId` variable and you activate the timer. The code in Listing 7.1 uses an `Interval` period of `12000`, which should be 12 seconds. However, on my emulator it turns out to be more like 45 seconds. Feel free to adjust this time value for something more realistic, as you see fit.

The rest of the code should look almost identical to the way it looked the last time you looked at it. The other major difference is the use of a new Boolean variable, `surveyAborted`, which tests whether the survey has been aborted. I'll explain in a minute why you need that.

3. Create the code for the tick event handler, as shown in Listing 7.2.

LISTING 7.2 `SurveyV1\PocketSurvey\frmMain.cs`
The `timer_Tick` Method and the `AbortSurvey` Method

```
private void timer_Tick(object sender, EventArgs e)
{
  if (currentQuestionId == lastQuestionId)
  {
    this.Invoke( new EventHandler(AbortSurvey));
  }
  else
  {
    lastQuestionId = currentQuestionId;
  }
}

private void AbortSurvey(object sender, EventArgs e)
{
  surveyAborted = true;
  dsRun.RejectChanges();
  if (blankForm != null)
  {
    blankForm.Close();
  }
  // in the span of one timer tick, the current question has not changed
  MessageBox.Show("Current survey has been aborted due to timeout.",
    "Timeout Expired",
    MessageBoxButtons.OK,
    MessageBoxIcon.Exclamation, MessageBoxDefaultButton.Button1);
  this.Close();
  Application.Exit();
}
```

There are a couple interesting things going on with this code. For example, the issues you have to get around with this timer in this Compact application are the same issues that you would experience on a standard Windows Forms application.

The first thing that might look odd is that instead of directly calling the `AbortSurvey` method, you're actually using the `Invoke` method instead. The important thing to remember is that a timer is made possible by the fact that a background thread is being used. This thread is woken up, and it invokes the `Tick` event handler at a timed interval. This provides an excellent method of performing tasks at certain times. The problem is that this thread is not the same thread that is associated with the main user interface. As a result, things you do to the main user interface from a background thread aren't guaranteed to work properly, if at all. The `Invoke` method uses a delegate to invoke the method indicated on the main user interface thread. This gets rid of any ambiguity and prevents method calls from failing. I tried the code in Listing 7.2 without using `Invoke`, and I could not get the main form to close, no matter how hard I tried.

With the code in Listing 7.2 in place, someone can start taking the survey and walk away from the device or give it back to a survey administrator. The person will not have to be concerned with aborting the survey, as it will happen automatically. If you want to make the survey abort silently and simply return to the most recently opened window on the Pocket PC, you can simply remove the `MessageBox` method call.

Note the use of the `surveyAborted` flag. The main problem is that when you use the `Close` method of a form, it doesn't actually shut down the form right away. All the currently running threads are told to finish what they're doing. In this case, an active thread is running a loop that iterates through the questions in a survey profile. Therefore, if you just tell the form to close, the code in the loop will execute and display the next question, even though you want the form to shut down. To account for this, you set a flag, `surveyAborted`. Inside the loop, you check to see whether this flag has been set. If it has, you break out of the loop and allow the method to exit cleanly without displaying any further question prompts. Without this little bit of code, the user would have to finish the survey to get the survey to close—and that would completely defeat the purpose of the code. Figure 7.1 shows the new timeout message.

FIGURE 7.1
The new timeout message.

STEP-BY-STEP GUIDE: Enhancing the User Interface Elements

As mentioned at the beginning of this chapter, actually using your own application is very helpful to you as a developer. Use your application the way you expect your users to use it, and you will be able to see places they might get frustrated or confused—or even places that simply don't work the way they should.

One such area in the PocketSurvey application has to do with user input. There are a few places where it is just not very convenient for users to enter data. In fact, some parts of the application make it almost difficult for users to enter data.

For example, when the application prompts the user for a ranked value, it simply displays an empty text box. This is just screaming for an improvement. You know the minimum value and the maximum value because the scale of the rank is defined on the question itself.

If you need the user to input a numeric value and you know the range of that value, then the best bet is to actually use a `TrackBar` control. This is especially useful in this situation because on a Pocket PC it's far easier to drag a `TrackBar` control than it is to pull up the software keyboard and press the correct number.

There are a couple things you need to do in order to create a `TrackBar` control on the dynamic form for a single-response, numeric rank question. Follow these steps to implement some of the user interface elements:

1. Pass the rank scale values from the main loop to the method in the `DynaFormHelper` class that actually creates the form. The method call to create the dynamic form should look like this:

```
rankHigh = ((question["RankScaleHigh"] == DBNull.Value) ||
            (question["RankScaleHigh"] == null))
             ? 0 : (int)question["RankScaleHigh"];

rankLow = ((question["RankScaleLow"] == DBNull.Value) ||
           (question["RankScaleLow"] == null))
           ? 0 : (int)question["RankScaleLow"];

DynaFormHelper.Initialize_DynaForm(
  blankForm, questionType,
  questionText, options,
  rankLow, rankHigh );
```

   `Initialize_DynaForm` does a little bit of test logic on the type of question and then calls another helper method to get the actual work done. In the case of a single-response, numeric rank question, the `Initialize_SingleNumericQuestion` method is invoked. This method as it stands now just creates a `TextBox` control and places it on the dynamic form.

2. Replace the code for the `Initialize_SingleNumericQuestion` method with the following code:

```
InitializeQuestion( blank, question );

TrackBar tb = new TrackBar();
tb.Minimum = scaleLow;
tb.Maximum = scaleHigh;
tb.Value = scaleLow;
tb.Location = new Point(8, 40);
tb.Width = 80;
tb.Height = 10;
blank.Controls.Add( tb );
```

This is actually a fairly simple procedure. You just create a `TrackBar` control, set the `Minimum` and `Maximum` values to the corresponding scale values for the question, and then place the control on the dynamic form.

When the `TrackBar` control is actually on the form, you need to modify the code that obtains the user responses from a given form. That code is in the `frmBlank` form. A property called `Response` invokes the `determine_Response()` method.

3. Create a new version of the `determine_Response()` method that takes into account the new `TrackBar` control. The following is the code for that new method:

```
private string determine_Response()
{
  string response = "";

  switch (questionType)
  {
    case QuestionType.ChoiceListMultipleAnswers:
    response = build_CheckboxResponse();
    break;
    case QuestionType.ChoiceListNumericalRank:
    response = build_TextboxResponse();
    break;
    case QuestionType.Essay:
    // do nothing
    break;
    case QuestionType.MultipleChoiceSingleAnswer:
    response = build_RadioButtonResponse();
    break;
    case QuestionType.SingleResponseNumericalRank:
    response = build_TrackbarResponse();
    break;
  }
  return response;
}
```

You can see that instead of invoking `build_TextboxResponse` for a single-response, numeric rank question, you are calling a new function called `build_TrackbarResponse()`.

4. Create the new `build_TrackbarResponse` method, as shown here:

```
private string build_TrackbarResponse()
{
  string response = "";
  for (int i=0; i<Controls.Count; i++)
  {
    if (Controls[i] is TrackBar)
    {
      response = ((TrackBar)Controls[i]).ToString();
    }
  }
  return response;
}
```

This method finds the appropriate `TrackBar` control on the dynamic form and then returns the numeric value indicated by the slider's position. Figure 7.2 shows the new `TrackBar`-based input control.

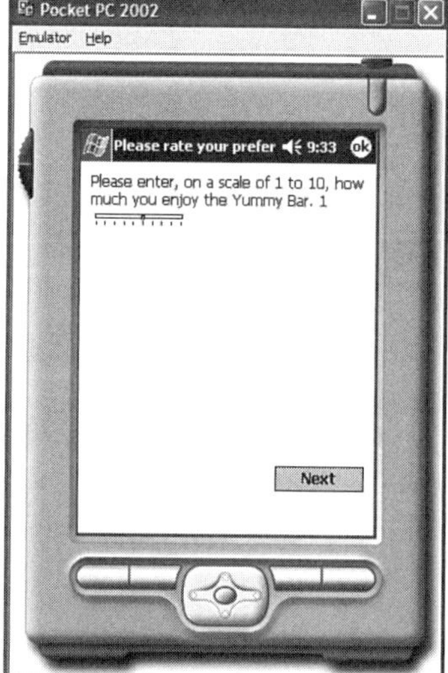

FIGURE 7.2
The new `TrackBar` input control on the dynamic form.

User Interface Enhancements for Accessibility

You are probably already aware of some of the user interface issues that exist because of the limited form factor of Pocket PC devices. Some Pocket PC devices might be fairly easy for some people to use, but other people might have trouble seeing and reading the text at the default size. In addition, devices such as Smart Phones have an even smaller form factor and can sometimes be even more difficult to view and read.

There isn't much you can do to change the form factor of a handheld device, but you can make an effort to make things easier to read and more accessible to people who might not be able to make out smaller letters on a handheld device.

The easiest thing you can do is make the fonts for your application bigger. The bigger the font, the easier it is to read from a distance and the easier it is for people with eyesight difficulties to see. The problem is that if the font is bigger, it takes up more space on the screen. And if it takes up more space, less of it can be displayed without getting cut off.

The don't want to cut off half of your text just to make the fist half more readable. To get around this, you need to figure out how to increase the text size and not increase the amount of screen real estate that the text consumes. The easiest way to accomplish this is to make sure that the text is in a scrollable region.

Using a scrollable region allows you to set a large amount of text and have it displayed in a limited amount of space. Users can then scroll through the remaining text by clicking the buttons on a scrollbar, using the arrow keys, or using the Page Up and Page Down keys.

The simplest and most available scrollable region for containing text, of course, is the `TextBox` control. If you replace some of your static text controls on forms with a read-only `TextBox` control, you automatically gain the ability to scroll through the text and allow users to select some or all of the text in the control.

The following quick step-by-step guide takes you through replacing a static text control with a scrollable, read-only `TextBox` control that has an enlarged font for accessibility.

STEP-BY-STEP GUIDE: **Increasing Font Size for Accessibility**

The following steps walk you through the fairly simple process of replacing a static text control with a dynamic control that consumes the same amount of screen space yet can display text in much larger fonts without cutting off or losing any of the original text string:

1. Open `SurveyV1\PocketSurvey\DynaFormHelper.cs`.
2. Go down to the `Initialize_Question` method and replace its contents with the following lines of code:

```
TextBox tbQuestion = new TextBox();
tbQuestion.Text = question;
tbQuestion.Location = new Point(8,8);
tbQuestion.Width = blank.Width - 10;
```

```
tbQuestion.Height = 30;
tbQuestion.ReadOnly = true;
tbQuestion.Multiline = true;
tbQuestion.Font = new Font("Tahoma", 10.0f, FontStyle.Regular);
blank.Controls.Add( tbQuestion );
```

As you can see, there's nothing overly complex about this new code. All you're doing is creating a `TextBox` control instead of creating a `Label` control. The font size is 10 in this example, but you could easily bump that up more if you wanted the font size to be bigger and more readable.

As I'm sure you've already noticed, several areas of the PocketSurvey application are suffering because there isn't enough room to display all the text required. Conveniently, I've left those areas of the PocketSurvey application in a state that is just begging for enhancement. Consider it your challenge to find all the places in the application where text is being cut off and modify them so that there is enough room for that amount of text and so that there is enough room for virtually *any* text in that location. It might be difficult, but I'm sure you'll find a way to take care of it. The key isn't in finding a difficult piece of code to write; the key is in finding the right GUI design that supports text of virtually any size. Figure 7.3 shows the new question form with the new `TextBox` control. You can see that no matter how long the question is, the user can keep scrolling to see all the text, even when the font size is large.

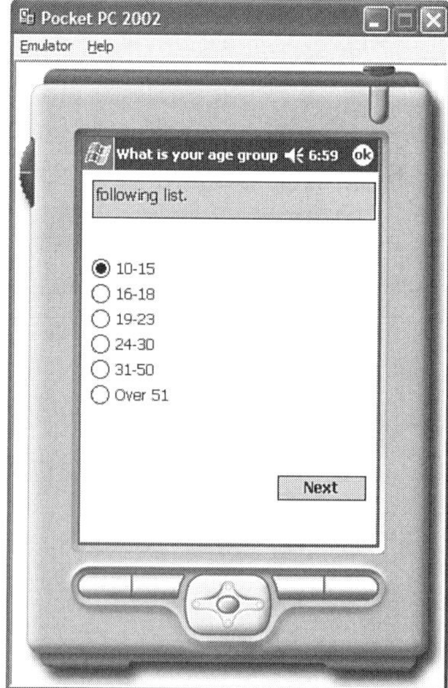

FIGURE 7.3
The PocketSurvey GUI, with a new text box control replacing static text.

Respondent Feedback and Additional Auditing

Another issue with the PocketSurvey application that comes up through use and testing is the issue of accountability. The way the application works in its original form, every single response sheet that it creates is anonymous. In addition, the person taking the survey has no way of identifying which survey he or she took or what his or her responses were should the need ever arise.

Apparently in some cases there is a legal need for the respondent to be able to obtain the answers he or she supplied on a survey, to be able to prove what he or she did or did not say in a response. To make this possible, you have to record who each respondent is, and you have to be able to give the respondents the information they need to identify themselves and the survey they took.

To provide this functionality, you can ask the user if he or she would like to remain anonymous after answering the questions. If the user chooses yes, the application does exactly what it did before. However, if the user chooses no, the respondent is prompted for his or her name and address. After the user completes this personal information, he or she is given the ID of the survey and his or her own respondent ID, which can be used in the future to identify the user and his or her response sheet if necessary.

STEP-BY-STEP GUIDE: Implementing Additional Respondent Feedback and Auditing

The following steps take you through the process of creating some additional feedback and auditing capabilities for the `PocketSurvey` application:

1. Create the input form that will prompt the user for his or her name and address. Figure 7.4 is a screenshot of the designer, with the new form (called `frmRespondant`) open.

   As you can see, there is room for the respondent's first and last names, street address, city, state, zip code, and country. As with all well-designed input forms, you want to create a set of properties that expose the important values you're editing. In this case, you need a property to expose the value of each of the text boxes on the form. You wan to have such a property because it's good design practice to never allow a control on a form to have any outside visibility; this also makes it easier to fit forms into a good workflow.

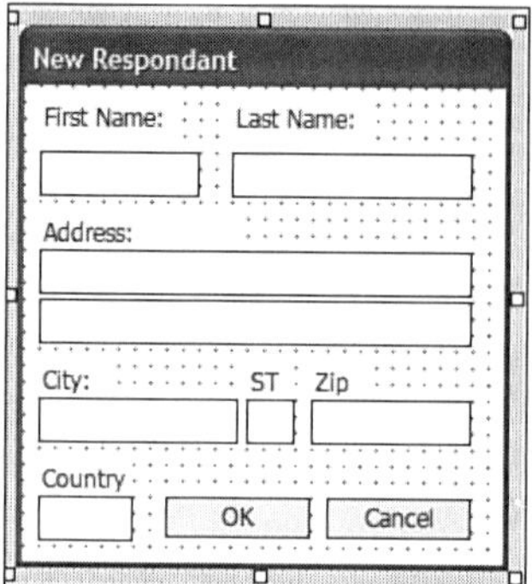

FIGURE 7.4 The `frmRespondant` input form.

2. Add the following code to `frmRespondant` to expose the appropriate properties:

```
public string FirstName
{
  get
  {
    return txtFirstName.Text;
  }
}

public string LastName
{
  get
  {
    return txtLastName.Text;
  }
}

public string Address
{
  get
  {
    return txtAddress1.Text;
  }
}
```

```
public string Address2
{
  get
  {
    return txtAddress2.Text;
  }
}


public string City
{
  get
  {
    return txtCity.Text;
  }
}

public string State
{
  get
  {
    return txtState.Text;
  }
}

public string Zip
{
  get
  {
    return txtZip.Text;
  }
}

public string Country
{
  get
  {
    return txtCountry.Text;
  }
}
```

These are all read-only properties that expose an IntelliSense-aware set of data. If you decided to make the controls on this form more complex, you would simply modify the inside of the property definition, and you wouldn't have to worry about damaging any code that uses this form.

When the input form has been created and you have properties that you can use to read the values the user supplied, you are ready to modify the code to ask the user if he or she wishes to remain anonymous.

3. To round out the rest of the code, insert the following code immediately after the `timer = null;` line of code in the `btnStart_Click` event handler method:

```
if (MessageBox.Show("Remain anonymous?",
  "Respondant Identification",
  MessageBoxButtons.YesNo, MessageBoxIcon.Question,
    MessageBoxDefaultButton.Button1) == DialogResult.No)
{
  // obtain respondant's identification information,
  // store it in the DataSet
  // and provide them with feedback concerning the survey.
  frmRespondant respForm = new frmRespondant();
  if (respForm.ShowDialog() == DialogResult.OK)
  {
    // store respondant ID data
    DataRow respondant = dsRun.Tables["Respondants"].NewRow();
    respondant["FirstName"] = respForm.FirstName;
    respondant["LastName"] = respForm.LastName;
    respondant["Address"] = respForm.Address;
    respondant["Address2"] = respForm.Address2;
    respondant["City"] = respForm.City;
    respondant["State"] = respForm.State;
    respondant["Zip"] = respForm.Zip;
    respondant["Country"] = respForm.Country;
    dsRun.Tables["Respondants"].Rows.Add( respondant );
    int newRespId = (int)respondant["ID"];
    newSheet["RespondantID"] = newRespId;

    MessageBox.Show( string.Format(
    "Thank you for submitting your responses.
```

```
ÂThe Survey ID is {0}, " +
        "and your Respondant ID is {1}.\n\r" +
    "You may need those values in the future.",
    (string)dsProfile.Tables["Profile"].Rows[0]["GlobalID"],
    newRespId.ToString()),
    "Thank You", MessageBoxButtons.OK, MessageBoxIcon.None,
        MessageBoxDefaultButton.Button1);
  }
}
```

In this section of code, first you ask the user whether he or she would like to remain anonymous. If the user chooses not to remain anonymous (that is, the user clicks Cancel), you call `ShowDialog` on the respondent data entry form. If the respondent chooses to remain anonymous, by clicking OK on that form, you can add the respondent to the data set and associate the respondent's ID with the current response sheet.

Finally, just before the survey is complete, you display the survey's ID and the respondent's ID to the user so that they can keep the information for whatever reason they might have. Because the data set gets all its information from the schema, you know that if you simply insert a new row into the `Respondants` table, that row will be assigned a new, unique number. That number is then associated with the current response sheet. Finally, just before the method completes, the changes to the current run are saved, just as they were before the recent changes.

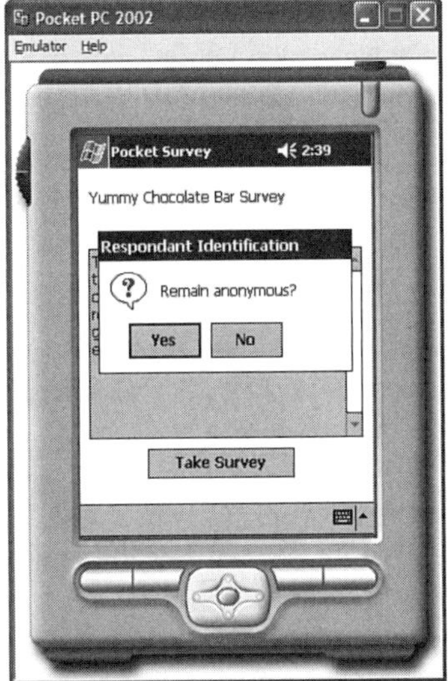

FIGURE 7.5
The Remain anonymous? prompt dialog.

FIGURE 7.6

The identity confirmation prompt.

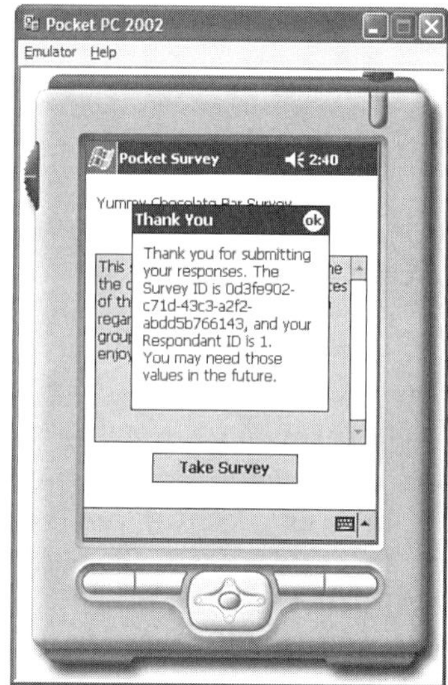

Recording the Time Taken to Answer a Question

Along the lines of providing additional feedback and auditing facilities, this section shows you one of the many things you can do to provide additional information to the people analyzing the survey.

One of the pieces of information that might be useful to people analyzing survey results is the amount of time taken to complete each of the questions.

Your first instinct might be to make use of the timeout timer. However, there are a couple problems with that. First, the timer ticks only every 12 seconds (or at whatever interval you've defined). If you use this timer to record the time taken to answer a question, the resolution will only be down to 12-second intervals.

Second, you will not be able to accurately determine the exact moment that the user finished answering the question without doing some code changes that you might not otherwise want to do.

An easier way to get this done would be to simply record the current time when the input form is displayed and then record the time when the input form is submitted. The difference between those two times is the elapsed time it took to answer that particular question, and you can then add that information to the data set. Listing 7.3 shows the new click event handler for starting a new survey, complete with the code to determine the elapsed time taken to answer questions.

LISTING 7.3 `SurveyV1\PocketSurvey\frmMain.cs`

The `btnStart_Click` Revised Event Handler, with Elapsed Time Code

```
private void btnStart_Click(object sender, System.EventArgs e)
{
  SAMS.Survey.Studio.Library.QuestionType questionType;
  string questionText;
  int rankHigh;
  int rankLow;
  DateTime timeStarted;
  DateTime timeFinished;
  double elapsedTime;

  try
  {
   surveyAborted = false;
   DataRow newSheet = dsRun.Tables["ResponseSheets"].NewRow();
   newSheet["DateEntered"] = DateTime.Now;
   newSheet["Source"] = "PocketSurvey";
   dsRun.Tables["ResponseSheets"].Rows.Add( newSheet );

   lastQuestionId = (int)dsProfile.Tables["Questions"].Rows[0]["ID"];
   timer = new System.Windows.Forms.Timer();
   timer.Tick +=new EventHandler(timer_Tick);
   timer.Interval=12000;
   timer.Enabled = true;
   // for each question in the profile, prompt the user for a response
   // then store the responses in a new run
   foreach ( DataRow question in dsProfile.Tables["Questions"].Rows )
   {
      currentQuestionId = (int)question["ID"];
      // obtain the question type
      questionType =
        (SAMS.Survey.Studio.Library.QuestionType)((int)question["Type"]);
      questionText = (string)question["LongText"];
      int choiceListId = (int)question["ChoiceListId"];
      string[] options = null;
      if (choiceListId > 0)
      {
        DataRow[] items =
          dsProfile.Tables["ChoiceListItems"].Select("ChoiceListId=" +
          choiceListId.ToString());
        options = new string[ items.Length ];
```

LISTING 7.3 SurveyV1\PocketSurvey\frmMain.cs
The `btnStart_Click` Revised Event Handler, with Elapsed Time Code (continued)

```
        int i=0;
        foreach (DataRow item in items)
        {
          options[i] = item["Description"].ToString();
          i++;
        }
    }

    // grab the options (if any)
    blankForm = new frmBlank();
    blankForm.Text = question["ShortDescription"].ToString();
    rankHigh = ((question["RankScaleHigh"] == DBNull.Value) ||
                (question["RankScaleHigh"] == null)) ? 0 :
                   (int)question["RankScaleHigh"];
    rankLow = ((question["RankScaleLow"] == DBNull.Value) ||
               (question["RankScaleLow"] == null)) ? 0 :
                  (int)question["RankScaleLow"];
    DynaFormHelper.Initialize_DynaForm(
       blankForm, questionType, questionText, options,
       rankLow, rankHigh );
    timeStarted = DateTime.Now;
    if (blankForm.ShowDialog() == DialogResult.OK)
    {
      timeFinished = DateTime.Now;
      // do something with the result
      string response = blankForm.Response;
      DataRow newResponse = dsRun.Tables["Responses"].NewRow();
      newResponse["QuestionId"] = (int)question["ID"];
      newResponse["SheetId"] = (int)newSheet["SheetId"];
      newResponse["ResponseData"] = response;
      newResponse["ResponseTime"] = (TimeSpan)(timeFinished - timeStarted);
      dsRun.Tables["Responses"].Rows.Add( newResponse );
    }
    if (surveyAborted)
      break;

    }
    timer.Enabled = false;
    timer = null;
```

LISTING 7.3 SurveyV1\PocketSurvey\frmMain.cs
The `btnStart_Click` Revised Event Handler, with Elapsed Time Code
(continued)

```
if (MessageBox.Show("Remain anonymous?",
    "Respondant Identification", MessageBoxButtons.YesNo,
    MessageBoxIcon.Question,
    MessageBoxDefaultButton.Button1) == DialogResult.No)
{
  // obtain respondent's identification information, store it in the DataSet
  // and provide them with feedback concerning the survey.
  frmRespondant respForm = new frmRespondant();
  if (respForm.ShowDialog() == DialogResult.OK)
  {
   // store respondent ID data
   DataRow respondent = dsRun.Tables["Respondants"].NewRow();
   respondent["FirstName"] = respForm.FirstName;
   respondent["LastName"] = respForm.LastName;
   respondent["Address"] = respForm.Address;
   respondent["Address2"] = respForm.Address2;
   respondent["City"] = respForm.City;
   respondent["State"] = respForm.State;
   respondent["Zip"] = respForm.Zip;
   respondent["Country"] = respForm.Country;
   dsRun.Tables["Respondants"].Rows.Add( respondent );
   int newRespId = (int)respondent["ID"];
   newSheet["RespondantID"] = newRespId;

   MessageBox.Show( string.Format(
    "Thank you for submitting your responses. The Survey ID is {0}, "+
    "and your Respondant ID is {1}.\n\r" +
    "You may need those values in the future.",
    (string)dsProfile.Tables["Profile"].Rows[0]["GlobalID"],
    newRespId.ToString()),
    "Thank You",
    MessageBoxButtons.OK, MessageBoxIcon.None,
    MessageBoxDefaultButton.Button1);
  }
}

if (!surveyAborted)
{
```

LISTING 7.3 `SurveyV1\PocketSurvey\frmMain.cs`
The `btnStart_Click` Revised Event Handler, with Elapsed Time Code
(continued)

```
      dsRun.AcceptChanges();
      dsRun.WriteXml( @"\Program Files\PocketSurvey\CurrentRun.svr" );
    }

  }
  catch (Exception ex)
  {
    dsRun.RejectChanges();
    MessageBox.Show( ex.Message, "Error",
      MessageBoxButtons.OK, MessageBoxIcon.Exclamation,
      MessageBoxDefaultButton.Button1 );
  }
}
```

STEP-BY-STEP GUIDE: Customization and Branding

So far you've made a few interesting changes to the PocketSurvey application. Some of them have made the application more reliable, and others have made it more thorough and have potentially made you less legally responsible for potential issues that might arise.

While using the application, you might think that the main screen looks a little bland. In addition, it might be nice if whatever company is using this application (presumably, you're making the application to sell to more than one customer) were able to place its own corporate logo and branding on the main window of PocketSurvey.

Your first instinct might be to think, "That's easy; I'll just put some variables in a `.config` file and just use that to point to the logo and branding text." Unfortunately, our instincts are not always right or practical. In this case, the problem is that the Compact Framework *does not* implement `System.Configuration.ConfigurationSettings`. I've never gotten a complete explanation about why this is so, but there is no native support for configuration files in the Compact Framework.

The Compact Framework does, however, contain support for XML documents. Follow these steps to enable customization and branding in the `PocketSurvey` application:

1. Create a small XML file that contains the information needed to customize the look of the main page to fit with whatever corporate style is required at the time. The XML file should look like the following:

```
<?xml version="1.0" encoding="utf-8" ?>
<CorporateSettings>
  <Logo filename="\Program Files\Pocketsurvey\Logo.bmp"/>
  <Greeting>Welcome to PocketSurvey by QuestionCorp!!</Greeting>
</CorporateSettings>
```

   This is just a simple XML document that contains a path to the filename of the corporate logo and some text to display for the application's greeting before a user takes the survey. Given this particular format, you could expand what you're doing here to include more customizations, such as font sizes, typefaces, colors, or even culture settings for surveys in different languages.

2. In the `Form_Load` event handler, add a few lines of code that retrieve those settings from the configuration XML file and store them for use later:

```
XmlDocument doc = new XmlDocument();
doc.Load(@"\Program Files\Pocketsurvey\CorporateSettings.xml");
corpFilename =
  doc.DocumentElement.ChildNodes[0].
      Attributes["filename"].Value;
corpGreeting = doc.DocumentElement.ChildNodes[1].InnerText;
doc = null;
```

   You might be wondering why you don't use something like `SelectNodes` or `SelectSingleNode`. Unfortunately, this is yet another limitation of the Compact Framework. The implementation of `XmlDocument` in the Compact Framework is far more limited than the implementation of `XmlDocument` in the standard .NET Framework. Rather than mess around with other ways of loading the document, you can just load the document and grab the nodes because you know the order in which they appear in the document. For something more efficient, and more reliable, you can use something that lets you specify the node name—something that supports XPath expressions.

3. To make room for the new elements, you can shrink the `TextBox` control that contains the survey description and put a `PictureBox` control on the main form. The following lines of code set up the new picture and label controls with the information gathered from the configuration file:

```
pbLogo.Image = new System.Drawing.Bitmap( corpFilename );
lblCorpGreeting.Text = corpGreeting;
```

That's all there is to it. By putting a few values in an XML file, you're able to give the customer the ability to configure his or her own devices with any logo and greeting message. For the purposes of testing, I've added the `Logo.bmp` and `CorporateSettings.xml` to the PocketSurvey project with the type `Content` so that they will be deployed whenever I build the project (see Figure 7.7).

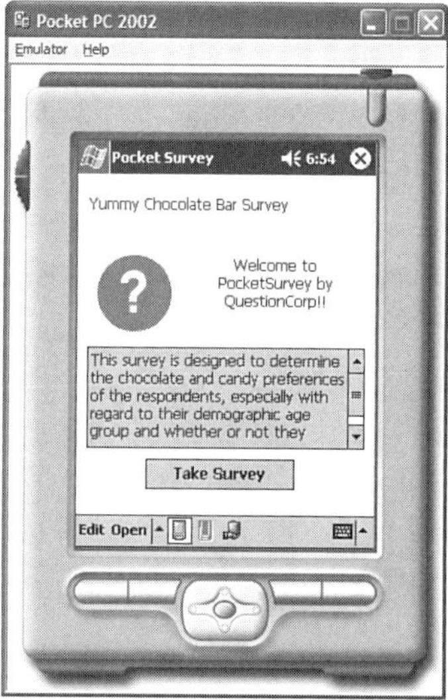

FIGURE 7.7
The new corporate logo and greeting.

As an additional challenge related to corporate branding and settings, take the code shown in the "Increasing Font Size for Accessibility" section, earlier in this chapter, and make the font size a corporate option in the XML file. Just create a new option in the XML file called `CorporateFontSize` and use that value whenever a new question is rendered on a blank form. This will allow you to conduct runs in multiple conditions where sometimes it might be better to use smaller or larger fonts, depending on the situation.

Moving On

This chapter continues the theme of customization and tweaking to improve an application and extends it to the PocketSurvey application. As mentioned earlier in this chapter, just because an application compiles doesn't mean that it is ready for release. In fact, even after you test an application and users get hold of it, you might find that some of your requirements were off or not needed. There may even be times when you realize that there should have been some features in the application that you didn't build.

In cases like this, you have to go back into the application to poke and prod and make the changes. If you followed good design patterns and coding practice guidelines for the original application, making tweaks and customizations should never be a painful process.

This chapter takes a look at customizing the PocketSurvey application and giving the customer the ability to customize the application with graphics and custom text.

A little bit of effort to improve and extend an application goes a long way and will do a lot to please your customers and provide them with the features they need and want in order to be productive.

Improving the Code of the Survey Development Suite

CHAPTER 8

So far in this book you have done quite a few things. You've taken a look at the existing code for all three of the applications in the Survey Development Suite, located flaws in design and requirements building, and customized and tweaked the code to improve the usability, scalability, and reliability of the applications. This chapter covers the following:

- Speeding up Object-Relational Mapping (ORM) code
- Making use of the `IDisposable` interface
- Asynchronous Web service access
- Smart client auto-update features

Improving the Survey Development Suite Code

In this chapter, you're not going to concern yourself with the design or business requirements. In fact, you won't be adding any new features to or even analyzing the design of the Survey Development Suite. This chapter is all about going over the existing code and making it better. In essence, you can think of this chapter as the results of a peer code review. You've handed your code to our peers, as frightening as that prospect may be, and they've come back and told you what you can do to improve the performance of the application and the elegance of the code.

In addition to peer reviews by other programmers, you can also use automated testing tools. There are a variety of unit test tools that you can use, as well as profilers that analyze how well the code is performing; these tools can give you ideas about how to improve the elegance and efficiency of the code.

In keeping with the theme "Just because it compiles doesn't mean its done," this chapter looks at code that works perfectly fine without errors, and you'll spend some time looking at ways to make it work better, faster, and more reliably.

STEP-BY-STEP GUIDE:
Speeding Up ORM Code

In Chapter 3, "Exploring the Code of the Survey Development Suite," I showed you the code that drives the entire ORM layer. Essentially, have XML documents map object instance properties to stored procedure parameters. In addition to the property maps, information shows how to relate those mappings to and from the database (for example, which stored procedures to invoke). When the code instantiates a `SqlRelator` object, that object in turn calls a method called `FetchTypeMap`. `FetchTypeMap` is actually defined by the abstract base class `ObjectRelator` because it is required by all ORM operations, regardless of the destination database. This method uses reflection to figure out what assembly from which the type itself was loaded. When the code figures that out, it looks in the appropriate assembly's manifest for a resource stream that contains the XML document named `ORM.xml`. This document contains all the information required to translate (or map) instances of the given type to the SQL Server database.

At first glance (without discussing the merits of pure ORM versus procedural data access), this might seem like a fairly good solution to the problem. However, if you look a little deeper, you may notice that there is something wrong. Each and every time `SqlRelator` is used, it goes through all the reflection code to load the type, find the type's assembly, load the XML document from the assembly's manifest, and so on. All this gets a little repetitive and will probably have a significant performance impact on the application under high load. You might be thinking that the code is fine on its own because the assembly is already in memory, so there's no need to cache it. While it is true that the assembly is in memory (it has to be in order for you to have a reference to the type of the variable you loaded from that assembly), you still have to use reflection to sift through the assembly's manifest, retrieve the XML stream, load the stream into an XML document, and then populate class instance data. This extra work might not seem obvious with just one or two concurrent users, but in a high-load system, something like this can become a large bottleneck.

Fortunately, you can narrow the entire process down to a single method, `FetchTypeMap`. Thankfully, when I was writing the original application, I managed to subdivide the tasks enough to be able to simply modify a few lines of code in a method without affecting other areas of the application.

This next set of instructions will show you how to speed up the ORM code by caching the `ORMTypeMap` instance that you retrieve the first time you load it. Subsequent requests will return the existing class instance and will not require the use of reflection or an XML document traversal. Listing 8.1 illustrates the new `FetchTypeMap` method. There is only one step for this step-by-step guide:

1. Replace the old `FetchTypeMap` method with the code shown in Listing 8.1.

LISTING 8.1 `SurveyV1\ObjectRelationalDb\ObjectRelator.cs`
The New `FetchTypeMap` Method of the `ObjectRelator` Class

```
protected ORMTypeMapping FetchTypeMap( IRelatable relatee )
{
  SystemTrace.MethodStart( MethodBase.GetCurrentMethod() );
  Type t = relatee.GetType();
  if (typeMaps.ContainsKey(t))
  {
    return (ORMTypeMapping)typeMaps[t];
  }
  else
  {
    Assembly sourceAssembly = t.Assembly;
    string resourceName = t.Namespace + ".ORM.xml";

    XmlDocument xDoc = new XmlDocument();
    StreamReader xmlRaw = new
      StreamReader(
        sourceAssembly.GetManifestResourceStream( resourceName ) );
    xDoc.Load( xmlRaw );

    string query = "//type[@fullname='" + t.FullName + "']";
    XmlNode typeMapNode = xDoc.DocumentElement.SelectSingleNode( query );
    if (typeMapNode != null )
    {
      ORMTypeMapping typeMap = new ORMTypeMapping( typeMapNode );
      typeMaps.Add( t, typeMap );
      return typeMap;
    }
    else
    {
      SystemTrace.TraceError("Failed to load type map for {0}", t.FullName);
      ExceptionManager.Publish(
        new NullReferenceException("Unable to fetch type map for " + t.FullName));
    }
  }
  return null;
}
```

In Listing 8.1, the `ObjectRelator` class has been modified to contain a new static, private member called `typeMaps`. This variable is of type `Hashtable`. The thing I like about the `Hashtable` type is that you can use any kind of object as the key and store any object in the value. It is far more than just a simple string-indexed collection. As such, it is perfect for your need to store instantiated `ORMTypeMapping` classes related to individual `Type` objects. If the type being related is located in the hashtable, the corresponding `ORMTypeMapping` is returned to the caller. Otherwise, the reflection and XML code will be invoked just as it was before the modification. With this new code in place, after some sustained operation, most of the types that the application uses frequently will be in the cache, and the system will not slow down due to reflection until the next application restart.

As with all modifications, you need to rebuild the application and run it through a few tests to satisfy yourself that it is still working properly. The last thing you need is to make the application break or work worse than before as a result of the enhanced code.

Making Use of `IDisposable`

One of the concepts that a lot of programmers seem to have trouble getting a firm grasp on is the concept of *nondeterministic finalization*. Those of us who grew up writing code for DOS, especially in C, know the tedium that is the allocation and de-allocation of memory for every string, array, and class in an application. In that model, programmers are forced to dispose of the memory used by objects as soon as they objects are no longer in use to preserve memory and application efficiency. Improper finalization in those programs generally results in what is fondly referred to as a *memory leak*.

With the creation of managed environments or runtimes such as Java and the .NET Framework, programmers were finally able to throw away `malloc()`, and they didn't have to worry about disposing of the memory associated with object pointers. It truly was a memory-handler's nirvana. Or was it?

Nondeterministic finalization essentially means that unlike what happens when you dispose of a class instance in C++ (immediate invocation of the destructor), something less obvious takes place. Instead of a destructor being called immediately, a finalizer is called. However, the finalizer is called at the convenience of the runtime's garbage collector (GC), not at the convenience of the programmer. Depending on system conditions at the time, a fairly long period could pass between when you set the class instance to `null` and when the memory for that class is actually reclaimed by the GC.

For the most part, we programmers are perfectly happy to let the runtime GC take care of the housekeeping for us. In most situations the GC knows best, can figure out when it should be reclaiming memory and when is the most opportune time to make a pass through memory, and can pick up the trash and get rid of it. However, there are some times when we, as programmers, might want more control over the process.

Let's say you have an object instance. This object instance is holding on to some extremely expensive resources. These resources could be unmanaged resources, possibly pointers obtained through P/Invoke operations, or they could be database connections and so on. If you want an application to run as tightly as possible, with the smallest possible memory footprint, you might consider manually controlling the de-allocation of your own objects.

This means that instead of simply letting our objects go out of scope and letting the GC handle it, you need to manually call `Dispose` on the objects that have expensive resources associated with them.

You can't simply call `Dispose` on your object. In order to be able to call `Dispose` on your class instances, you need to implement the `IDisposable` interface. This interface is more of a marker than anything else, containing only one method: `Dispose`.

A custom implemented `Dispose` method should do two things. First, if the `Dispose` method was invoked by the GC (through the finalizer method), it should *not* attempt to destroy managed resources because they might not be there in order to be destroyed. Second, if the `Dispose` method is invoked explicitly by programmer code, then it should attempt to dispose of all managed resources immediately. This particular model is a design pattern that Microsoft has used in many samples illustrating `IDisposable` on MSDN and other materials.

A perfect guinea pig for implementing `IDisposable` is the `SqlRelator` class. This class maintains a reference to a `SqlConnection` class instance throughout its lifetime. If you want things to run as tightly as possible, you might want to make sure that the connection is disposed of manually by calling the `Dispose` method from all code that uses the `SqlRelator` class.

The following few methods illustrate just how easy it is to implement the `IDisposable` interface (added to the `SqlRelator` class):

```
public void Dispose()
{
  Dispose(true);
  GC.SuppressFinalize(this);
}

private void Dispose(bool disposing)
{
  if (!this.disposed)
  {
    if (disposing)
    {
      // dispose of managed resources
      conn.Dispose();
      conn = null;
    }
    // If applicable, dispose unmanaged resources here.
    disposed = true;
  }
}

~SqlRelator()
{
  Dispose(false);
}
```

As you can see, the code is fairly simple, and this template can be reused over and over with virtually any class over which you want to exert tight finalization control. In this case, the only managed resource is a `SqlConnection` class, so the illustration isn't as obvious as it could be. The use of `IDisposable` might be more meaningful if `SqlRelator` were holding on to more unmanaged resources that require special function calls to properly dispose.

The beauty of using the `IDisposable` interface is that now you can wrap the invocation of the `SqlRelator` class in the `using` keyword. This will make the compiler automatically generate the `Dispose` statements for you when the variable goes out of scope. You can modify the `Validate` method on the User class as follows, to illustrate the new way in which you can call the new, revised SqlRelator class:

```
public int Validate()
{
  using (SqlRelator sr = new SqlRelator())
  {
    sr.Relate( this, "Validate" );
    return this.UserId;
  }
}
```

This code doesn't take up much more space than the original version of it, and now there's an implicit Dispose in the use of that object. This might not have a huge impact on the application as a whole, but if you implement the IDisposable interface in the appropriate places and you know what resources the application holds that could benefit from on-time destruction, you can improve the stability and memory footprint of the application.

Asynchronous Web Service Access

When you use Visual Studio .NET to create a reference to a Web service, it does you the tremendous favor of building a proxy class. This proxy class contains methods that look exactly like the contract signature, as defined by the Web service in its WSDL (Web Services Description Language). It does something extra, as well. In addition to providing synchronous methods that have the same signature as the signature defined by the service's WSDL, the proxy also contains asynchronous methods.

These asynchronous methods allow you to initiate a call to the Web service and leave the main user interface thread free to handle events, respond, and continue rendering. For testing, you probably haven't yet seen any reason to use asynchronous methods. All your methods seem to run pretty fast, and the user interface never seems locked up.

However, what if there is a network problem? If there is a problem connecting to the Web server and you're using a synchronous method, your entire application could appear "locked up" for several minutes, until the underlying network plumbing gives up and issues a timeout error. Even if the network is working properly, a large result set can take a long time to transmit, parse, and load into a proper method result.

During this time, if you make synchronous calls, the entire application user interface is locked up and unresponsive.

What you can do is use both synchronous and asynchronous methods. To the end user, it will appear as if the application is doing something, but the application won't be unresponsive. The user will be able to click and move around and do what he or she wants with the user interface. While that is taking place, the application will be running an asynchronous method without blocking the main user interface. This is an elegant approach to integrating a Web services back end with a Windows Forms application.

STEP-BY-STEP GUIDE:

Asynchronous Web Service Access

The following steps walk you through the process of converting a synchronous Web service access model to an asynchronous access model:

1. To upgrade your Web service invocations to asynchronous calls, you first need to create a "progress" form. This is a simple form that does nothing but display a message to the user that a request to the Web service is being processed. This gives the end user an indication that something is taking place without locking up the user interface and making the user think that the application is broken or hung. To create this form, just add a new form to Survey Development Studio and call it `frmServiceComm`. You can put a little networking icon on the form and a little message explaining what is going on. You can also set the border style to dialog and turned off all the control boxes. You can set the `TopMost` flag to `true`, to keep it visible even if the user moves the main window around.

2. Modify the login routine to make it asynchronous. The following is the old login method in the `RepositoryClient` helper class:

```
public static void Login(string userName,
    string password)
{
  clientUserName = userName;
  clientPassword = password;

  PerformLogin();
  reloginTimer = new Timer(3600000); // every hour
```

```
    reloginTimer.AutoReset = true;
    reloginTimer.Elapsed +=
      new ElapsedEventHandler( OnTimerElapsed );
    reloginTimer.Start();
  }
```

This looks pretty straightforward. In fact, there's nothing you need to change in this code. You still want all this behavior to be retained in the asynchronous invocation. Remember, the only thing you really want to accomplish is to avoid the user interface locking and to display a message to the user that you're communicating with the Web service.

3. Before you take a look at the new asynchronous code, it might be good to have a quick refresher on asynchronous method calls. Essentially, the proxy is allowing you to provide it with a delegate when you begin the invocation of a Web service method. This delegate is a `CallBack` method that will be invoked when communication with the Web service has completed. Essentially, you're telling the Visual Studio .NET–generated proxy, "Go ahead and call the Web service, and let me know when you're done. You can reach me *here*." The *here* in that statement is the `CallBack` method you provide.

4. Take a look at a new version of the `PerformLogin` method, which has been rewritten to take advantage of asynchronous invocation:

```
private static void PerformLogin()
{
  svcProgress = new frmServiceComm();
  svcProgress.Show();
  IAsyncResult loginResult =
    loginService.BeginLoginUser(
      clientUserName, clientPassword,
      new AsyncCallback( FinishPerformLogin ), null );
}

private static void FinishPerformLogin(IAsyncResult oRes )
{
  userToken = loginService.EndLoginUser( oRes );
  if (userToken != "")
    loggedIn = true;
  else
```

```
      loggedIn = false;
    svcProgress.Close();
    svcProgress.Dispose();
    if (OnLogin != null)
    {
      OnLogin( clientUserName, clientPassword );
    }
  }
```


The quick rundown of what's going on here starts with IAsyncResult. You're invoking the BeginLoginUser asynchronous method instead of the synchronous LoginUser method. Just like the regular invocation, you pass in the user's name and password. In addition, you pass in a new AsyncCallback delegate, which is special delegate used for asynchronous method invocation. The method you indicate will be called when the invocation of the LoginUser method on the Web server has completed and a result has been obtained. Figure 8.1 shows the message the user sees when the new asynchronous login method is being used.

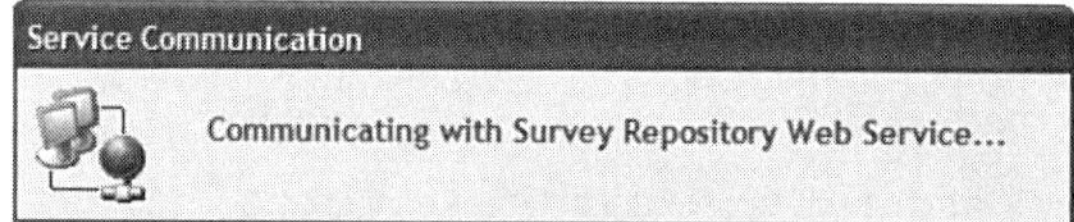

FIGURE 8.1 The Service Communication dialog.

In the previous implementation, you just called LoginUser, which returns a user token if the username and password are valid. Otherwise, it returns an empty string. In that same implementation, you test the return value, set a Boolean loggedIn flag accordingly, and call all the registered OnLogin event handlers.

In the new implementation, you are doing exactly the same things. The only difference is that instead of doing it at the time of the method call, you're actually performing all those operations at the time of asynchronous method *completion*. The difference is key here. Instead of the one line of code blocking the entire user interface until it returns, you're free to go about your business while the call takes place. Even when the call returns and invokes your delegate, nothing in the main user interface thread is blocked.

Asynchronous Versus Synchronous Method Calls

You might be wondering why go to all this trouble just to free up the user interface thread? Well, for simple testing scenarios or debugging, synchronous method calls may in fact be easier and a better choice than asynchronous calls. However, I would venture to say that a production application that makes use of Web services should *never* use synchronous method calls. Even if the application forces a user interface block, the underlying calls to the Web service should be asynchronous. These calls introduce more reliability, stability, and elegance into an application. You want your users to feel as though the interaction with the Web service is second nature and built into the application. At no point should an application that is interacting with an HTTP-based back end feel slow, sluggish, stuck, or unresponsive. All those behaviors would make users think the application is broken. Very few people will think the application is doing something useful when it sits still for three minutes, waiting for a network timeout. Did I mention that if someone looks at your application in Task Manager while it is waiting for a network timeout, they will in fact see "Not Responding," even if everything is working properly?

Some of the things covered in this book you can certainly treat as optional. However, one point that I feel extremely strong about is accessing a Web service. If a Windows Forms application is going to access a Web service and it will be used by anyone except yourself, it should do so in a smooth, elegant, reliable, asynchronous fashion.

After preaching all the merits of asynchronous Web service access, I feel compelled to point out a few caveats. The first and foremost is thread safety. Whenever you introduce the ability for an application to do something in the background while the user is doing something in the foreground, you run the risk of doing something unintended. For example, in the current implementation, the user can actually queue up a few hundred requests to log in to the application if he or she feels like it.

This application is partially set up to solve this problem. All the requests to the Web service are going through a static-only class that serves as an additional wrapper around the Visual Studio .NET–generated proxy. If you add a semaphore (state machine status variable) to the class that indicates the current operation being performed, you can actually have other operations either abort or wait to complete. By serializing the requests to the Web service, you prevent the user from making multiple (and possibly conflicting) requests of the Web service at the same time. This chapter doesn't go over that code, but you can feel free to add it on your own if you feel like an additional challenge.

Another issue that arises with asynchronous server access that the new code doesn't address is the concept of timeouts. As I said earlier, if the network is unavailable and you make a synchronous call, you can be stuck waiting for the protocol stack to time out for as many as three full minutes. Obviously, this isn't the desired result, so you switch to an asynchronous call. The problem is, if the method call never returns, you could be sitting there *forever* instead of for three minutes. In a way, you might have made the situation worse.

To keep the application stable, reliable, and elegant, you can insert an additional timer. What you could do is start a timer when you make the initial asynchronous request. If the timer elapses before the method call returns with a full result, you can pop up a message to the user, indicating that the request to the Web service timed out. The user would know what went wrong and would probably not think the application was broken. Instead, the user might be prompted to check his or her network connectivity or the availability of the Web server itself. These kinds of additions make an application far more agile and more tolerant of unexpected conditions. Applications that expect the perfect working environment all the time are anything but professional.

Adding a Smart Client Auto-Update Feature

If you've been keeping up-to-date with articles, publications, and the overall buzz on the Internet, you've probably heard the phrase *smart client* already. What is a smart client? Unfortunately, there is no really good clear-cut definition of exactly what a smart client is. In essence, you can think of smart clients as clients that can operate in online and offline modes and that are capable of updating themselves when new versions of the software come out.

Quite a few examples are available on the Internet for how to create a smart client. One of the key factors in the examples you might see is the use of `Assembly.LoadFrom`. This is probably the single most crucial method involved in creating a smart client. When you use this method on an Internet URL (as opposed to a URI that indicates a local filename), the assembly you're referencing as a parameter is actually downloaded from the Internet and placed in the download cache. The next time you make this call, if the file on the Internet has not changed since it was placed in the download cache, it will not be downloaded again.

So, how do you use this information to create a smart client? The general idea is to create a loader application. This application is a very small, compact little application that does nothing but load the real application from the Internet.

The problem I have with `Assembly.LoadFrom` is that in its current form (version 1.1 of the .NET Framework), it actually throws an exception if you attempt to load an assembly from the Internet and you are not connected to the Internet. Even if you happen to have a copy of the file in the download cache, the method call to `LoadFrom` will throw an exception if the URL cannot be reached. In the upcoming release of the .NET Framework (codenamed "Whidbey"), a new technology called ClickOnce deployment will make all this completely automatic.

That doesn't seem like very smart behavior for a smart client, does it? You have two options: You can either wait until Visual Studio Whidbey comes out and take advantage of ClickOnce deployment or you can add a little bit of intelligence to `Assembly.LoadFrom` on your own.

At this point, waiting for Whidbey to release just isn't an option (regardless of how much fun using ClickOnce deployment will be). So far we've been assuming that the Survey Development Studio application has been installed by an administrator or by the user, probably using a Microsoft Installer (`.msi`) file of some kind. As a result, we don't have to worry about Internet deployment for the original application.

Let's add a bit of logic to the loader application. Instead of just blindly attempting to load a DLL from a URL, you can make two attempts. If the attempt to load the DLL from a URL fails (no network connection, regardless of the contents of the download cache), then you can try to load the DLL directly from the local drive, presumably from the installation directory.

This two-phase approach to dynamic loading gives you some extreme flexibility. Administrators only have to place updated files on the central Web server in a download directory, and Survey Development Studio clients will automatically obtain the newest version when the client starts up. If a client's Internet connection becomes unavailable for some reason, the dynamic loader will use the preinstalled local version of the assembly as a back up.

STEP-BY-STEP GUIDE: Creating an Auto-Updating Application Loader

In theory, an auto-updating application loader sounds great. Follow these steps to implement it:

1. Convert the Survey Development Studio Windows Forms application into a class library. This essentially converts it from an executable into a simple container for classes that can be accessed over the Internet via the `LoadFrom` method. To do this, right-click the `SurveyStudio` project and change the output type from `Windows Application` to `Class Library`. Recompile the project, and you see that it has produced `SAMS.Survey.Studio.DLL` instead of `SAMS.Survey.Studio.EXE`.

2. Make the Survey Development Studio application (now contained in a DLL) available for remote access via your Web server. To do this, you can create a directory called `downloads` directly under the `inetpub` directory.

3. Copy the entire contents of Survey Development Studio's `bin\debug` directory (including the satellite directories containing the Hindi DLLs you created in Chapter 6, "Customizing Survey Development Studio") to the new download directory.

4. Make sure that the directory security is configured properly. Using the IIS administration console, make sure that the directory does *not* allow execution, or you won't be able to properly download the assembly.

5. As fun as it might be to jump right in and start coding the loader, there is one more thing you need to do. It has to do with code access security. If you load an assembly from the Internet via `Assembly.LoadFrom`, that assembly's code access security permissions are obtained from the permissions given to the Internet domain for your machine or enterprise. If everything is set up according to the defaults, the code will not be able to access files from the Internet due to an insufficient trust level. This will cause the loader application to fail, even if the IIS security is configured properly. To fix this problem the easy way, select Start, Settings, Control Panel, Administrative Tools and then open .NET Wizards and choose the Trust an Assembly Wizard. Navigate to the `SAMS.Survey.Studio.DLL` assembly and click Next. Instead of just trusting that one assembly, select the radio button indicating that

you want to trust all assemblies with the same public key, and uncheck the Include Version Number check box. When prompted for the trust level, choose Full Trust. Obviously, in a production environment, you need to provide the minimal level of trust possible. (If you have already modified your computer policy to automatically grant a higher level of trust to .NET assemblies—something that should be done only in a test environment—you will not see these dialogs and you will not have to increase the trust.)

Finally, now that the download directory is set up and all code having the public key associated with the strong name is fully trusted, you can get to work on the Survey Development Studio loader application.

6. Add a new project to the main solution and call it `StudioLoader`. This new project is a Windows Forms application. Set the default output filename and default namespace to `SAMS.Survey.Studio.Loader`.

   Figure 8.2 illustrates what the main form of the application (called `frmMain`) looks like in the Visual Studio .NET designer.

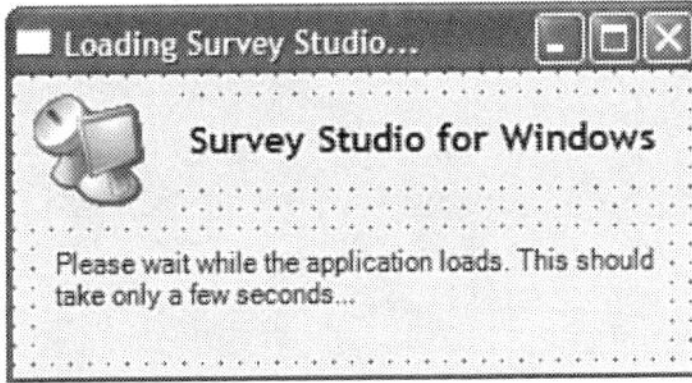

FIGURE 8.2
The main form of the Survey Development Studio loader application.

   The flow of the application is fairly straightforward. Instead of using the standard `Application.Run( new frmMain() )` inside the `Main` function, you're going to use some logic and the `Assembly.LoadFrom` method to try to find the main form of `SurveyStudio`, and then instead of passing the local `frmMain` instance to the `Application.Run` method, you'll pass the instance you retrieved either from the Internet or from the local installation directory.

7. Listing 8.2 shows the contents of the `Main` method of the `SurveyStudio` loader's `frmMain` class. Before compiling this code, make sure that you've set the `AssemblyKeyFile` attribute on the loader's `AssemblyInfo.cs` file so that it will have the same public key as the one you set to Full Trust earlier in the chapter.

LISTING 8.2 `SurveyV1\SurveyStudio\frmMain.cs`
The Constructor for the `frmMain` Class

```
[STAThread]
static void Main()
{
  frmMain main = new frmMain();
  main.Show();

  string url = ConfigurationSettings.AppSettings["LoaderURL"];

  Assembly surveyAssembly;
  Type formType;
  Form downloadedForm;

  try
  {
    surveyAssembly =
      Assembly.LoadFrom( url );
    formType = surveyAssembly.GetType("SAMS.Survey.Studio.frmMain");
    downloadedForm = (Form)System.Activator.CreateInstance( formType );
    if (downloadedForm != null)
    {
      main.Close();
      main = null;
      Application.Run( downloadedForm );
    }
    else
    LoadLocal(main);
  }
  catch (Exception ex)
  {
    try
    {
      LoadLocal(main);
    }
    catch (Exception ex2)
    {
      MessageBox.Show( ex2.ToString(), "Failed to Load Survey Studio");
    }
  }
}
```

LISTING 8.2 SurveyV1\SurveyStudio\frmMain.cs
The Constructor for the `frmMain` Class
(continued)

```
static void LoadLocal(frmMain main)
{
  string localurl = ConfigurationSettings.AppSettings["LocalFile"];

  Assembly surveyAssembly = Assembly.LoadFrom( localurl );
  Type formType = surveyAssembly.GetType("SAMS.Survey.Studio.frmMain");
  Form downloadedForm = (Form)System.Activator.CreateInstance( formType );
  if (downloadedForm != null)
  {
    if (main != null) main.Close();
    MessageBox.Show(
      "Survey Studio loaded from local installation " +
      " (Internet connection unavailable)",
      "Loaded Survey Locally",
      MessageBoxButtons.OK,
      MessageBoxIcon.Information);
    Application.Run( downloadedForm );
  }
}
```

The “magic” that makes this all work is a three-step process. The first step is obtaining a reference to an assembly somewhere on the Internet (or on the local filesystem) with `Assembly.LoadFrom`. This method accepts a URI indicating an assembly. The second step is calling `GetType` on that assembly to obtain a reference to the `frmMain` class. The third step that puts it all together is using `Activator.CreateInstance` to obtain an instance of the `frmMain` class of the remotely loaded assembly.

8. Notice that there are two configuration settings at work here. These settings dictate the URL from which the Survey Development Studio assembly is requested via the Internet, as well as the full path from which to load Survey Development Studio in case the Internet connection is unavailable. These settings are stored in the `App.config` file as follows:

```
<?xml version="1.0" encoding="utf-8" ?>
<configuration>
```

```
  <appSettings>
   <add key="LoaderURL"
      value="http://localhost/download/SAMS.Survey.Studio.DLL"/>
   <add key="LocalFile"
      value="C:\documents and settings\Kevin S Hoffman\
➥My Documents\Visual Studio Projects\SurveyV1\SurveyStudio\
➥bin\Debug\SAMS.Survey.Studio.DLL" />
  </appSettings>
</configuration>
```

To test the behavior of the application and to make sure that it is actually doing what you think it's doing, run a couple of quick tests. First, make sure that IIS is running, rebuild the loader application, and open it in a new debug instance. If things are running properly, you should see the loading "splash" screen for a brief moment and then you should see the familiar main form of the Survey Development Studio application.

It would be nice if you could verify for sure exactly what is going on throughout the execution. You could add some trace messages fairly easily, but there is an even easier way. The .NET Framework SDK ships with a tool called `GACUTIL` that not only allows you to examine the contents of the global assembly cache but lets you examine the contents of the download cache. As I said earlier, every time you download an assembly via the Internet through `Assembly.LoadFrom`, the assembly is cached in the download cache so that you have a local copy. By using the `GACUTIL` utility, you can prove that on the last execution of the loader application you did indeed store the Survey Development Studio assembly in the download cache. Figure 8.3 shows a screenshot of the `GACUTIL` utility examining the download cache.

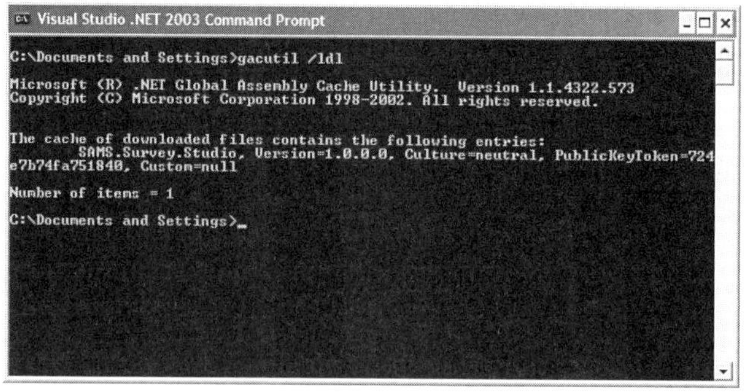

FIGURE 8.3

Using the `GACUTIL` utility to examine the download cache.

```
Visual Studio .NET 2003 Command Prompt
C:\Documents and Settings>gacutil /ldl

Microsoft (R) .NET Global Assembly Cache Utility.  Version 1.1.4322.573
Copyright (C) Microsoft Corporation 1998-2002. All rights reserved.

The cache of downloaded files contains the following entries:
        SAMS.Survey.Studio, Version=1.0.0.0, Culture=neutral, PublicKeyToken=724
e7b74fa751840, Custom=null

Number of items = 1

C:\Documents and Settings>_
```

The first half of the "really smart" client is working perfectly. When you have a solid Internet connection and the Web server is working properly, you can successfully download the newest version of Survey Development Studio from a download directory. If an administrator were to copy a new version of Survey Development Studio out to the download directory, the loader client would be aware of it, and you would get the new version of the application.

The second half of the plan was to provide for a fall-back alternative in case the Internet connection isn't available. In this case, the application loads the `SAMS.Survey.Studio.DLL` file from a local directory rather than the Internet. To simulate a broken Internet connection or a malfunctioning Web server, simply turn off IIS for the default Web site. This will essentially block the loader application from being able to download from the Internet and will force it to load the local backup. Figure 8.4 shows a dialog box that indicates the local backup being used.

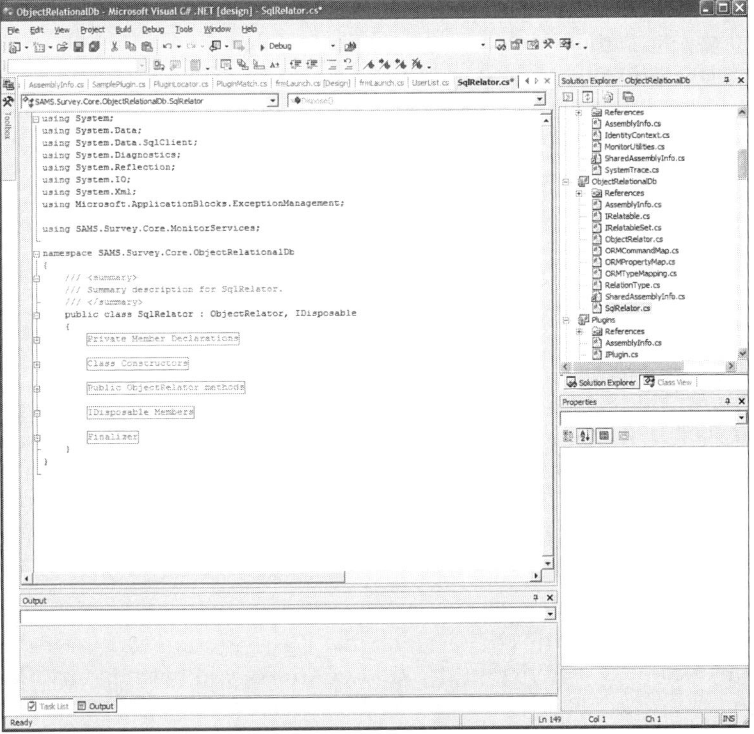

FIGURE 8.4

A dialog indicating that the local backup was used instead of the live Internet download.

So now you've seen how to tweak and improve code to turn a mild-mannered Windows Forms application into a module that can be the target of a smart client loading application. Again, you've increased the reliability, stability, and maintainability of the application with what can be considered a small amount of effort.

One thing that this smart client does not do is overwrite the local installation copy (the alternate fall-back) when it detects a newer version that was obtained via Internet download. I'll leave that as an exercise for you to complete on your own. It should be a fairly straightforward task to add that kind of functionality on top of the framework that you've built so far.

Making Code Maintenance and Documentation More Efficient

A common misconception among developers is that after you've written the code and it compiles and passes all the tests assigned to it, that piece of code is done. Unfortunately, this isn't the case. Developers need to take certain steps to organize their code to make it easier to read. The following sections cover some of the techniques that developers can use to make the task of reading, organizing, and maintaining the code they write easier and more efficient. The following are some of the techniques:

- Defining code regions
- Using XML comments
- Building user documentation from XML comments

Defining Code Regions

Using code regions helps logically organize related sections of code, making the code easier to read, maintain, and edit. Code regions work by providing named sections of code that can be collapsed or expanded at will, like a tree view. In C# a code region is started with the `#region` statement and finished with an `#endregion` statement.

If you have done much development in Visual Studio .NET 2003, you have probably seen the code regions that Visual Studio .NET creates automatically, depending on the kind of project you have open at the time.

You can use code regions to organize related properties, members, and methods into named sections that make the code more accessible. If you have a lot of related code that doesn't all fit on a single page, being able to expand and collapse regions of that code makes the code much easier to navigate and edit.

To see how you can simplify your code by using code regions, take a look at the source code for the `SqlRelator` class, shown in Listing 8.3, which has no region identifiers. Next, you'll add regions to the code and take a look at how much simpler it looks within Visual Studio .NET.

LISTING 8.3 `SurveyV1\ObjectRelationalDb\SqlRelator.cs`
The SqlRelator Class, Without `#region` Markers

```
using System;
using System.Data;
using System.Data.SqlClient;
using System.Diagnostics;
using System.Reflection;
using System.IO;
using System.Xml;
using Microsoft.ApplicationBlocks.ExceptionManagement;

using SAMS.Survey.Core.MonitorServices;

namespace SAMS.Survey.Core.ObjectRelationalDb
{
  /// <summary>
  /// Summary description for SqlRelator.
  /// </summary>
  public class SqlRelator : ObjectRelator, IDisposable
  {
    private SqlConnection conn;
    private bool disposed = false;

    public SqlRelator()
    {
      SystemTrace.MethodStart( MethodBase.GetCurrentMethod() );
      conn = new SqlConnection(
         System.Configuration.ConfigurationSettings.AppSettings["DefaultDSN"] );
    }
```

LISTING 8.3 `SurveyV1\ObjectRelationalDb\SqlRelator.cs`
The SqlRelator Class, Without `#region` Markers
(continued)

```
public override void Relate( IRelatable relatee, RelationType relationType )
{
  SystemTrace.MethodStart( MethodBase.GetCurrentMethod() );
  Relate( relatee, relationType.ToString() );
}



public override void Relate( IRelatable relatee, string relationKey )
{
  SystemTrace.MethodStart( MethodBase.GetCurrentMethod() );
  ORMTypeMapping typeMap = FetchTypeMap( relatee );
  ORMCommandMap cmdMap = typeMap.GetMapByName( relationKey );
  SqlCommand cmd = BuildCommandFromTypeMap( relatee, typeMap , relationKey );
  conn.Open();
  if (cmdMap.ReturnsMultiple)
  {
    SqlDataAdapter da = new SqlDataAdapter( cmd );
    IRelatableSet relateSet = (IRelatableSet)relatee;
    da.Fill( relateSet.ResultSet );
  }
  else
  {
    cmd.ExecuteNonQuery();
  }
  AssignOutputValuesToObject( cmd, relatee, typeMap, relationKey );
  conn.Close();
}

private void AssignOutputValuesToObject(
 SqlCommand cmd, IRelatable relatee,
 ORMTypeMapping typeMap, string relationKey )
{
  SystemTrace.MethodStart( MethodBase.GetCurrentMethod() );
  ORMCommandMap ocm = typeMap.GetMapByName( relationKey );
  foreach (object ob in ocm.PropertyMaps)
  {
```

LISTING 8.3 `SurveyV1\ObjectRelationalDb\SqlRelator.cs`
The SqlRelator Class, Without `#region` Markers
(continued)

```
        ORMPropertyMap propMap = (ORMPropertyMap)ob;
        if (( propMap.DataDirection == ParameterDirection.Output) ||
          ( propMap.DataDirection == ParameterDirection.InputOutput ) )
        {
          PropertyInfo prop;
          Type t = relatee.GetType();
          prop = t.GetProperty( propMap.MemberName );
          if (prop != null)
          {
            if ( cmd.Parameters[ propMap.Parameter ].Value != DBNull.Value)
            {
              prop.SetValue( relatee, cmd.Parameters[ propMap.Parameter ].Value, null );
            }
          }
          else
          {
            ExceptionManager.Publish(
              new NullReferenceException("Missing member " +
                t.FullName + "." + propMap.MemberName) );
          }
        }
      }

    }

    private SqlCommand BuildCommandFromTypeMap(
      IRelatable relatee, ORMTypeMapping typeMap,
      string relationKey )
    {
      SystemTrace.MethodStart( MethodBase.GetCurrentMethod() );
      ORMCommandMap ocm = typeMap.GetMapByName( relationKey );
      if (ocm != null)
      {
        SqlCommand cmd = new SqlCommand( ocm.StoredProcedure, conn );
        cmd.CommandType = CommandType.StoredProcedure;
        foreach (object ob in ocm.PropertyMaps)
        {
```

LISTING 8.3 SurveyV1\ObjectRelationalDb\SqlRelator.cs
The SqlRelator Class, Without #region Markers
(continued)

```
          ORMPropertyMap propMap = (ORMPropertyMap)ob;
          SqlParameter newParam = CreateParameterFromPropertyMap( propMap );
          if ((newParam.Direction == ParameterDirection.Input) ||
              (newParam.Direction == ParameterDirection.InputOutput) )
          {
            SetParameterValue( newParam, relatee, propMap.MemberName );
          }
          cmd.Parameters.Add( newParam );
        }
       return cmd;
      }
      else
      {
        ExceptionManager.Publish(
          new NullReferenceException(
            "No such command mapping: " + typeMap.FullName + ":" + relationKey) );
      }
      return null;
    }

    private SqlParameter CreateParameterFromPropertyMap( ORMPropertyMap propMap )
    {
      SystemTrace.MethodStart( MethodBase.GetCurrentMethod() );
      SqlParameter param = new SqlParameter();
      param.ParameterName = propMap.Parameter;
      param.SqlDbType = propMap.SqlDataType;
      param.Direction = propMap.DataDirection;
      if (propMap.Size != -1)
        param.Size = propMap.Size;
      return param;
    }

    private void SetParameterValue(
      SqlParameter param,
      IRelatable relatee, string member )
    {
      SystemTrace.MethodStart( MethodBase.GetCurrentMethod() );
      PropertyInfo propInfo;
      Type t = relatee.GetType();
```

LISTING 8.3 `SurveyV1\ObjectRelationalDb\SqlRelator.cs`
The SqlRelator Class, Without `#region` Markers
(continued)

```
      propInfo = t.GetProperty( member );
      if (propInfo != null )
      {
        param.Value = propInfo.GetValue( relatee, null );
      }
      else
      {
        SystemTrace.TraceError("Read failed on member {0} on type {1}",
          member, t.FullName);
      }
    }


    public void Dispose()
    {
      Dispose(true);
      GC.SuppressFinalize(this);
    }

    private void Dispose(bool disposing)
    {
      if (!this.disposed)
      {
         if (disposing)
         {
           // dispose of managed resources
           conn.Dispose();
           conn = null;
         }
         disposed = true;
      }
    }

    ~SqlRelator()
    {
      Dispose(false);
    }

  }
}
```

Making Code Maintenance and Documentation More Efficient

The code in Listing 8.3 should look familiar; you've seen it in previous chapters. However, it could definitely be made to look much more organized. Listing 8.4 shows how you can add code regions to this code.

LISTING 8.4 `SurveyV1\ObjectRelationalDb\SqlRelator.cs`
The `SqlRelator` Class, Decorated with Code Regions

```
using System;
using System.Data;
using System.Data.SqlClient;
using System.Diagnostics;
using System.Reflection;
using System.IO;
using System.Xml;
using Microsoft.ApplicationBlocks.ExceptionManagement;

using SAMS.Survey.Core.MonitorServices;

namespace SAMS.Survey.Core.ObjectRelationalDb
{
  /// <summary>
  /// Summary description for SqlRelator.
  /// </summary>
  public class SqlRelator : ObjectRelator, IDisposable
  {
    #region Private Member Declarations
    private SqlConnection conn;
    private bool disposed = false;
    #endregion

    #region Class Constructors
    public SqlRelator()
    {
      SystemTrace.MethodStart( MethodBase.GetCurrentMethod() );
      conn = new SqlConnection(
        System.Configuration.ConfigurationSettings.AppSettings["DefaultDSN"] );
    }
    #endregion
```

LISTING 8.4 SurveyV1\ObjectRelationalDb\SqlRelator.cs
The SqlRelator Class, Decorated with Code Regions
(continued)

```
#region Public ObjectRelator Methods
public override void Relate( IRelatable relatee, RelationType relationType )
{
  SystemTrace.MethodStart( MethodBase.GetCurrentMethod() );
  Relate( relatee, relationType.ToString() );
}

  public override void Relate( IRelatable relatee, string relationKey )
{
  SystemTrace.MethodStart( MethodBase.GetCurrentMethod() );
  ORMTypeMapping typeMap = FetchTypeMap( relatee );
  ORMCommandMap cmdMap = typeMap.GetMapByName( relationKey );
  SqlCommand cmd = BuildCommandFromTypeMap( relatee, typeMap , relationKey );
  conn.Open();
  if (cmdMap.ReturnsMultiple)
  {
    SqlDataAdapter da = new SqlDataAdapter( cmd );
    IRelatableSet relateSet = (IRelatableSet)relatee;
    da.Fill( relateSet.ResultSet );
  }
  else
  {
    cmd.ExecuteNonQuery();
  }
  AssignOutputValuesToObject( cmd, relatee, typeMap, relationKey );
  conn.Close();
}

private void AssignOutputValuesToObject(
  SqlCommand cmd, IRelatable relatee,
  ORMTypeMapping typeMap, string relationKey )
{
  SystemTrace.MethodStart( MethodBase.GetCurrentMethod() );
  ORMCommandMap ocm = typeMap.GetMapByName( relationKey );
  foreach (object ob in ocm.PropertyMaps)
  {
```

LISTING 8.4 `SurveyV1\ObjectRelationalDb\SqlRelator.cs`
The `SqlRelator` Class, Decorated with Code Regions
(continued)

```
        ORMPropertyMap propMap = (ORMPropertyMap)ob;
        if (( propMap.DataDirection == ParameterDirection.Output) ||
           ( propMap.DataDirection == ParameterDirection.InputOutput ) )
        {
          PropertyInfo prop;
          Type t = relatee.GetType();
          prop = t.GetProperty( propMap.MemberName );
          if (prop != null)
          {
            if ( cmd.Parameters[ propMap.Parameter ].Value != DBNull.Value)
            {
              prop.SetValue( relatee,
                cmd.Parameters[ propMap.Parameter ].Value, null );
            }
          }
          else
          {
            ExceptionManager.Publish(
              new NullReferenceException("Missing member " +
                t.FullName + "." + propMap.MemberName) );
          }
        }
      }

    }

    private SqlCommand BuildCommandFromTypeMap(
      IRelatable relatee, ORMTypeMapping typeMap,
      string relationKey )
    {
      SystemTrace.MethodStart( MethodBase.GetCurrentMethod() );
      ORMCommandMap ocm = typeMap.GetMapByName( relationKey );
      if (ocm != null)
      {
        SqlCommand cmd = new SqlCommand( ocm.StoredProcedure, conn );
        cmd.CommandType = CommandType.StoredProcedure;
        foreach (object ob in ocm.PropertyMaps)
```

LISTING 8.4 `SurveyV1\ObjectRelationalDb\SqlRelator.cs`
The `SqlRelator` Class, Decorated with Code Regions
(continued)

```
        {
          ORMPropertyMap propMap = (ORMPropertyMap)ob;
          SqlParameter newParam = CreateParameterFromPropertyMap( propMap );
          if ((newParam.Direction == ParameterDirection.Input) ||
              (newParam.Direction == ParameterDirection.InputOutput) )
          {
            SetParameterValue( newParam, relatee, propMap.MemberName );
          }
          cmd.Parameters.Add( newParam );
        }
       return cmd;
      }
      else
      {
        ExceptionManager.Publish(
          new NullReferenceException(
            "No such command mapping: " + typeMap.FullName + ":" + relationKey) );
      }
      return null;
    }

    private SqlParameter CreateParameterFromPropertyMap( ORMPropertyMap propMap )
    {
      SystemTrace.MethodStart( MethodBase.GetCurrentMethod() );
      SqlParameter param = new SqlParameter();
      param.ParameterName = propMap.Parameter;
      param.SqlDbType = propMap.SqlDataType;
      param.Direction = propMap.DataDirection;
      if (propMap.Size != -1)
        param.Size = propMap.Size;
      return param;
    }

    private void SetParameterValue(
      SqlParameter param,
      IRelatable relatee, string member )
    {
```

LISTING 8.4 `SurveyV1\ObjectRelationalDb\SqlRelator.cs`
The `SqlRelator` Class, Decorated with Code Regions
(continued)

```
    SystemTrace.MethodStart( MethodBase.GetCurrentMethod() );
    PropertyInfo propInfo;
    Type t = relatee.GetType();
    propInfo = t.GetProperty( member );
    if (propInfo != null )
    {
      param.Value = propInfo.GetValue( relatee, null );
    }
    else
    {
      SystemTrace.TraceError("Read failed on member {0} on type {1}",
        member, t.FullName);
    }
  }
  #endregion

  #region IDisposable Members
  public void Dispose()
  {
    Dispose(true);
    GC.SuppressFinalize(this);
  }

  private void Dispose(bool disposing)
  {
    if (!this.disposed)
    {
       if (disposing)
       {
         // dispose of managed resources
         conn.Dispose();
         conn = null;
       }
       disposed = true;
    }
  }
  #endregion
```

LISTING 8.4 `SurveyV1\ObjectRelationalDb\SqlRelator.cs`
The `SqlRelator` Class, Decorated with Code Regions
(continued)

```
    #region Finalizer
    ~SqlRelator()
    {
      Dispose(false);
    }
    #endregion
  }
}
```


Now let's look at what the Visual Studio .NET 2003 IDE looks like when the code from Listing 8.4 is loaded. With just a few lines of typing into the Visual Studio .NET IDE, you can make things much easier on any programmer who might have to look at or maintain your code in the future. Figure 8.5 shows the Visual Studio .NET IDE, looking at the `SqlRelator.cs` code file that has been decorated with code regions.

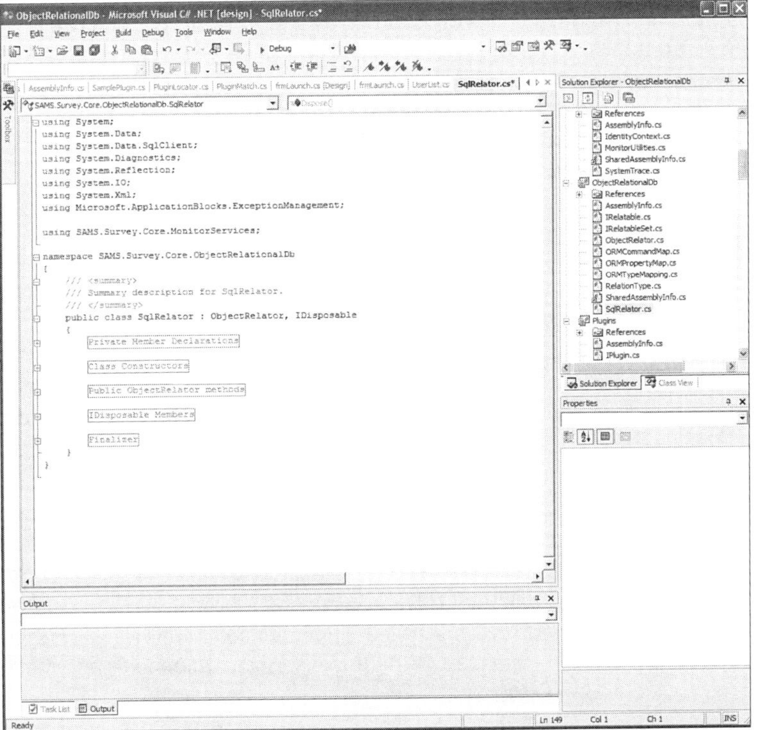

FIGURE 8.5
The Visual Studio .NET 2003 IDE, looking at a region-decorated code file.

Using XML Comments

XML comments are a structured form of code comments that Visual Studio .NET and other third-party programs can use to create reports and documentation. You'll see some of the tools that utilize XML comments shortly. First, let's take a look at what you can do with an XML comment.

The simplest XML comment is one that you've probably seen countless times before—the default comment that appears on top of each new class you create:

```
/// <summary>
/// Summary description for Class1
/// </summary>
```

The XML comment is indicated by the triple-slash (///) comment character. The standard C# comment is indicated with two slashes or a slash and an asterisk (/*). When the compiler sees the triple-slash comment, it extracts the XML from within the comment and stores it alongside relevant type information in an external XML file that can then be used by Visual Studio .NET and other third-party tools.

XML comments wouldn't be all that helpful if the only thing you could use them for was to provide summary information. In fact, Microsoft has quite a few XML tags that you can use to add enhanced, structured comments to code. Table 8.1 contains some of the most popular XML comment tags.

TABLE 8.1 Common XML Comment Tags

XML Comment Tag	Description
`Code`	The text within the code tag in an XML comment is flagged as code. Different formatting tools treat this tag differently.
`Param`	The `param` tag indicates a method parameter. The `name` attribute indicates the name of the parameter. The inner text indicates the description. Here's an example: `<param name="inValue">Input Value 1</param>`.
`Seealso`	The `seealso` tag references another member by means of the `cref` attribute. The member name indicated by `cref` must be fully qualified to establish a link between the two members.
`Summary`	This is a typical summary comment. It can apply to classes, attributes, variables, members, and methods.

TABLE 8.1 Common XML Comment Tags (continued)

XML Comment Tag	Description
`Remarks`	The `remarks` tag is used to add supplemental information about a type that might not belong in the type's short description.
`List`	The `list` tag is used to create a formatted list of items within an XML comment.
`Returns`	The `returns` tag indicates the return value of the method to which this XML comment is attached.
`Example`	The `example` tag is used to contain some code that illustrates an example of how to use the particular type to which the XML tag applies.

Listing 8.5 shows one of the `Relate` method overloads that has been decorated with XML comments.

LISTING 8.5 `SurveyV1\ObjectRelationalDb\SqlRelator.cs`
The `SqlRelator` Class' `Relate` Method, with XML Comments

```
/// <summary>
/// The Relate method performs all of the work to relate a particular object
/// instance to the database or vise versa. Several helper methods are used
/// to make this method work. Eventually this method will call a stored procedure
/// within the database as indicated by XML meta-data that will perform the
/// actual data operation.
/// <example>
/// The following example illustrates how to use the Relate method
/// <code>
/// SqlRelator sr = new SqlRelator();
/// MyRelatable myObject = new MyRelatable();
/// myObject.SomeData = 25;
/// sr.Relate( myObject, "InsertData");
/// </code>
/// </example>
/// </summary>
/// <param name="relatee">
/// An object that implements IRelatable,
/// its members map to stored procedure parameters</param>
```

LISTING 8.5 SurveyV1\ObjectRelationalDb\SqlRelator.cs
The SqlRelator Class' Relate Method, with XML Comments (continued)

```
/// <param name="relationKey">A string indicating how the relation is to take place</param>
public override void Relate( IRelatable relatee, string relationKey )
{
  SystemTrace.MethodStart( MethodBase.GetCurrentMethod() );
  ORMTypeMapping typeMap = FetchTypeMap( relatee );
  ORMCommandMap cmdMap = typeMap.GetMapByName( relationKey );
  SqlCommand cmd = BuildCommandFromTypeMap( relatee, typeMap , relationKey );
  conn.Open();
  if (cmdMap.ReturnsMultiple)
  {
    SqlDataAdapter da = new SqlDataAdapter( cmd );
    IRelatableSet relateSet = (IRelatableSet)relatee;
    da.Fill( relateSet.ResultSet );
  }
  else
  {
    cmd.ExecuteNonQuery();
  }
  AssignOutputValuesToObject( cmd, relatee, typeMap, relationKey );
  conn.Close();
}
```


In the project configuration section of Visual Studio .NET 2003, you can go to configuration settings and set the filename of the XML comments file to something appropriate. (I called mine `xmlcomments.xml`, but you can call it anything you like.) When you rebuild the project, you will notice that this file appears in the `doc` subdirectory below your project's main directory.

Building User Documentation from XML Comments

You can do several things with the XML comments file that Visual Studio .NET produces. The first and easiest thing you can do is use Visual Studio .NET 2003 to create comment Web pages. To do this, in the Build menu, you choose Build Comment Web Pages. For this example, you can just select the `ObjectRelationalDb` project and put the files in a suitable temporary folder.

Figure 8.6 shows the Web page produced by the Visual Studio .NET comment XSLT stylesheets.

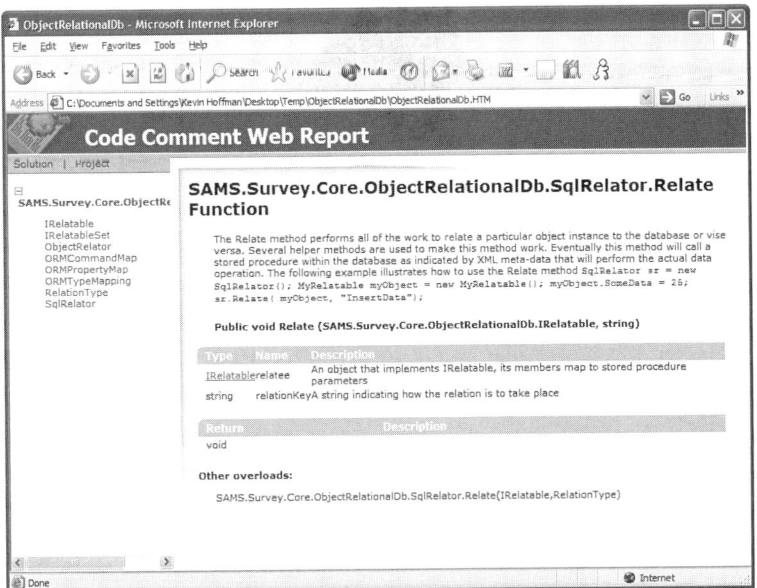

FIGURE 8.6
The HTML that Visual Studio .NET 2003 produces when compiling comment Web pages.

The second, and my favorite, thing that you can do with the XML comment file is produce an HTML help file that looks nearly identical to the help contained in the MSDN library for the .NET Framework. You can accomplish this with a tool called NDoc that is available through open-source licensing from SourceForge.net (`http://sourceforge.net/projects/ndoc`).

NDoc allows you to create documentation project files. Each of these project files contains a list of assemblies that you want to document, as well as the list of XML comment files produced by Visual Studio .NET for those assemblies. You can set any number of configurable options, and you can then build the help file, which results in an extremely robust, searchable, indexed, organized MSDN-style document for your application. Figure 8.7 shows a sample of this built output (a `.chm` file).

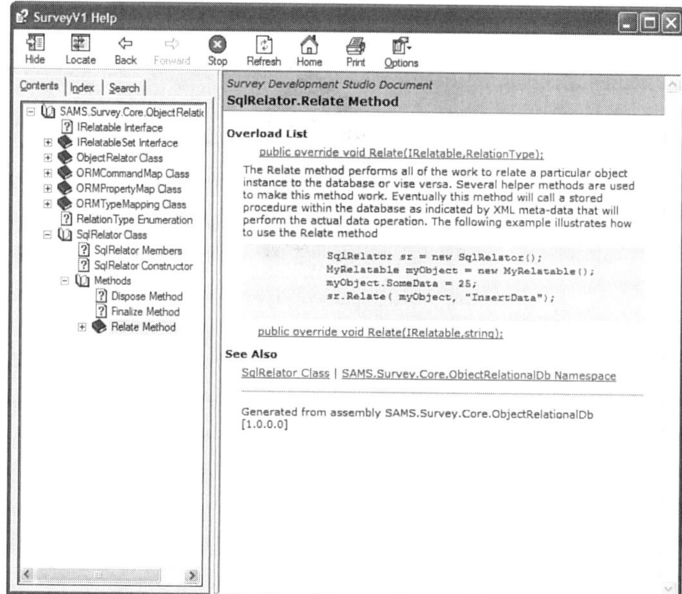

FIGURE 8.7

The `.chm` MSDN-style output produced by the NDoc application for the `SqlRelator` Class `Relate` method.

Moving On

This chapter is all about improving the code that you already have. At first you looked at a few ways in which you can speed up the application and improve reliability. After digging deep into the code and enhancing it from the bottom level upward, you took a look at how to turn an entire, complete Windows Forms application into an assembly that can be used as the target for an auto-updating smart client. Finally, this chapter looks at ways to improve the code that drives the application by exploring code regions and XML comments. At this point, you should be ready to create some challenging new features to the Survey Development Suite.

Extending the Survey Development Suite

9

CHAPTER

When you first opened this book and started reading, you had access to a fully functioning application suite. This application suite contained a Web service, a Windows Forms application, and a Compact Framework application that can run on an iPAQ or another PocketPC mobile device.

Instead of wasting your time with hundreds of pages of source code listings, I decided to spend your time more constructively. So far in this book you have looked at how the existing Survey Development Suite works and taken note of some of the design and architecture points that you might be able to use for your own applications.

After becoming familiar with the architecture, design, and functionality of the existing application, you moved on to something more detailed. You took a look at how to improve the code's performance, reliability, and stability. In addition, you took a look at some possible customizations that might make the user experience more robust.

In this chapter, you're going to work on extending the application. At this point, the application that you're working with is much more solid and the features are more well rounded than the version of the application that comes on this book's CD. There is always room for improvement. Instead of improving on features that are already have built in to the application or adding things that really should have been there in the first place, in this chapter I challenge you to create completely new features to the application. This chapter takes a look at the following:

- Creating a survey analysis API
- Dynamic image generation with ASP.NET and GDI+
- Creating a pie chart control
- Building the Survey Analysis Web site

Not only will this chapter help you continue to learn more about C#, the .NET Framework, and ASP.NET, but it will help you with a very important skill: working with and adding to existing code. Sooner or later, every programmer has to work with code he or she didn't write, and the better you are at handling it the better off you will be in the long run.

What new feature should you add to the Survey Development Suite? The application handles just about everything: survey input from the desktop, survey response from the PocketPC, and survey repository/storage via the Web service. However, there is one thing that the application does not handle at all: survey analysis. Somehow, we've managed to get all the way through building the application, and it doesn't provide any means of analyzing surveys.

This chapter challenges you to add your own analysis features to the Survey Development Suite. It provides some sample code, some direction, and some hints on what might work best, but the final code will be completely up to you. I find that code I write myself to experiment or learn something is far more memorable and far more useful to me than code I find in other people's samples or in a text book.

Creating a Survey Analysis API

There are a couple different ways that you can go about adding the survey analysis functionality to the Survey Development Suite. You could just start creating a GUI for analyzing the surveys and attach the appropriate statistics code in the code-behind of a Web page. Another option would be to create some new forms in the Windows Forms application and embed the statistical code in that application.

Although these methods will get the job done, they aren't the best designs. I'd like you to completely isolate the analysis logic from the GUI. This will allow any portion of the Survey Development Suite—not just the Web site or the Windows Forms application—to perform analysis.

The basic idea behind creating the survey analysis API has to do with deciding what constitutes an analysis. I managed to escape the statistical analysis classes in college, so I won't be able to help you create anything all that complex. However, I do know a few things about survey analysis.

As an example, let's look at a question that has a single response available from a list of choices. It is a standard multiple-choice question that everyone is familiar with. If you were going to analyze the question, you might want to look at the demographic groups. The survey profile allows for certain multiple-choice questions to be flagged as demographic classifiers. Let's say that you want to know how each demographic group on the survey profile responded to the question. The results you'd expect to see in a GUI might be several pie charts. Each pie chart would show the breakdown of each demographic group for that particular answer.

To make the example clearer, let's say that the survey has two questions. The first question asks the respondent's age and is a demographic indicator. The second question asks the person's favorite color.

Figure 9.1 illustrates some sample pie charts that might result from this two-question survey.

Instead of embedding the code to create these pie charts directly into a Web site or a Windows application, you can create a GUI-agnostic API that analyzes surveys created by the Survey Development Studio application.

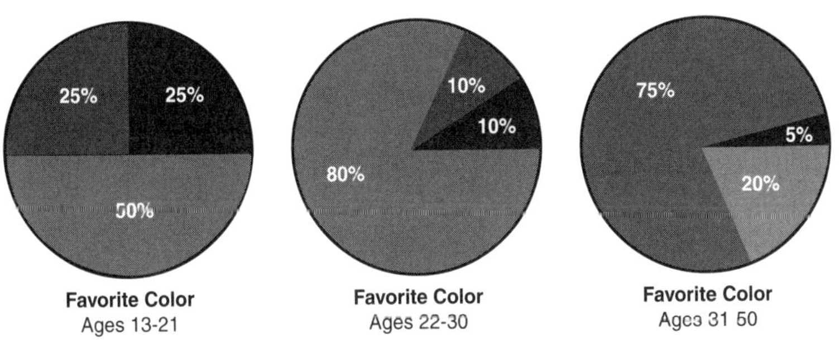

FIGURE 9.1
Sample pie charts resulting from survey analysis.

Taking a look at Figure 9.1, try and come up with an object model to represent the analysis data that you want to create. Obviously, you've got what looks like a collection of pie charts. Equally as obvious is that each pie chart is made up of a collection of wedges. From here, it should be pretty straightforward to design some kind of object model to represent the results of an analysis without regard to the method by which that analysis is rendered to the user. Take a look at Figure 9.2, a quick first attempt at the object model for storing survey result analysis in pie chart form.

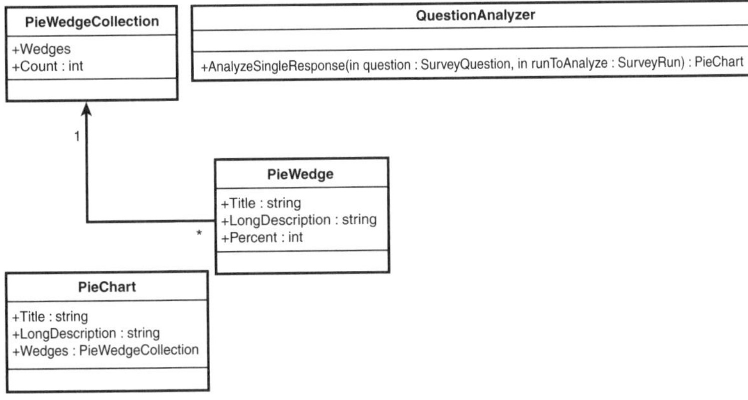

FIGURE 9.2
A survey analysis object model.

There are a couple incredibly useful advantages to using this object model, but I'll keep those a surprise until a little bit later. For now, let's take a look at the code implementation of the custom `PieChart` class, and the `Wedge` class, and the `WedgeCollection` class.

CODE TOUR: The PieChart Class

The `PieChart` class sits at the top of the hierarchy. It contains a collection of wedges, a title, and a description (see Listing 9.1).

LISTING 9.1 `SurveyV1\SurveyAnalysis\PieChart.cs`
The PieChart Class

```
using System;

namespace SAMS.Survey.SurveyAnalysis
{
public class PieChart
{
  private WedgeCollection wedges;
  private string title;
  private string longDescription;

  public PieChart()
  {
    wedges = new WedgeCollection();
  }

  public WedgeCollection Wedges
  {
    get
    {
      return wedges;
    }
    set
    {
      wedges = value;
    }
  }

  public string Title
  {
    get
    {
      return title;
    }
```

LISTING 9.1 `SurveyV1\SurveyAnalysis\PieChart.cs`
The `PieChart` Class
(continued)

```
    set
    {
      title = value;
    }
  }

  public string LongDescription
  {
    get
    {
      return longDescription;
    }
    set
    {
      longDescription = value;
    }
  }
 }
}
```


CODE TOUR:
The `Wedge` Class

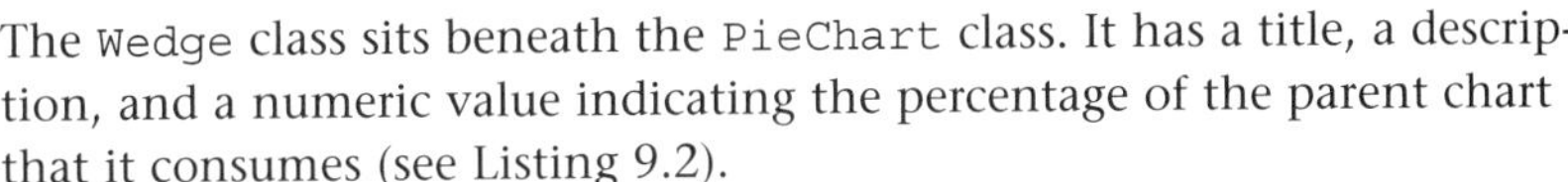

The `Wedge` class sits beneath the `PieChart` class. It has a title, a description, and a numeric value indicating the percentage of the parent chart that it consumes (see Listing 9.2).

LISTING 9.2 `SurveyV1\SurveyAnalysis\Wedge.cs`
The `Wedge` Class

```
using System;

namespace SAMS.Survey.SurveyAnalysis
{
  public class Wedge
  {
```

CODE TOUR: **The Wedge Class**

LISTING 9.2 SurveyV1\SurveyAnalysis\Wedge.cs
The Wedge Class
(continued)

```
    private string title;
    private string longDescription;
    private int percent;

    public Wedge()
    {
      title = "(Untitled)";
      longDescription = "(No Description)";
    }

    public Wedge( string newTitle, string newLongDescription, int newPercent )
    {
      title = newTitle;
      longDescription = newLongDescription;
      percent = newPercent;
    }

    public int Percent
    {
      get
      {
    return percent;
      }
      set
      {
    percent = value;
      }
    }

    public string LongDescription
    {
      get
      {
    return longDescription;
      }
      set
      {
```

LISTING 9.2 SurveyV1\SurveyAnalysis\Wedge.cs
The Wedge Class
(continued)

```
    longDescription = value;
      }
    }

    public string Title
    {
      get
      {
    return title;
      }
      set
      {
    title = value;
      }
    }
  }
}
```

CODE TOUR: The WedgeCollection Class

The `WedgeCollection` class is, as I'm sure you've guessed, a class that represents a collection of pie wedges (see Listing 9.3). It inherits from `CollectionBase`, a class provided by the .NET Framework in the `System.Collections` namespace.

LISTING 9.3 SurveyV1\SurveyAnalysis\WedgeCollection.cs
The WedgeCollection Class

```
using System;
using System.Collections;


namespace SAMS.Survey.SurveyAnalysis
{
  public class WedgeCollection : CollectionBase
  {
```

LISTING 9.3 SurveyV1\SurveyAnalysis\WedgeCollection.cs
The WedgeCollection Class
(continued)

```
    public virtual void Add( Wedge wedge )
    {
      this.List.Add( wedge );
    }

    public virtual Wedge this [int index]
    {
      get
      {
    return (Wedge)this.List[index];
      }
    }
  }
}
```


The PieChart Class, the Wedge Class, and the WedgeCollection Class

Listings 9.1–9.3 are pretty straightforward. The only really interesting things to look at are the Wedge constructor and the custom collection class. The Wedge constructor allows you to supply all the properties at once so that you can create a new Wedge instance inline. You'll see how that becomes handy shortly. The other interesting piece of this code is the WedgeCollection class. You simply inherit from CollectionBase and force a typecast on the individual items in the list when retrieved.

The following little bit of sample code illustrates how to use the PieChart and WedgeCollection classes:

```
PieChart chart = new PieChart();
chart.Title = "New Chart";
chart.LongDescription = "This is a new chart";
chart.Wedges.Add( new Wedge("Wedge 1", "This is a wedge", 50) );
chart.Wedges.Add( new Wedge("Wedge 2", "This is another wedge", 50) );

XmlSerializer xs = new XmlSerializer( chart.GetType() );
xs.Serialize( Console.Out, chart );
Console.Readline();
```

In addition, you can serialize the PieChart instance to the console output to examine how the collection looks when serialized.

As you can see, the convenient constructor addition on the Wedge class lets you create a wedge inline while you're adding the wedge to the collection of pie charts. The XML that is output to the console looks like this:


```
<?xml version="1.0" encoding="IBM437"?>
<PieChart
  xmlns:xsd="http://www.w3.org/2001/XMLSchema"
  xmlns:xsi="http://www.w3.org/2001/XMLSchema-instance">
  <Wedges>
    <Wedge>
      <Percent>50</Percent>
      <LongDescription>This is a wedge</LongDescription>
      <Title>Wedge 1</Title>
    </Wedge>
    <Wedge>
      <Percent>50</Percent>
      <LongDescription>This is another wedge</LongDescription>
      <Title>Wedge 2</Title>
    </Wedge>
  </Wedges>
  <Title>New Chart</Title>
  <LongDescription>This is a new chart</LongDescription>
</PieChart>
```


The fact that a pie chart serializes so well into an XML output format makes it easy for you to turn the analysis API into a Web service. This can come in handy if, at some later date, you want to expose the service to the Survey Development Studio application.

At this point you have the object model to store the pie charts, and you have a project in your solution (SurveyAnalysis) that contains all these classes.

The challenge for you is to create some survey analysis business logic and use that logic to create instances of the PieChart class. You've already built the object model to store pie charts in a GUI-agnostic fashion. If you feel like experimenting, you can write the AnalyzeSingleResponse method. Feel free to build it however you like. (The implementation I had in mind when I created the design was for the method to return an array of PieChart instances.)

Dynamic Image Generation with ASP.NET and GDI+

Now that you have the business logic in place (or some of it, anyway), you can worry about how to actually render what you need. Before we talk about creating the ability to render pie charts, let's take a quick look at how to build dynamic images with ASP.NET. There are a couple different ways to accomplish it, but my favorite—and the one I think is the simplest and most efficient—is to create a page that is responsible for rendering the binary image data directly to the response stream.

As you're probably aware, the client's browser determines what to do with the information it is receiving by examining the `content-type` header. If the content is standard HTML, the browser renders the Web page as it normally does. However, if the content is an image, the browser collects all the bytes and renders the page in a graphic format.

The key to the method I use for generating images is to create an ASP.NET page that places rendered images on the output stream. You can then reference this page in an HTML `<img>` tag from a normal Web page, and it will appear inline as if it were an image loaded normally from the Internet.

In order to create the images you're going to be outputting, you need to make use of GDI+. Thankfully, you can use all of the GDI+ code in the code-behind of an ASP.NET page. The following sample of code creates a test image and then renders it to the browser by sending it to the output stream:

```
namespace SAMS.Survey.RepositoryV1
{
  public class GenerateChart : System.Web.UI.Page
  {
    private void Page_Load(object sender, System.EventArgs e)
    {
      using (Bitmap bmp = new Bitmap( 300, 200,
        PixelFormat.Format24bppRgb ) )
    {
      Graphics g = Graphics.FromImage( bmp );

      g.Clear( Color.Black );

      g.DrawString( "This is dynamic" ,
        new Font("Tahoma", 12, FontStyle.Bold),
        Brushes.White, new PointF(10,10) );
```

```
      Response.ContentType = "image/gif";

      bmp.Save( Response.OutputStream, ImageFormat.Gif );
     }

    }
  }
}
```

By navigating to the URL of the dynamic image generation page in Internet Explorer, we get the image shown in Figure 9.3.

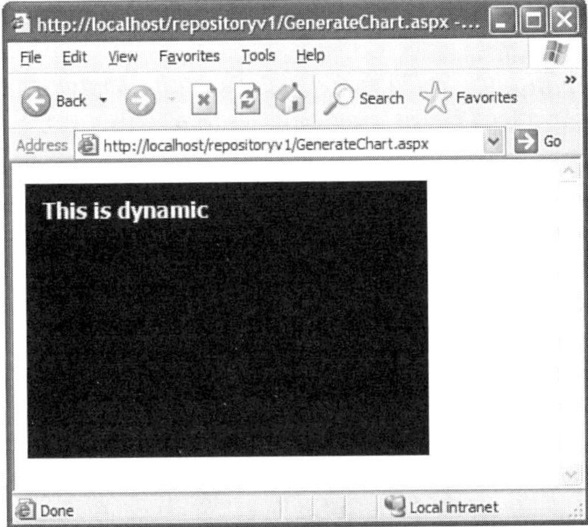

FIGURE 9.3

An image generated dynamically by ASP.NET.

Instead of navigating to the page itself, you could also reference the page in an image tag:

```
<img src="http://localhost/RepositoryV1/GenerateChart.aspx"
   alt="Chart" />
```

This allows you to create an exterior format page and reference the dynamically generated images through `<img>` tags. In addition, you can pass to the chart-generation page parameters such as information on the question to analyze.

CHALLENGE: Creating a Pie Chart Control

This code challenge takes the previous code a little bit further. You need to take the knowledge you now have about creating images on-the-fly with GDI+ and ASP.NET and apply it to creating pie charts.

There are a couple tasks you need to figure out how to do. First, you need to draw the circle for the pie chart. After you have the circle, you need to draw a line from the center of the circle to the outside edge. The angle of that line will be determined by the percentage of the circle that the particular wedge takes up.

I am not all that good with geometry. However, the key to drawing a piece of a wedge is in knowing that the percentage of the wedge is the same as the percentage of 360 degrees consumed by the wedge. If the wedge is 50%, then you know it consumes 180 degrees. Therefore, you start with the first wedge and continue around the circle, adding `(percentage / 100) * 360` degrees to the current angle. Some more geometry will give you the length of the radian line coming out of the center of the pie graph.

Fortunately, the point of this exercise is to create a page that renders an image in response to a set of user-supplied data. This is the goal, so you don't have to worry too much if your pie chart isn't the best ever; you're not building a commercial charting control.

DON'T REINVENT THE WHEEL, BORROW SOMEONE ELSE'S

One other option here is to simply invoke a third-party charting library to create the bitmap for you in response to the pie data. After you have an image created by the third-party charting library, you can simply place the image on the response output stream.

Now that you know the hard way to create a pie chart, let's take a look at a little shortcut that GDI+ provides: the `FillPie` method. The `FillPie` method of the `Graphics` class actually fills a pie wedge. All you have to do is specify a brush, the starting x and y coordinates of the upper-left corner of the bounding rectangle in which the pie wedge will be drawn, a width, a height, and the starting angle and the sweep (or width) angle. With that information, the `FillPie` method creates a perfect pie wedge for you. I've already given you the statement that creates the value that you use for the `sweepAngle` parameter (remember that there is a ratio between the width of the wedge in percentage and the width of the wedge in degrees).

Building an Analysis Web Site

So far in this chapter you've taken a look at one way to represent pie chart data in a portable, XML-serializable fashion that you can use with a GUI-agnostic business logic layer. In addition, you learned some techniques for creating dynamic, on-the-fly images using ASP.NET, code-behind pages, and GDI+. Finally, I challenged you to create your own chart-building code, using the techniques outlined in this chapter. If you've already done so, you're well on your way to becoming a master of the information covered in this chapter.

CHALLENGE: Building the Survey Analysis Web Site

The final challenge to you for this chapter is to create a Web site that provides analysis features. This Web site can be as simple or as complex as you want, but there are some features that I think would not only rank pretty high on the cool meter but would be extremely helpful in teaching you some of the most valuable programming skills illustrated in this book.

I suggest that you create a Web site that allows users to browse through the survey profiles contained within Survey Repository. Because you already have a Web service that does this, you can simply create a new site that consumes the Survey Repository Web service or you can add on to the site in the `RepositoryV1` project.

After the user selects a profile and selects one of the runs associated with that profile, he or she should be taken to an analysis screen. From there the user can choose a question to analyze, using the analysis logic discussed earlier. You can add a few `QueryString` parameters, such as `profileId` and `runId`, and a few other pieces of information to the `GenerateChart.aspx` page, and then it can be used to create pie charts based on data stored in Survey Repository.

Using the information you already have on consuming Web services, creating ASP.NET pages, and creating dynamic graphics and working with pie charts, you should be able to create a very powerful analysis tool without much effort. In addition, you can work within the constraints of the existing system and allow only certain users to run analysis reports and work with other functions.

CHALLENGE: Implementing Plug-in Modules for Survey Development Studio

One of the best ways that you can extend your own application is to allow other developers to extend your application for you. Currently, application modifications (often called "mods"), enhancements, skins, and extensions are extremely popular. Among certain demographic groups, consumers consider an application to be broken if it can't be extended with mods, plug-ins, or skins.

There are multitudes of ways in which you can allow an application to be extended. Some applications enable you to completely reconfigure the user interface. Sometimes this is accomplished with a configuration file that indicates colors, fonts, images, and pixel coordinates. Popular applications that can have skins applied include media players and instant messengers.

Another way that you might be able to extend an application is with plug-ins. By allowing other developers to create pluggable modules that snap into your application, you give them the ability to enhance your application and add functionality that you might not have originally considered. Creating an application that supports plug-ins is a great way to increase the community involvement around an application and extend its lifetime.

In order to create an application that supports plug-ins, there are three different sets of code that you need to consider:

- **Your application code**—This set of code is the code you write in your own application that enables the enumeration and invocation of plug-ins written by third parties.
- **The plug-in API**—This set of code is code that you write that creates an API that enables third parties to create their own plug-ins.
- **The third-party plug-in**—Although you don't have to write the code for the plug-in yourself, you should definitely familiarize yourself with the process of creating one. This enables you to streamline the process and make the necessary functionality available to plug-in authors.

The Plug-in API

In order to figure out what you need to include in a plug-in API, you need to figure out exactly how your plug-ins are going to work. In general, there are two different design patterns for plug-ins:

- **Context plug-ins**—This type of module embeds itself seamlessly within a particular area of the application's functionality, and the application generally provides it with the information it needs.
- **Standalone plug-ins**—This is the most common type of plug-in module. *Standalone*, in this case, means that the plug-in is simply installed into the application, and it is invoked from some kind of plug-in menu in a central location rather than being embedded within a particular piece of the application.

Combinations of these two patterns are available today, but for the most part, these two designs cover the majority of plug-in applications. The pattern illustrated for this particular challenge is the standalone plug-in.

The API for this plug-in is pretty basic. You, as the application developer, provide a library that contains at the very least a single interface. For this application, I'm calling that interface `IPlugin`, but you can call it anything you like. In addition to that interface, you can contain any other classes and interfaces that you think will help the plug-in developer create his or her plug-in. Functionality often found in such API libraries includes helper functions for deciphering proprietary data and methods for accessing information shared in memory, data sources, configuration information, and user preferences.

The first thing you should include in your plug-in API is the plug-in interface. This interface is a marker that indicates to your main application that a class found in a library is actually a plug-in written for your application. Not only is the interface used for a marker, but it is used for telling plug-in developers exactly what they can and cannot do and for providing a standard contract to which all third-party developers must conform. Listing 9.4 shows the sample `IPlugin` interface.

LISTING 9.4 `SurveyV1\Plugins\IPlugin.cs`
The `IPlugin` Interface

```
using System;
using System.Windows.Forms;

namespace SAMS.Survey.Plugins
{
  /// <summary>
  /// Marker interface for a Plugin class
  /// </summary>
  public interface IPlugin
  {
    string PluginName { get; }
    string Author { get; }
    string Description { get; }
    string Version { get; }

    void Launch();
  }
}
```

At first glance, there doesn't seem to be anything all that interesting about this interface. The first thing to notice is the four public members. The main application uses these members to identify a plug-in that your application finds on disk. This particular interface provides facility for supplying a name, an author, a description, and a version. More information can obviously be included if you find that your application has need for more information. There is also a method in this interface, called `Launch`. As you might expect, this method is called by the main application to launch the plug-in.

So far this interface looks pretty simple. It gives you a marker that identifies a single class as a class that implements not just *any* `IPlugin` interface but *your* `IPlugin` interface, defined by your plug-in API. However, it doesn't give you the ability to quickly sort through a directory of plug-in modules and construct a list of available plug-ins that can be displayed to the end user. For a standalone plug-in implementation, a list like this is mandatory because there is no other way for the user to find and execute plug-ins. To iterate through all the available plug-ins, you need to use some reflection and create a few more helper classes, which you'll see shortly.

Before we get to that, let's take a look at a class that implements the `IPlugin` interface. If you're following along, just create a new project called `SamplePlugin`. It is a C# class library project. Listing 9.5 shows the source for the `SamplePlugin` class that I created in this new class library project.

LISTING 9.5 `SurveyV1\SamplePlugin\SamplePlugin.cs`
The `SamplePlugin` Class, an Implementor of `IPlugin`

```
using System;
using System.Windows.Forms;
using System.Runtime.Remoting;
using SAMS.Survey.Plugins;

namespace SAMS.Survey.SamplePlugin
{
  [Serializable()]
  public class SamplePlugin :
     System.MarshalByRefObject, IPlugin
  {
    public SamplePlugin()
    {

    }
    #region IPlugin Members
```

LISTING 9.5 `SurveyV1\SamplePlugin\SamplePlugin.cs`
The `SamplePlugin` Class, an Implementor of `IPlugin`
(continued)

```
    public string Description
    {
      get
      {
        return "This is a sample Plugin";
      }
    }

    public void Launch()
    {
      frmLaunch launchForm = new frmLaunch();
      launchForm.ShowDialog();
    }

    public string Author
    {
      get
      {
        return "Kevin Hoffman";
      }
    }

    public string PluginName
    {
      get
      {
        return "Sample";
      }
    }

    public string Version
    {
      get
      {
        return "1.0.0.0";
      }
    }

    #endregion
  }
}
```

All the properties defined by the `IPlugin` interface return string constants in the `SamplePlugin` implementation. You could change this if you like. For example, you could make the version dynamic and have it return the version number of the plug-in assembly itself. In addition, you could change the name and description of the plug-in to indicate whether the customer has paid for, or registered, his or her copy of the plug-in.

The `Launch` method is called by the main application to invoke the plug-in. This particular sample plug-in creates an instance of a new form and displays it as a modal dialog. The implications here are pretty staggering: A third-party developer could create an entire application full of Windows Forms classes, embed those in an assembly, and attach that entire application to yours as a plug-in module. When you think about it this way, it almost seems silly not to write your application as one that is aware of plug-ins.

Now that you have a plug-in interface and a class that implements that interface, you can start putting together the code that will glue everything together into one single, cohesive piece of software.

Earlier I mentioned that enumerating the list of available plug-ins is tricky. It is actually tricky in a couple ways. The first is that you must use reflection to accomplish it. Using reflection adds a level of complexity to the project, but it is by no means impossible to use. The second involves the efficient use of memory.

In order to obtain the author, name, description, and version information for each `IPlugin`-implementing class that your application finds in a directory full of DLLs, you need to create an instance of that class. Any time you create an instance by using the normal methods, the assembly in which that class is defined is loaded into memory and *will never be unloaded until your application exits*. For a simple Windows Forms client application, this might not be too big of a concern for you. However, what if the application that is searching for plug-ins is an ASP.NET Web application? Consuming an unknown amount of memory on a Web server can be a really bad thing.

As you might already know, the AppDomain class represents an abstraction of an application domain, an enclosed area in which a .NET Framework application executes. The reason for this particular memory issue is that after an app domain loads an individual assembly, that assembly cannot be removed from the app domain. To avoid your main application having to have all these assemblies in memory just to list them, even if it's not going to use them, you need to do a little bit of reflection trickery.

This trickery is to create a new `AppDomain` instance that will then be used to obtain the list of plug-in modules available; then the `AppDomain` instance *can be discarded when you're done with it.* When you have the `AppDomain` instance created, you can make use of a helper class that will do the work of finding all the plug-ins and returning information about each one. This helper class is called `PluginLocator`, and it is in the `SAMS.Survey.Plugins` assembly. Listing 9.6 shows this class's definition.

LISTING 9.6 `SurveyV1\Plugins\PluginLocator.cs`
The `PluginLocator` Class

```
using System;
using System.Collections;
using System.Reflection;

namespace SAMS.Survey.Plugins
{
  [Serializable()]
  public class PluginLocator
  {
    public PluginLocator()
    {
    }

    public ArrayList FindPlugins( string path )
    {
      ArrayList results = new ArrayList();

      string[] files = System.IO.Directory.GetFiles(
        path, "*.*");
      foreach (string file in files )
      {
        Assembly asm = Assembly.LoadFrom( file );
        foreach (Type t in asm.GetTypes())
        {
          foreach (Type iface in t.GetInterfaces())
          {
            if (iface.Equals(typeof(IPlugin)))
            {
              // add the plugin data to the results
              IPlugin plug =
               (IPlugin)Activator.CreateInstance( t );
```

LISTING 9.6 SurveyV1\Plugins\PluginLocator.cs
The PluginLocator Class
(continued)

```
                    PluginMatch pm = new PluginMatch();
                    pm.Author = plug.Author;
                    pm.Version = plug.Version;
                    pm.Name = plug.PluginName;
                    pm.Description = plug.Description;
                    pm.SourceFile = file;
                    pm.TypeName = t.FullName;
                    results.Add ( pm );
                }
            }
        }
      }
      return results;
    }
  }
}
```


The PluginLocator class contains a single method, FindPlugins. This method is called and returns an array list that contains instances of the PluginMatch class. One extremely important thing to keep in mind is that this class will be running in a *completely separate* AppDomain instance from your main application. This means that not only this application, but anything that it returns, must be serializable by the .NET Framework or inherit from MarshalByRefObject because any communication between your application and the PluginLocator class will be done across AppDomain instance boundaries.

Another thing to note is the nested loops. The outer loop iterates through all the files found in the directory indicated by the path parameter. Within that is a loop that iterates through each type contained in that file. Finally, the innermost loop iterates through the list of interfaces implemented by the current type. If one of those interfaces is the IPlugin interface, an instance of that type is created, and the information about the plug-in is stored in a PluginMatch instance. Listing 9.7 shows the PluginMatch class. Note that this class is also serializable because it is being returned in an array list to the main application.

LISTING 9.7 SurveyV1\Plugins\PluginMatch.cs
The PluginMatch Class

```
using System;

namespace SAMS.Survey.Plugins
{
  [Serializable()]
  public class PluginMatch
  {
    public string Name;
    public string Description;
    public string Author;
    public string Version;
    public string SourceFile;
    public string TypeName;
  }
}
```


PluginMatch is a pretty simple class. The only really interesting thing about it is that I've decorated it with the Serializable attribute.

Let's recap for a minute: You've got a Plugins library that contains the plug-in API. At the moment, that library contains a PluginLocator class, a PluginMatch data-helper class, and the IPlugin interface. You also have another library (SamplePlugin) that contains a class that implements the IPlugin interface. Now you have two more tasks to complete before your plug-in infrastructure will be complete: Enumerate the plug-ins from the main application, using the helper class and a "scratch" AppDomain instance, and then launch the plug-in from your application.

Enabling Plug-in Support in an Application

The code in Listing 9.8 illustrates how to create a new AppDomain instance, invoke the helper class, and use the results to populate a ListView control.

LISTING 9.8 SurveyV1\SurveyStudio\frmPluginList.cs
The frmPluginList Constructor

```
public frmPluginList()
{
  InitializeComponent();
```

LISTING 9.8 SurveyV1\SurveyStudio\frmPluginList.cs
The frmPluginList Constructor
(continued)

```
  try
  {
    AppDomain ad = AppDomain.CreateDomain(
      "PluginLoader");
    PluginLocator pluginLocator =
    (PluginLocator)ad.CreateInstanceFromAndUnwrap(
    Application.StartupPath + @"\SAMS.Survey.Plugins.dll",
      "SAMS.Survey.Plugins.PluginLocator");
    ArrayList plugins = pluginLocator.FindPlugins(
      System.Configuration.ConfigurationSettings.AppSettings["PluginPath"]);
    foreach (PluginMatch pm in plugins)
    {
      ListViewItem lvi = new ListViewItem();
      lvi.Text = pm.Name;
      lvi.SubItems.Add( pm.Description );
      lvi.SubItems.Add( pm.Author );
      lvi.SubItems.Add( pm.Version );
      lvi.Tag = pm.SourceFile + "," + pm.TypeName;
      lvPlugins.Items.Add( lvi );
    }
    AppDomain.Unload( ad );
  }
  catch (Exception ex)
  {
    MessageBox.Show(this, ex.ToString(), "Failed to load Plug-in");
  }
  finally { }
}
```


The frmPluginList method accomplishes quite a bit in a small amount of code. At first, a new AppDomain instance, called PluginLoader, is created. Then, an instance of the PluginLoader class is created and marshaled from the new AppDomain instance. When the code has that instance, the code calls the FindPlugins method. The array list result is then examined and converted into items in a ListView control. Finally, the recently created PluginLoader AppDomain instance is removed from memory, taking with it all the assemblies loaded during its search of the plug-in directory.

Now you've set up the plug-in API, you've created a sample plug-in (and hopefully copied that assembly to the plug-in path defined in the application's configuration file), and you have a form that displays a list of all the available plug-ins. The only thing left to do is add the code to launch the plug-in. That code is shown in the `btnLaunch_Click` event handler in Listing 9.9.

LISTING 9.9 SurveyV1\SurveyStudio\frmPluginList.cs

The `btnLaunch_Click` Event Handler

```
private void btnLaunch_Click(object sender, System.EventArgs e)
{
  string source = (string)lvPlugins.SelectedItems[0].Tag;
  string[] sourceArr = source.Split(',');

  string sourceFile = sourceArr[0];
  string typeName = sourceArr[1];

  Assembly asm = Assembly.LoadFrom( sourceFile );
  Type t = asm.GetType(typeName);
  IPlugin plug = (IPlugin)Activator.CreateInstance( t);
  plug.Launch();
}
```

The `btnLaunch_Click` event handler loads the plug-in into the current `AppDomain` instance and then calls the `Launch` method on the instance. You could rewrite this method to make use of another temporary `AppDomain` instance as a small challenge.

This isn't the end of the challenge, however. What you have now is enough code to create a simple standalone plug-in that does something in response to a request to be launched. To take this challenge to the next level, I challenge you to adapt this code and create some contextual plug-ins. Create a plug-in that shows up only while you're editing a survey profile. After that, create a plug-in that shows up only while you're editing a survey run or when you're editing contacts.

To make something like this work, you'll need to do a few things. The first is to modify the `IPlugin` interface so that you can determine the context in which the plug-in should be run. Second, you'll need to determine some way to exchange data between the main application and the plug-in in a bidirectional fashion.

For example, let's say that you write a plug-in that shows up in the Plug-ins menu on the Survey Profile Editor form. This plug-in creates a very high-quality rich-text document that contains all the questions and possible answers. This plug-in allows you to create printed survey profiles for people to read and respond to. How do you get the profile data to the plug-in? If you think about the fact that you're using remoting (even if it doesn't look like it) to invoke the plug-in, the answer might become clear.

By using a `CallContext` variable, you can place information on the `CallContext` variable and invoke whatever method you need on the plug-in. You can be guaranteed that the plug-in method and all subsequent methods will have access to that data. Because of this, the plug-in can then examine and/or modify the data. When the plug-in is done with the data, you can write code that takes the data back off the `CallContext` variable and commits those changes within the main application.

If you think about contextual plug-ins and all the various techniques that I've illustrated related to plug-ins, the possibilities are endless. By adding the ability for your application to be extended, customized, and enhanced by others in ways you might not be aware of at design time, you open an entire world of potential customers, support, and community for your application that might not have otherwise been available.

Moving On

One of the main goals of this book is to give you an opportunity to work with an existing application—something not many books on the market provide. This approach gives you real, hands-on experience in designing new features, customizing existing features, troubleshooting, enhancing, and debugging existing code.

After having completed the challenges in this chapter and working through all the code outlined throughout the book, you can be confident that you have taken part in all the major activities of a developer working on ASP.NET and .NET Framework applications in the real world today. You have designed new features and analyzed the performance and stability of existing features with regard to customer preference and need. You have modified existing code to make it run faster and cleaner. In addition, you have coded new features, both using existing code provided by someone else and by creating your own completely new add-ons to an existing application. The experience provided by this book should help you in your job as a .NET programmer or give you new insight into .NET programming for your hobby.

Index

A

B

C

How can we make this index more useful? Email us at indexes@samspublishing.com

D

E

F

G-H-I

J-K-L

M

N

O

P

How can we make this index more useful? Email us at indexes@samspublishing.com

Q-R

How can we make this index more useful? Email us at indexes@samspublishing.com

S

How can we make this index more useful? Email us at indexes@samspublishing.com

T

U

V-W

X-Y-Z

What's on the CD-ROM

The companion CD-ROM contains all of the source code for the examples developed in the book, and Microsoft's .NET Framework 1.1 Redistributable and Software Development Kit.

Windows Installation Instructions

1. Insert the disc into your CD-ROM drive.
2. From the Windows desktop, double-click the My Computer icon.
3. Double-click the icon representing your CD-ROM drive.
4. Double-click on `start.exe`. Follow the on-screen prompts to access the CD-ROM information.

NOTE

If you have the AutoPlay feature enabled, `start.exe` will be launched automatically whenever you insert the disc into your CD-ROM drive.

License Agreement

By opening this package, you are also agreeing to be bound by the following agreement:

You may not copy or redistribute the entire CD-ROM as a whole. Copying and redistribution of individual software programs on the CD-ROM is governed by terms set by individual copyright holders.

The installer and code from the author(s) are copyrighted by the publisher and the author(s). Individual programs and other items on the CD-ROM are copyrighted or are under an Open Source license by their various authors or other copyright holders.

This software is sold as-is without warranty of any kind, either expressed or implied, including but not limited to the implied warranties of merchantability and fitness for a particular purpose. Neither the publisher nor its dealers or distributors assumes any liability for any alleged or actual damages arising from the use of this program. (Some states do not allow for the exclusion of implied warranties, so the exclusion may not apply to you.)

Microsoft .NET Framework 1.1 Redistributable and Software Development Kit

This program was reproduced by Sams Publishing under a special arrangement with Microsoft Corporation. For this reason, Sams Publishing is responsible for the product warranty and support. If your disc is defective, please return it to Sams Publishing, which will arrange for its replacement. PLEASE DO NOT RETURN IT TO MICROSOFT CORPORATION. Any product support will be provided, if at all, by Sams Publishing. PLEASE DO NOT CONTACT MICROSOFT CORPORATION FOR PRODUCT SUPPORT. End users of this Microsoft program shall not be considered "registered owners" of a Microsoft product and therefore shall not be eligible for upgrades, promotions or other benefits available to "registered owners" of Microsoft products.

NOTE: This CD-ROM uses long and mixed-case filenames requiring the use of a protected-mode CD-ROM Driver.